Vrije Universiteit Brussel

FACULTY OF ENGINEERING
Department of Electronics and Informatics (ETRO)

Best-Practice Framework for Developing and Implementing e-Government

Thesis submitted in fulfilment of the requirements for the award of the degree of
Doctor in de ingenieurswetenschappen (Doctor in Engineering) by

Abdelbaset Rabaiah

June 2009

Advisor(s):   Prof. Dr. Eddy Vandijck
                 Prof. Dr. Farouk Musa

Print: DCL Print & Sign, Zelzate

© 2009 Abdelbaset Rabaiah

2009 Uitgeverij VUBPRESS Brussels University Press
VUBPRESS is an imprint of ASP nv (Academic and Scientific Publishers nv)
Ravensteingalerij 28
B-1000 Brussels
Tel. ++32 (0)2 289 26 50
Fax ++32 (0)2 289 26 59
E-mail info@vubpress.be
www.vubpress.be

ISBN 978 90 5487 000 5
Legal Deposit D/2009/11.161/053

ABSTRACT

Governments struggle to implement electronic government (e-government) seeking out some potential values. Such values have internal as well as external benefits. On the internal level, e-government promises better, faster and more convenient internal operation. Better management of resources is likely to reduce costs and bureaucratic burden causing a boast to internal efficiency. Citizens and businesses, as a result, will receive better and faster response from the government. Service delivery is believed to become more agile. Cost and time savings would also be felt by citizens and businesses. The internal and external efficiencies would reflect on the society at large. Transparency, accountability, social inclusion and political participation are highly likely to be enhanced. Furthermore, the established technological infrastructure might accelerate the general development within a country. Without legal, organisational and operational reforms e-government is not likely to function properly to its full potential. This reform will surely result in better overall governance and healthier society. On the global level, e-government can provide cooperative tools to fight cybercrime and terrorism that know no national borders. Cross-national electronic exchange of information assures better response to pressing issues and global challenges.

The quest for e-government realisation is not all honey and roses. Major political, social, legal, organisational, economic and technical challenges have to be overcome throughout the process. Besides, e-government is still a work in progress. Governments worldwide are piloting e-government initiatives. There is no common approach to tackle e-government. Many countries have developed their own ways in developing and implementing e-government. Aims, contents, focus...etc. can vary even for the same domain. In this study, I have analysed the experiences of e-government implementation across (21) countries. The intention was to see if there was a global convergence in the basic concepts of e-government. I sought to measure to what degree there was a consensus on every concept. I started from no presumed conclusion about the existence or otherwise of such a global convergence. The structured case approach and comparison analysis have let evidence immerge. In fact, the findings tell us that there is much in common. The differences mentioned above do not dismiss the fact that governments, worldwide, face similar challenges and that they tend to implement comparable solutions. Concepts regarding service delivery, internal and external efficiency and government networking were found to be very much in common across sample governments.

The convergence of evidence has gradually originated a *best practice strategic framework of e-government*. This framework represents a missing link in all national strategies of e-government. It is advocated to form the core of any national e-government strategy. Besides, the analysis that led to the formulation of the framework has revealed a lack in literature on this very important domain of e-government. The presence of such a framework is shown to introduce a great value to e-government programmes. The proposed framework incorporates very important elements and principles. It has desirable characteristics and features that can add value to an e-government strategy. Unlike previous studies, the proposed framework defines strategic building blocks of e-government based on real-life implementations of e-government of the countries reviewed. This strategic framework possesses modular design. It is flexible, customisable and extensible. In putting this framework together, I took into consideration commonalities, trends, best practices in addition to relevant work of other scholars.

That framework was built for the strategic level of e-government. Nonetheless, it did not answer many of the pressing questions of how to develop a sustainable e-government that is flexible, interoperable and manageable. The next step on the agenda of my research was to figure out a proper technical model that can underpins the framework. The dissertation originates the *federated model of e-government*. This model was designed from the start to achieve better manageability, flexibility, sustainability, cost reduction, and security of e-government. Many studies have responded to technology platform integration and standardization. In my view, this is most rewarding for governments that do not have yet an IT infrastructure and that are only planning to establish one. Most governments, however, already have disparate systems in place. Each of these systems is usually built to serve a particular department that has predefined requirements. In most cases, there is a lack of vision of integration as decisions upon technologies are taken by the Local Governments (LGs). In firms, though, the decision is mostly central and any new system or platform with a typical size is normally planned to be interoperable. In democracies, LGs have autonomous status. Resistance to change can be more evident than in businesses. There is also a tendency to keep information private. This hinders much of the integration efforts. Also the cost for integration and rebuilding the IT infrastructure with the new standards can be awfully far above the ground. That said; it could be better and cheaper to adopt a different approach. "Encapsulation" of e-government can face far less resistance and demand much lower costs. This idea has a lot in common with Object-Oriented methodologies that are already applied in many businesses. The objective was to introduce a model that materializes this idea of encapsulation. The model, per se, is technology independent, yet the dissertation offers a workable technical implementation. The model should be perceived as a managerial as well as a technical tool that aims at the simplification of the implementation of e-government programmes.

This dissertation does not end without the introduction of some opportunities for the Less Developing Countries (LDCs). Such opportunities can be considered in order to effect some efficiencies in their e-government programmes. The dissertation shows that a learning and a considerate government should be motivated enough to spearhead the ICT development through its e-government programme. Towards the end of the dissertation, particular benefits of e-government for LDCs are highlighted. It clarifies how LDCs in particular can utilise the developed strategic framework of e-government. It has also introduced some simple and cheap yet sufficiently effective technologies that can potentially enhance e-government in LDCs. Although many of the presented technologies were not originally built for e-government, they can still be utilised to achieve more for quite less. Governments in LDCs are urged to adopt and promote the use of these technologies for more efficient governance. This part is not directly related to the major contributions of this dissertation. Its presence, however, will add even more value to the dissertation.

ACKNOWLEDGEMENTS

At last, I have a sigh of relief to have come to this page. Upon finalising this dissertation, I realised that writing a PhD thesis is quite demanding. Developing a sound argument to promote my contributions was indeed challenging. Uncertainty about the outcome was nerve breaking. Assessing pertinence of the different sections and the flow of ideas to convey a stronger message was as hard. However, continuous support from people around me has relieved much of my stresses and helped guide me through the process. I feel very much indebted to the inspiration, support and patience of many people to whom this thesis owes it existence.

First off, I would like to express my deep sense of indebtedness to my wife Abeer who has supported me and has endured much with me during that last five years. Despite their young age, my two sons Moh'd and Amre have had their share of endurance. Though being so much far a way at home, my mother and father have kept inspiring me. I know with absolute certainty that I would not have been so eager to finish my studies without their inspiration and support.

I would like to express my sincere gratitude to Professor Eddy Vandijck, the promoter and the friend, for his continued support and active guidance during every stage of my research. He brought me certainty when I was in doubt and provided me with fresh ideas when there was an impasse. I highly appreciate his valuable comments, corrections, suggestions and encouragement, which have made my contributions more solid and professional.

Many thanks to Professor Edmond Torfs who has supported me at the earliest stages of my PhD study at the Vrije Universiteit Brussel (VUB). I also thank him for the valuable suggestions that have enhanced the quality of this dissertation. In addition, I would like to thank Professor Farouk Musa for his directions during my case study back home and for all the efforts that he made to come to the VUB and participate in the defense. Many thanks go to Mr. Peter Strickx from FEDICT who have provided me with valuable insights and hands-on experience on technical implementations in e-government in Belgium.

To Prof. Dr. Philippe Lataire, president of the jury, Prof. Dr. Rik Pintelon, the vice-president, Prof. Dr. Jacques Tiberghien, and jury members Prof. Dr. Martin Timmerman, Prof. Dr. François Heinderyckx, thank you all for dedicating the time to read the dissertation and for the valuable comments you provided me with.

I would like to thank the Arab American University (AAU) for the financial and logistic support they provided me with and the Erasmus Mundus project, later on, for their scholarship.

Finally, yet importantly, I would like to thank my colleagues and friends at both the ETRO and MOSI research groups with whom I spent joyful and happy times.

TABLE OF CONTENTS

LIST OF FIGURES

LIST OF TABLES

"There is nothing more difficult to plan, more doubtful of success, nor more dangerous to manage than the creation of a new system. For the initiator has the enmity of all who would profit by the preservation of the old system and merely lukewarm defenders in those who would gain by the new one."

(Machiavelli, 1513)

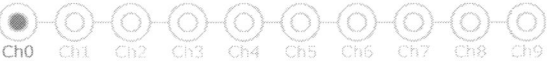

CHAPTER 0:   EXECUTIVE SUMMARY

0.1   Scope and Problem Formulation

e-Government, in general, addresses performance problems that have long persisted in government organisation and operation. e-Government has become an essential tool for governance reform and modernisation. It also promises better quality and increased efficiency of public services. This study has revealed that a *"client-centric government"* has topped the list of strategic objectives of national e-government strategies. Putting client needs at the centre of government operation is thus a core aim of e-government. Redundant and overlapping activities of government agencies constitute major impediments to this aim. In many cases, clients attempting to obtain a service from the government could file a plethora of forms that request much of the same data. This is due to the poor and inefficient organisation and lack of coordinated operation across government agencies. One can thus imagine the redundant activities, reporting, processes, efforts, man-hours, incurred costs and time consumed to provide services to clients. For example nineteen government departments in the US operate the same (28) lines of business (e-US government strategy, 2002). In another example, a client willing to open a restaurant, bar or hotel in Amsterdam has to obtain licenses from more than eighteen authorities (HoReCa1, 2007). The HoReCa1 project promises savings of € 30.1 million in terms of administrative costs and burdens upon resolving these redundancies. e-Government is therefore a powerful tool that can potentially introduce efficiencies and cost savings. It utilises ICT channels to deliver low-coast services repetitively.

During the last decade, most world governments have been intensively involved in developing their own e-government programmes. Countries have had mixed experiences. Some governments were quite successful; others have faced major challenges that led to setbacks. Each country has addressed e-government differently. This is because e-government was and still is a work-in-progress. There is no well-established literature yet. In fact, despite the many important scientific contributions, e-government is still more of practice than theory. This lack of established common knowledge has resulted in many efforts being replicated. There are neither proven best-practice guidelines nor any reference frameworks that governments can fall back on in order to develop their e-government programmes. Had a valid e-government framework existed, it would have saved governments a lot of time, research, money and disappointments.

Nevertheless, important lessons have been learned during the last years of global engagement in e-government programmes. Innovations and best practice cases have surfaced. In addition, there have been numerous and insightful research contributions to build upon. This dissertation summarises and presents the findings of more than four years of research in best practice of e-government. The dissertation introduces a strategic framework of e-government and an underlying model of e-government development. The framework and its underlying model are flexible and generic to fit the different governments of the world.

Best-Practice Framework for Developing and Implementing e-Government   1

0.2   Research Questions

The scope and problem background formulated in the previous section gave rise to some important research questions. These questions are fundamental to this research as they provide focus on how to get the problem solved. Answering these questions has guided my research all through.

Several of the research questions were open-ended to some extent. This was necessary to facilitate a broader exploration and to let the focus emerge during the course of this extended study.

This research attempted to answer a fundamental question, *was there a global convergence in the planning and implementation of e-government? How does such a possible convergence look like?* In developing the generic strategic framework of e-government, I had to look at the commonalities in e-government across a relatively large group of countries. To make the framework even more representative, governments with varied characteristics had to be considered. With all the differences, *could it be possible to still find commonalities among these countries? How can generalisability of the framework be guaranteed?*

As the title of this dissertation suggests the sought framework should be based on best practice. I had to record and analyse numerous cases of best practice implementation in e-government. The question was *what exactly qualifies as best practice?* Furthermore, *what does best practice really mean in the context of e-government?*

Some relevant previous studies helped enhance the understanding of e-government as a concept. Still though, a gap remained. As described in the scope of the problem, this study is aimed at addressing this gap at the strategic level. Additionally, problem scope was fairly broad. This called for pursuing an explorative research methodology. It was challenging to choose a proper methodology that was not too subjective. *What was, objectively, the sort of things to look for in order to structure the framework? Are there key trends that may help develop a common framework? Will evidence emerge out of the numerous case studies?*

Uncertainty of the outcomes has always blanketed the research. Starting with no clues was generally a good strategy to achieve unbiased results. Yet it meant that more care had to be taken in every step of the research. Detailed description of why a particular methodology had to be chosen over another was crucial for automatic validation. Questions such as, *what should the framework include? How should it look like.* .and so on had to be rationalised.

Similar research questions regarding the underlying e-government development model had followed. *What qualities should the model exhibit? How could such a model be constructed? How could such a model live up to its promises?*

Research questions regarding the methodology have been answered in Chapter 2. The questions related to the development of the framework have been mostly answered in Chapters 4 and 5 and the remaining ones were answered in Chapter 6. Chapter 7 answers the research questions about the e-government development model "the federated model of e-government".

0.3   Summary of Main Goals and Contributions

Thanks to the nature of this research, there is a fairly wide range of contributions in this dissertation. As mentioned above, this is an exploratory type of research. During the quest for compiling relevant evidence, I have introduced new knowledge repeatedly. The main contributions, however, can be summarised as follows:

Providing insight on the research problem

The dissertation explores the gap in hitherto research regarding the research problem. The pertinent contributions of previous researchers are discussed as well. A distinction between the contributions in this dissertation and previous ones is clarified. Furthermore, the dissertation discusses and clarifies the different challenges that face the development of e-government. It provides a detailed description of the potential opportunities offered by the developed framework. It also discusses how this research distinguishes itself from previous approaches.

As mentioned above, this study is based on numerous case studies. Reference to relevant cases is made whenever necessary. Before new theories are introduced, available pertinent research is called in to check contradiction or agreement. This continuous linking between theory and practice provides more insight on the issues under discussion.

In developing the framework, a holistic approach was followed. Qualitative data are channeled into themes to build the basic concepts of the framework. The multi-dimensional exploration of the basic components (Chapter 5) from practice and theory gives a better understanding of e-government as a notion.

All of these have contributed to a better understanding of the research issue.

Introducing the strategic framework of e-government

This is a core contribution of this dissertation. The strategic framework of e-government is both novel and innovative. It is novel because it has never existed before neither in literature nor in practice. It is innovative because of the methodology followed in structuring it and the characteristics it exhibits. The dissertation discusses the likely benefits of the inclusion of such a framework in an e-government strategy. Notably, the title of the thesis reflects the fact that this framework is a core contribution.

Abstraction of e-government

To simplify development of e-government a special methodology was followed. This methodology calls for the abstraction of e-government. The discussion explores the fit between this methodology and the requirements of e-government development. The thesis concludes the nice fit between the two.

Introducing the federated model of e-government

The federated model of e-government is another major contribution of the dissertation. The model was based on the abstraction concept mentioned above. The technical implementation of the model is described in detail to prove the workability of the model. A similar case from practice is provided for validation and to confirm applicability.

Other contributions

In addition to the major objectives and contributions described above, there are other minor contributions. These contributions are byproducts of the explorative study. The contributions are either amelioration of current theories in e-government or genuine ones. These contributions include the following:

- *Government officials perception of "e-government".* The study draws a generalised understanding of e-government. This understanding has taken into account the different individual perceptions of the sample governments. Formulating such a perception is extremely important as it describes clearly how world governments perceive "e-government". Future studies may address shortcomings in this perception and introduce more elaborated understandings, for example.

- *Strategic objectives maturity model.* There are a number of models that describe e-government maturity based on integration level (e.g. Layne & Lee, 2001; Bhatnagar, 2004). In contrast, the developed maturity model is rather based on the strategic objectives of e-government. Just by looking at these objectives, one can decide which maturity level the government exhibits. The model identifies four maturity levels. This tool can help governments assess their position against other governments and figure out what objective(s) they need to seek in order to move to a higher maturity level.

- *Rule-based process design.* The dissertation introduces a new approach for e-government process implementation. It calls for a rule-based processes design. The necessity for this approach is described and clarified. The dissertation verifies applicability with a practical example.

- *Better understanding of the components of an e-government strategy.* The dissertation discusses in sufficient details the most prominent and common contents of an e-government strategy. This discussion comes after a broad study of the different versions of national strategies of e-government of some (21) countries. Comparative analysis was used to draw out conclusions. The dissertation originates a structure of a typical e-government strategy. The findings were used inter alia to structure the strategic framework of e-government. The structure of the generic strategy per se is still of great value to say the least.

- *Drivers of e-government.* Part of this dissertation is dedicated to articulate the real drivers behind e-government. These drivers are important to understand. They explain why governments tend to incept e-government programmes. As we shall see, part of these drivers was found to be coming from within governments themselves. Many other drivers portray external pressures on the government. The dissertation clarifies each of these external elements.

- *Pillars of e-government.* More attention is given to the critical success factors of e-government. The most important factors identified as critical by both practice and theory were considered to build a framework for the pillars of e-government. They were referred to as pillars because any failure in any of them may increase dramatically the chances of failure to the whole government programme.

- *Adding values to e-government.* What is the value of e-government? How can governments introduce value through e-government? What is the connection between value and strategic objectives? How does public value relate to focus areas and e-government? These questions are answered through a dedicated part of the thesis.

- *Particular opportunities for the Less Developed Countries (LDCs).* The dissertation argues the potential benefits of the developed strategic framework of e-government for any government. There are, however, particular opportunities for LDCs where e-government implementation is just starting. A whole chapter is dedicated for the discussion of these opportunities.

0.4   Thesis Outline and Structural Organisation

This thesis is organised into nine chapters. This chapter (Chapter 0) serves as an executive summary.

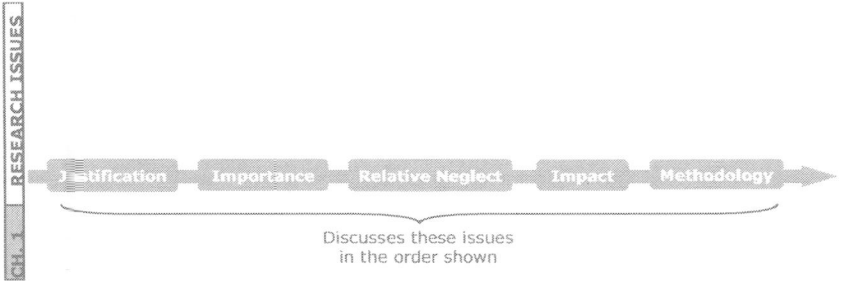

Figure 1: Overview of Chapter 1

Chapter 1 draws attention to some issues that are characteristic to this research. The chapter provides a proper justification of this research. In addition, it shows the importance of doing this particular research. Partly, it has to do with the relative neglect of previous research in the problem domain. The chapter also argues the potential impact of the outcomes. Finally, the chapter dedicates a large portion to describe the research methodology followed in order to answer the previously raised research questions. Figure 1 above gives an overview of the chapter. A real-life taste of the challenges facing e-government development is given in **Chapter 2**. Cases are pulled out from a number of countries. The chapter reviews some previous research to provide further recounts on these challenges. Adequate clarification of political, social, legal, organizational, economic and technical challenges is provided to allow the reader to gain a better understanding of the context of the research problem (Figure 2).

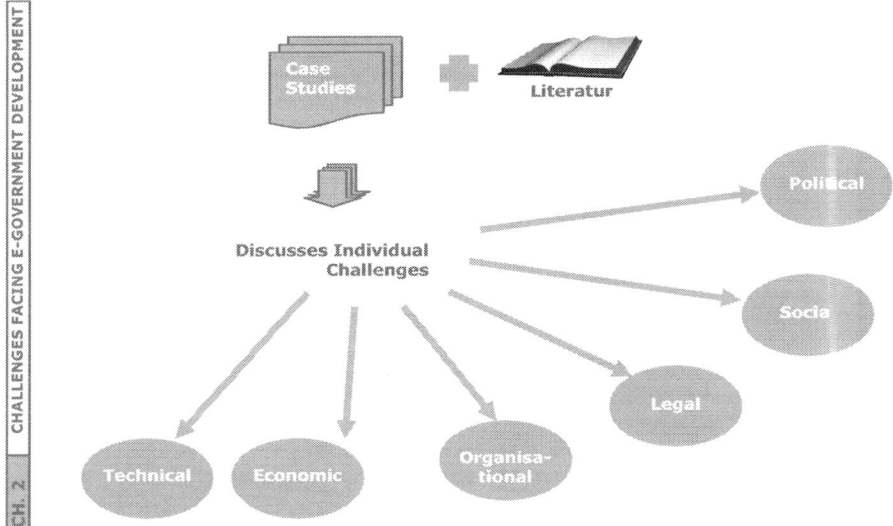

Figure 2: Overview of Chapter 2

A broad overview of e-government is presented in **Chapter 3** (Figure 3). This literature review covers the perception of e-government and its relationships to other initiatives.

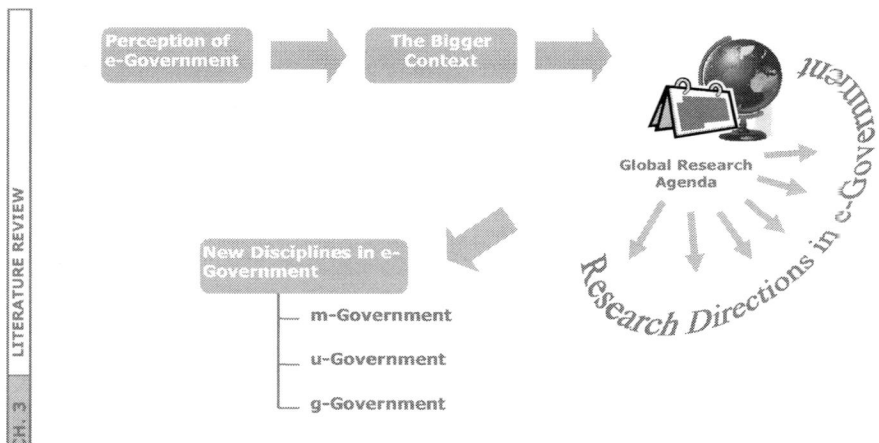

Figure 3: Overview of Chapter 3

The chapter portrays the trends in e-government research from a global perspective. Newly emerging disciplines of e-government are also provided towards the end of the chapter

A core chapter in this dissertation is **Chapter 4**. This chapter takes the reader into the systematic analysis that lead to structuring the strategic framework of e-government. In the process, the chapter introduces many important concepts. In addition, the chapter identifies best practice as a basis for the developed framework.

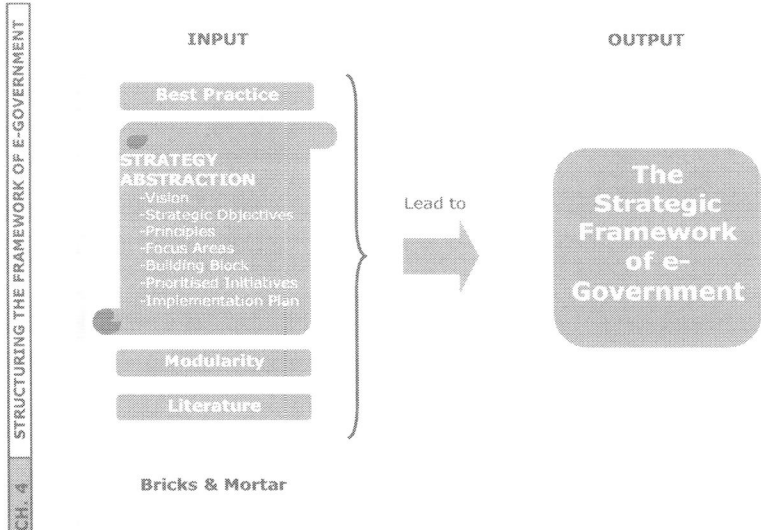

Figure 4: Overview of Chapter 4

It then presents the findings of the structured-case analysis of e-government strategies. The chapter conceptualises a generic abstraction of these strategies. It identifies the components needed to structure the framework (Figure 4).

As Figure 5 below depicts, **Chapter 5** culminates the findings presented in Chapter 4 with the introduction of the strategic framework of e-government. The chapter presents the nitty-gritty details of the framework and explains its different elements it incorporates. It also elucidates the layout and the general flow of the framework.

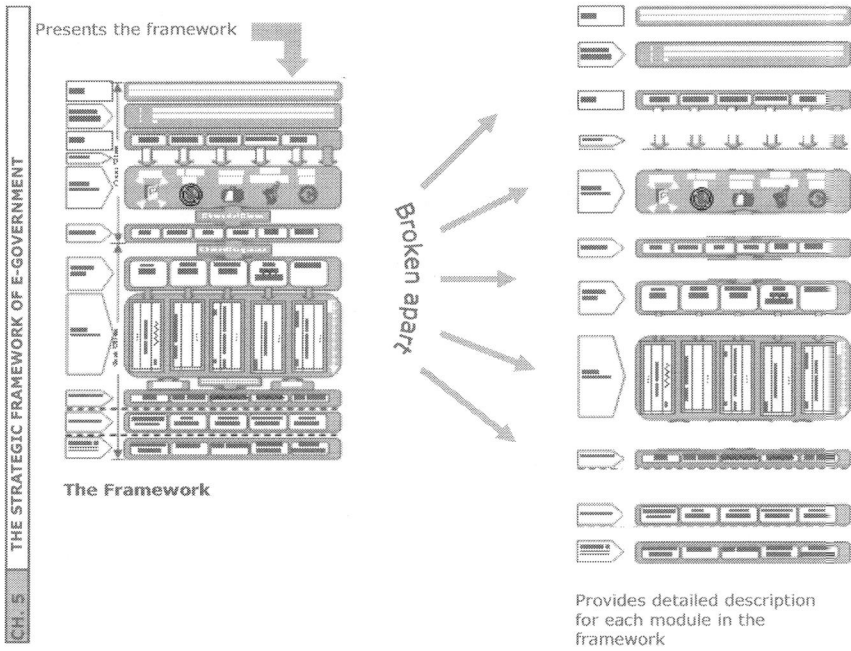

Figure 5: Overview of Chapter 5

Explanation of how to use the framework is offered in **Chapter 6**. The chapter explains the different symbols used in the framework (see Figure 6 below). Some of the symbols have different forms depending on certain constraints. The chapter also refers to some different possible implementations and customisations of the framework. Besides, the chapter identifies the potential users of the framework and illustrates how each group of users can utilise it. It also explores drivers and pillars of e-government. In addition, this chapter identifies the critical success factors of e-government. Finally, the chapter explains how to induce public value through the framework.

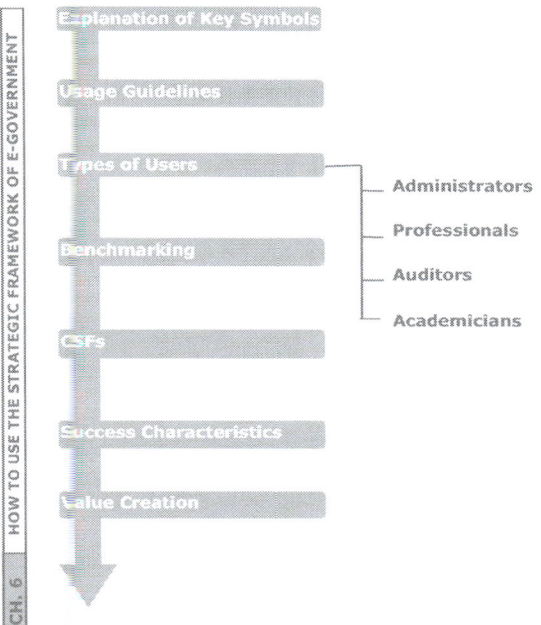

Figure 5: Overview of Chapter 6

Chapter 7 is another key chapter in the dissertation. It discusses development of e-government from a practical point of view (Figure 7).

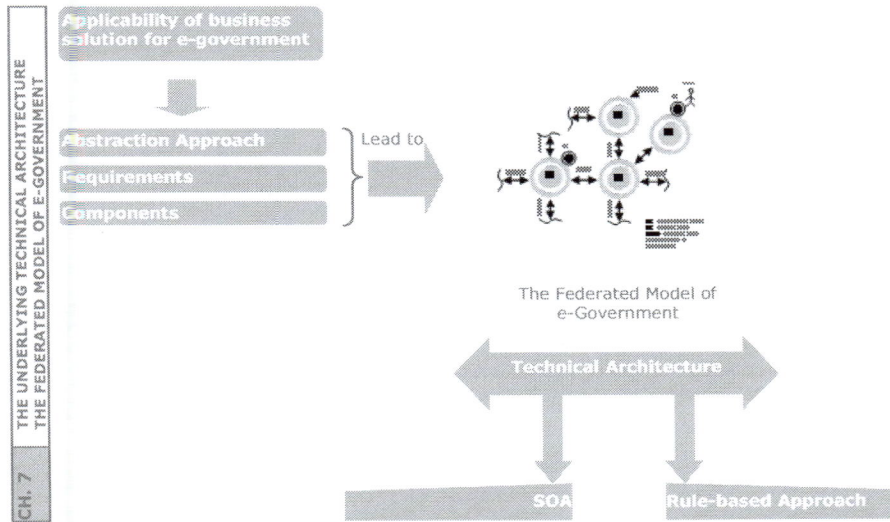

Figure 7: Overview of Chapter 7

This chapter introduces the second most important contribution in the dissertation. The federated model of e-government is presented here. This model is advocated to bring about a number of advantages. It addresses complexity, manageability, and risks associated with the development of e-government. The chapter provides an elaborated description of a technical implementation. Moreover, Chapter 7 gives further recounts on process design in e-government. It highlights the differences between business processes and government processes. Unfortunately, both types of processes have been addressed the same way by some researchers. The chapter proposes a new approach for implementing e-government. The new approach is based on rule-based programming.

This study presents new knowledge that is potentially beneficial for any government. However, there are particular opportunities for LDCs whose e-government programmes are just starting. Being from an LDC myself, I provided a discussion of the key characteristics of LDCs in **Chapter 8** (Figure 8). The chapter explicates how LDCs can use affordable technologies to incur more efficiencies.

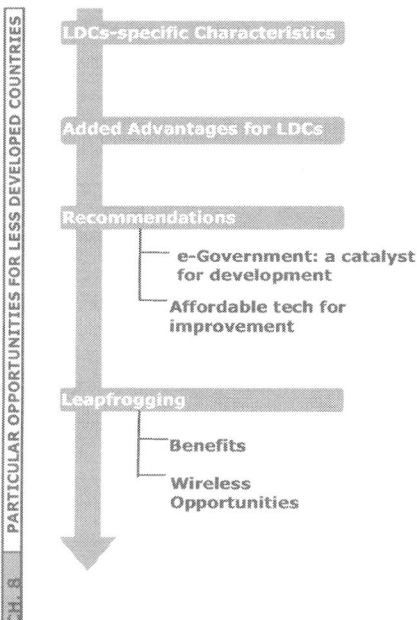

Figure 8: Overview of Chapter 8

Finally, **Chapter 9** concludes this thesis with a summary of the main findings and contributions to the body of knowledge (Figure 9). It then comments on implications of this research and the related findings for theory and practice. The chapter concludes with some recommendations for prospective future research and ends with some final remarks.

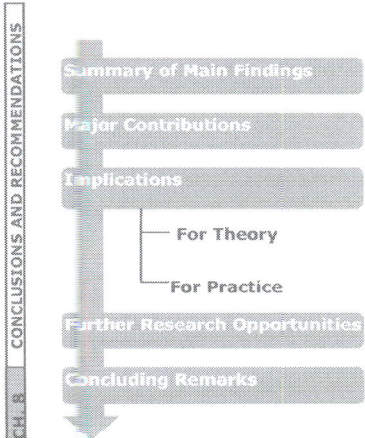

Figure 9: Overview of Chapter 9

Note: I have used "e-government" consistently to refer to "electronic government" throughout this dissertation. Other abbreviations used to refer to electronic government include eGovernment, e-gov and digital government.

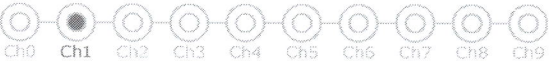

CHAPTER 1: RESEARCH ISSUES

1.1   Justification of the Research

World governments have achieved substantial progress in their e-government programmes during the last decade. e-Government has become a world phenomenon (Grant & Chau, 2005; Zhang, 2006; Mofleh & Wanous, 2008; Schuppan, 2009). Each government has developed its own strategy to meet the challenge. Nonetheless, e-government realisation in its full potential is still far from complete. Since it is still a work in progress, e-government is constantly evolving. e-Government strategies are updated fairly frequently. What was valid a few years ago may not be satisfactory today. This is mainly due inter alia to rapid debuts of newer technologies and ideas. Since an e-government strategy serves as a general guide to e-government realisation, it is absolutely crucial to keep it clear and simple.

Apart from suggestions from some researcher, there are no commonly established guidelines to write clear and simple strategies. Only few research studies (e.g. Heeks, 2006a) have provided guidelines for writing e-government strategies. Still though, no previous studies have been recorded to attempt to conceptualise e-government strategies in order to build a generic and structured one that incorporates the necessary basic elements for a successful implementation. This research delves into an exploratory study of real-life e-government strategies. It investigates the possibility of creating a typical e-government strategy.

An e-government strategy is a 'plan for e-government systems and their supporting infrastructure which maximises the ability of management to achieve organisational objectives' (Heeks, 2006). This plan is described in a top-level document that addresses strategic directions, goals, components, principles and implementation guidelines. The strategy should be understandable without any ambiguities. Such a strategy is considered a baseline and thus will be referred to quite often. Different versions of e-government strategies of (21) countries, in addition to that of the European Union, have been the subject of this study. These countries are Australia; Belgium; Denmark; Austria; Japan; Finland; France; Canada; Germany; Korea; Palestine; Singapore; Jordan; Egypt; UK; India; New Zealand; USA; Malaysia; Brazil and The Netherlands.

Choice of the list of countries was based on the availability of relevant published documentations. The countries with best-practice records were among the list. Many of the countries reviewed topped the score of e-government maturity. To make the list even more representative, I added some of the developing countries. Geographic variation was also taken into consideration. Thus, the list includes countries from all continents. This diversity is meant to provide a generalised perspective of these strategies during the study.

The question is now, *where should the analysis start?* Of course, one should build on the work of previous researchers. This is an essential requirement for valid scientific research. We will come to that later. First, let us see what we should look for from practice. The

---

following section discusses briefly the importance of studying *best practice* cases as an essential part in the analysis.

1.2   Why Best Practice?

It is now universally acknowledged that best practice is a major learning tool that accelerates progress (Undheim, 2008). Exchange of best practice has been systematically used worldwide. For example, the United Nations has built an e-government Readiness Knowledge Base. It incorporated best practice learning and knowledge sharing components (UNKB, 2007).

Similarly, the European Commission has established the good practice framework in e-government (European Commission, 2004). The objectives were to accelerate transfer of experiences and to re-use proven e-government solutions and provide a shared learning environment across Europe. The EC has recently established the ePractice.eu portal to publish best practice cases from around the EU member states. The portal includes cases in the fields of e-government, e-health and e-inclusion. It presents sixty best practice cases on average each month.

During my research, I found that governments tend to learn from each other. They introduce similar terminologies and principles in their national strategies. There have been instances in national e-government strategies where references of efforts of other governments have been made. For example, the u-Japanese strategy cited the Korean efforts in u-government. In fact, many governments look for best practices first. If no best practice in certain field is found then they innovate. This is wise enough not to recreate the wheel.

Since this study is deeply connected to practice (as is e-government in general), it has been natural to consult best practice before introducing new theories. Considering best practice and contrasting with previous research in building argument should arguably make the analysis more factual. Still though, *will the findings be relevant to practice?* This is what we will see in the next section

1.3   Importance

As has been mentioned in Chapter 0, a primary aim of this dissertation is to construct a strategic framework of e-government. This framework serves as a generic abstraction of an e-government strategy. Table 1 below assesses the presence or otherwise of such a framework in the national strategies of e-government of sample countries. Despite its simplicity and necessity as we shall see shortly, a strategic framework of e-government is missing from the majority of the reviewed e-government strategies. At lease, not in the way this dissertation is advocating.

Country	Presence	Relevant Diagrams
EU	No	
Australia	No	A representation of a connected government from a citizen point of view
Belgium	No	The elementary building blocks of FEDICT
Denmark	No	The E-Government Project Plan which categorises initiatives (sub-projects) into areas and relating them to strategic objectives
Austria	No	A collection of components of eGovernment
Japan	No	Outline of u-Japan Policy which sets current status, future vision, targets, measures implement, Major Actions
Finland	No	The vision and focus areas of the National Knowledge Society Strategy
France	No	The Vision of Development of Target System which depicts users, channels, basic components, and services
Canada	No	A representation of the Government Online Initiative which disqualifies as a strategic framework
Germany	No	There exists a figure which summarises fours areas of action: Portfolio, Process Chains, Identification, Communication Infrastructure
Korea	No	The e-Government Enterprise Architecture
Palestine	No	Labelled as Palestine E-Government Framework, it comprised: Vision, Objectives, Expected Outcomes, Application and Solution Portfolios, Enterprise Architecture, and Governance
Singapore	Yes *	It incorporates: Vision, Strategic Thrusts, Sub-Strategies, and Key Enablers
Jordan	No	E-GAF Architecture Building Blocks
Egypt	No	Implementation Framework for the E-Government Program
UK	No	Architectural model of how individual departmental and sectoral initiatives relate to the strategic framework and standards
India	No	
New Zealand	No	
USA	No	Integrated Business-Wide Government Architecture: Access Channels, Lines of Business, Internal Operations/Infrastructure, Value Chains
Malaysia	No	
Brazil	No	Structures and Relationships in the Field of Electronic Government: Users, Applications, Services, and Organisation
Holland	No	There is an Administrative framework for e-Government and a Framework of Basic technical Components

* Included strategic framework does not qualify as advocated

Table 1: Presence of an e-government strategic framework in e-government strategies (Compiled from national e-government strategies)

From Table 1 above, we see that the majority of the e-government strategies of sample countries are lacking a strategic framework. Some countries had included some relevant diagrams but they do not qualify as strategic e-government frameworks based on our description later on.

The presence of an e-government strategic framework could have certainly added value to e-government strategies of these countries as will be demonstrated. However, before going any further let us check any previous research that might have tackled the issue.

1.4   Relative Neglect by Hitherto Research

I have noticed a relative neglect of this strategic part of e-government despite its extreme importance. Soundness of an e-government strategy can be the difference between success and failure of the whole endeavour. Even in practice, many public authorities do not have any e-government strategy at all (Heeks, 2006a).

There have been a number of studies related to e-government strategies (e.g. Aichholzer, 2004; Bhatnagar, 2004; Chen et al, 2006; Heeks, 2006a; Shahkooh & Abdollahi, 2007). Most of these studies, however, shed some light on how e-government strategies should be like or how to plan those (Heeks, 2006a). However, none has discussed the importance of embedding a strategic framework. This is where my contribution fits. This study comes in to fill a gap in literature concerning e-government strategies.

Some other contributions sought to produce frameworks aimed at a better understanding of e-government as a concept. Each attempt tackled the complexity of e-government from a certain perspective. Methodologies and basis for these studies also varied. Grant & Chau (2006) and Wimmer (2002), for example, introduced frameworks to help understand e-government in its entirety. The framework of Sharma & Gupta (2003) was based on the work done be Heeks (2001), observation of few practical implementations by some countries (exclusively: USA, Canada, Singapore and India), and their own experience. The basic components of e-government Sharma & Gupta (2003) have stated were actually based on maturity levels of e-government implementation. Others (e.g. Miranda, 2000) thought of building blocks to be purely technical components (e.g. ERP, CRM…etc).

Wimmer (2002) on the other hand, perceived her framework as hodgepodge of different views of e-government, abstraction layers, and progress of public service. She argued that these perspectives provide better understanding and visualisation of e-government. Grant & Chau (2006) developed their e-government framework to help assess, categorise and classify e-government efforts. They started from few workable definitions of e-government to figure out the building blocks.

The drive behind developing e-government frameworks is the lack of mature documentation in literature (Sharma & Gupta, 2003). This paper comes in to address the lack of studies that advocate the inclusion of a *strategic* framework in e-government strategies. The contribution here is to produce a strategic framework of e-government that is both generic and best practice based. The word "strategic" in the title refers to the facts that it stems from the e-government strategy. Hence, my approach is rather different. I primarily relied on real-life strategies of e-government of many countries to produce the proposed framework. Thus, the end-product merits as both generic and best practice. In addition, I took relevant work of researchers mentioned above into consideration in structuring the framework. It is true that e-government strategies are driven by vision, political and economic factors and requirements of each individual country (Grant & Chau, 2006) yet I found a lot in common in all these facets.

Having seen the relative neglect of this vital research on this strategic level let us see the real impact of this contribution. The framework can have a strong impact on the validity and quality of e-government strategies. The following section discusses this potential impact.

1.5   Impact

Today, there is a lot of replication of efforts on the side of governments who look forward to incept e-government programmes. A comprehensive, well-designed framework and implementation methodology would save governments a lot of time, research, money and disappointments.

Sometimes a picture can convey more information than many pages of text. An e-government strategic framework is not meant to replace the detailed text of the e-government strategy but rather to serve as a quick alternative. This framework gives a lot of information at a glance, especially when it is drawn well to stress the main messages of the strategy (e.g. vision, strategic objectives…etc).

This makes it a perfectly useful tool in the hands of decision-makers. It is more convenient for politicians who are normally non-technical. It is always easier for them to handle graphical representations than huge tables, lengthy texts…etc.

Furthermore, a strategic framework gives a simplified yet a comprehensive conceptualisation of what the e-government strategy is all-about. It immediately shows the trends in e-government realisation. This is particularly important during discussions about e-government initiatives among stakeholders. Whenever the need arises to consult the strategy it might just be satisfactory to consult the framework first. In case further details are required then the complete strategy is always available. This can, in many cases, save time and efforts of delving into the full text of the strategy.

Being a comprehensive abstraction of the strategy, a strategic framework shows how different basic components fit together. It shows each component in relation to others. This makes planning and foreseeing of discrepancies a lot easier. Contradictions, misalignments, and inconsistencies with the general policies can be spotted easily.

For transparency reasons, people should know about their government initiatives and intentions. It is also important for a government to publish its accomplishments. The framework is easier to disseminate in brochures and handouts than the complete strategy. This can also save publishing costs.

The e-government strategic framework should convey the main message of the strategy (i.e. the strategic intent). The framework is very convenient for this purpose. This is because it is top-level representation of the strategic orientation in graphical format. Being a graphical visualisation, the strategic framework of e-government should neither be cluttered nor too complicated. Simplicity and easy interpretation is the power behind such a framework. Moving towards complexity decreases its usability and value. It is important, though, that the framework highlights the most important aspects of the e-government strategy. For example, it must include the government's focus and basic components of the e-government programme. The dissertation dedicates a large section to describe the methodology followed to put the framework together.

An e-government strategic framework has a relatively long-term scope and validity. In order to stay valid, it must respond to changes in the environment. Technology is ever changing at an accelerating pace. It is also frequent that simplification of procedure results in process re-engineering. Organisational structures within the government can also take place. These and many other changes in the environment must not invalidate the framework. It should be flexible enough to cope with them. One way to make a strategy more responsive is to make it as technology neutral as possible.

The proposed framework is "customisable". It is generic in nature and not constrained in some country-specific characteristics. Any country can utilise the proposed framework by populating it with its own visions, objective, initiatives…etc. Layout and the relationships within and among its different components can also be customised. Thereby, individual governments can still reflect their own focus and strategic agenda through local customisation of the framework.

A Strategic framework should serve as the bridge between regional and local strategies. In addition, it should also be extensible through detailed sub-strategies. For example, there could be a dedicated strategy for client centricity (e.g. Citizen Centric Government: Electronic Service Delivery Strategy for the Western Australian Public Sector…etc.)

Obviously all these requirements are challenging. Extra care will be taken to structure the framework. A valid methodology for building the framework is a first requirement. This is the subject of the next section.

1.6   Research Methodology

> *E-Government/e-Governance is a rapidly growing field, but one that is still immature and in search of defining boundaries, core focus, methods, and theories. There is a large and growing field of practice and a growing body of research, but a lack of and a strong need for, rigor and focus without which research cannot make a worthwhile contribution to practice.*
>
> E-Government Research Methods and Foundations Minitrack (Hawaii International Conference on System Sciences –HICSS 2006)

The lack of rigor and focus in e-government research is because e-government is a relatively new concept. It is still more practice than theory. My mission in this research is to explore the subject for purposes of putting together a framework that is generic and best practice. The domain I was exploring is complex in the sense that it is not just about one aspect (e.g. technology). It involves political, organisational, managerial, social, and technological issues.

In search for a research methodology, I had to choose rationally one that fulfils some basic requirements that are characteristic of this particular research problem. These requirements include:

- Support for deep exploration of the problem scope (which is fairly broad in this case)
- Allows to develop constructs and concepts from numerous cases of best practice of mostly text-based data

- Provides flexible data collection methodologies
- Supports structured comparative analysis

Broadly speaking, there are basically two major research methodologies: the traditional quantitative research and the less structured qualitative research.

Quantitative research stipulates that reality is not so problematic when conclusive results are feasible (Holliday, 2002). It is more concerned with the precise relationships among variables rather than exploring every possible variable (Easterby-Smith et al, 1992). Thus, quantitative research is simply insufficient to rely on in order to understand the intricacy of the current problem scope. Experience taught us that e-government failures are, in part, due to such complexity.

A rather deeper research methodology was required to find out the qualities that draw the main boundaries. Therefore, qualitative methodologies were followed to delve through the subject in a holistic fashion. Table 2 compares quantitative and qualitative research based on: activities; beliefs; steps; rigor; and declarations (Adapted from Holliday (2002).

Quantitative Research	Qualitative Research
Activities • Counts occurrences across a large population • Uses statistics and replication ability to validate generalisation from survey samples and experiments • Attempts to reduce contaminating social variables	• Looks deep into the quality of social life • Locates the study within particular settings which provide opportunities for exploring all possible social variables; and set manageable boundaries • Initial foray into the social setting leads to further and more informed explorations as themes and focuses emerge
Beliefs • Conviction about what it is important to look for • Confidence in established research instruments • Reality is not so problematic if research instruments are adequate or conclusive results are feasible	• Conviction that what it is important to look for will emerge • Confidence in an ability to devise research procedures to fit the situation and the nature of the people in it as they are revealed • Reality contains mysteries to which the researcher must submit and can do no more than interpret
Steps • Decide the focus first (e.g. testing a specific hypothesis) • Devise research instruments next • And finally approach the subject	• Explore inmportance in the subject (per se or because it represents an area of interest) • Explore the subject • Allow focus and themes emerge • Devise appropriate research instruments during the process
Rigor • Disciplined application of established rules for statistics, experiment and survey	• Principled development of research strategy to suit the scenario being studied as it is revealed

Declaration
• Details of the population in samples
• Questions in a survey questionnaire
• Which statistics
• Composition of groups in experiments
• Which variables are being included or
	• Choice of social setting:
	  o how it represents the research topic in its role in society
	  o how feasible (e.g. access)
	  o how substantial (e.g. duration,

Quantitative Research	Qualitative Research

excluded
 • What groups are exposed to in experiments
	depth, breadth)
	 • Choice of research activities:
	    o how they suit the social setting
	    o appropriateness to researcher (subject relationships)
	    o how they form coherent strategy
	 • Choice of themes and focus
	    o how they emerged
	    o why they are significant
	    o how far they are representative of the social setting

Table 2: Quantitative vs. Qualitative research methodologies (Source: Holliday, 2002)

As per the basic requirement for this research stated above, my research is primarily exploratory in nature. There were no relevant theories in the literature or in common practice that can be used as an initial starting point. Without such guidelines or established theory, I had to fathom my way through. It was necessary to follow a flexible methodology. Quantitative research is too structured to prove flexible to meet my research requirements.

Unlike quantitative research, which tries to control variables in the environment, I sought to explore all the variables in the domain. I started from an unbiased perspective. I did not know in advance, what the framework would look like or what constructs it would include. Qualitative research doctrine states that important variables will emerge as the study progresses. As important variables emerge, research procedures can be devised to fit the situation better. In quantitative research, on the other hand, the researcher has to set forth in advance what variables are to be tested. The importance of variables is preset. The most important ones are chosen. This was *not* an option for me as I wanted the focus themes to surface.

Figure 10 summarises the differences between quantitative and qualitative research methodologies.

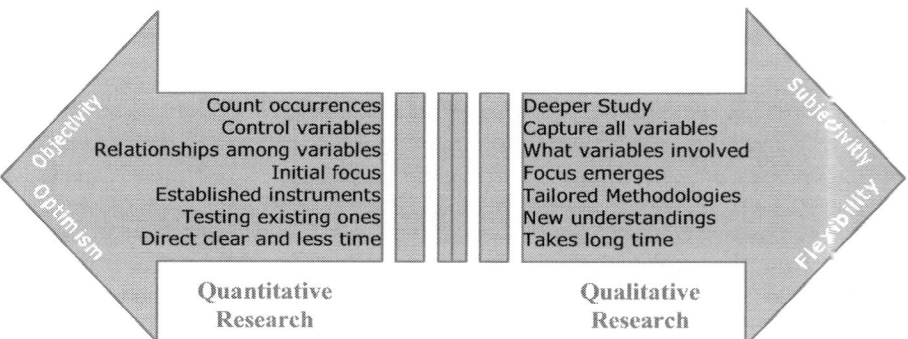

Figure 10: Qualitative vs. qualitative research methodologies (adapted from Holliday, 2002, Easterby-Smith et al, 1992)

Putting the two directions on balance and projecting them against the stated research requirements, made it obvious that a qualitative research was the main methodology to follow. This diagram should not mean that these two types of research could not be combined in one study. On the contrary, many studies have used both quantitative and qualitative research.

Normally researchers use qualitative research to start exploring a relatively new field. Once the basic constructs in this field become more obvious, they may use quantitative methodologies to assess relationships amongst the constructs.

In search for qualitative data, the emphasis was on those that carry the "best practice" tag. Naturally, the first place to look at was the best practice cases from around the world. In fact, arriving at "best practice" requires learning from successful case studies (Cornford & Smithson, 1996). Successful case studies yield critical learning, which can then be incorporated as "best practice" (Sharma, 2007). Thus, the core data-collection methodology in this research was case studies. A case study is 'an empirical inquiry that investigates a contemporary phenomenon within its real-life context, especially when the boundaries between phenomenon and context are not clearly evident' (Yin, 1994).

As Figure 11 shows case study is a valid methodology for both quantitative and qualitative research. Comparison of results to find methodologies aided in producing the sought generic framework. If two or more cases are shown to support the same theory, replication may be claimed" (Yin, 1993). In my quest, I studied, deeply, cases from (22) countries. I relied on convergence of evidence to produce the constructs that eventually led to structuring the framework.

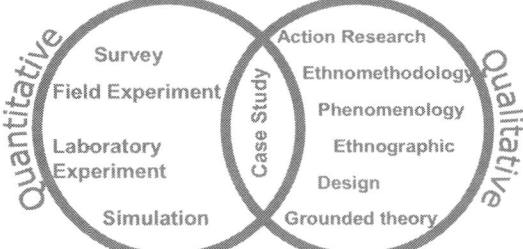

Figure 11: Research methodologies (developed from Myers, 1997; Silverman, 1993; Denzin, & Lincoln, 1994)

I analyzed collectively and comparatively the e-government strategies from various countries. In the process, I followed the *structured case study research approach* suggested by Plummer (2001). Plummer (2001) suggested that structured case study approach has the powers of interpretive (during data analysis) and positivist (through conceptual framework) epistemologies. Riedl et al (2007) advocated and implemented the structured case approach to build theory in e-government. They argued that this methodology draws the linkage between data and conclusion. They concluded the validity of the approach for theory and knowledge building. I estimated that this scientific research methodology fits well the nature of our research. I overlapped data analysis with data collection as Van Mannen (1988) and Glaser & Strauss (1967) suggested. This allowed me to make adjustments during data collection process. The added flexibility of data collection was important since I was not sure what data collected will become important in the course of my research. Figure 12 shows how important constructs have emerged during data collection and analysis. I started with no preset constructs or hypotheses. This was necessary to avoid any biased results.

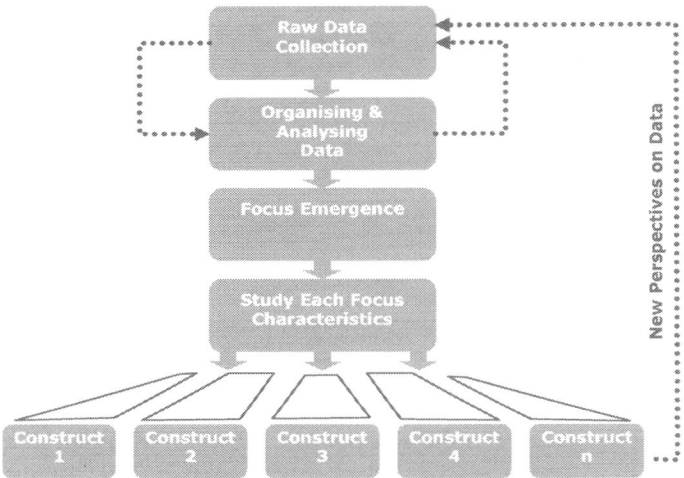

Figure 12: Emergence of constructs (based on Holliday, 2002; Van Mannen (1988) and Glaser & Strauss (1967

In building the e-government strategic framework, I have reviewed the available strategies as mentioned above. Many countries have already developed different versions of their strategies. New versions came out upon completion of a major phase of e-government implementation and the beginning of another. They may come also as a response to changes in the environment including government policies and new innovative technologies as seen in Figure 13 . In the course of my research, I reviewed all the different versions of the available e-government strategies.

As the figure shows, the policy cycle comprises six steps (Stone, 2001; Janssen et al, 2004; Heeks, 2006b). The first step is to add a response in the agenda (agenda setting) upon a change in the environment. This is followed by internal preparations for decision making which might involve many other steps including doing R&D for example. The decision is then taken. At this point, a new strategy is churned out. Once the strategy is prepared, it can then be implemented. Benchmarking implementation follows to measure performance and in some cases, updates to the strategy might take place. Finally, governments learn from their experience and lessons are documented.

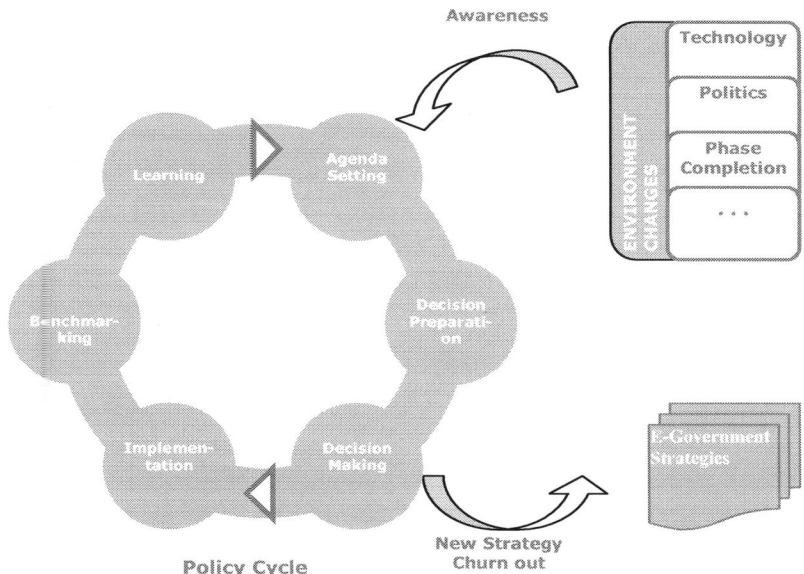

Figure 13: Churning out of new e-government strategies (developed from Stone, 2001; Janssen et al, 2004; Heeks, 2006b)

Figure 14 below gives an overview of the research methodology followed during my study. As the figure shows, I resorted to the structured case approach as mentioned above. I was essentially building a framework out of basically textual data. In the process, I conducted intensive and iterative cross case comparisons. Diversity among cases selected should not produce variation. My selection is affected, however, by available data. The goal behind selection of this particular group of countries was to replicate and extend the emerging generic framework. This helped validate the framework for different governments. I sought to enhance generalisability of the framework.

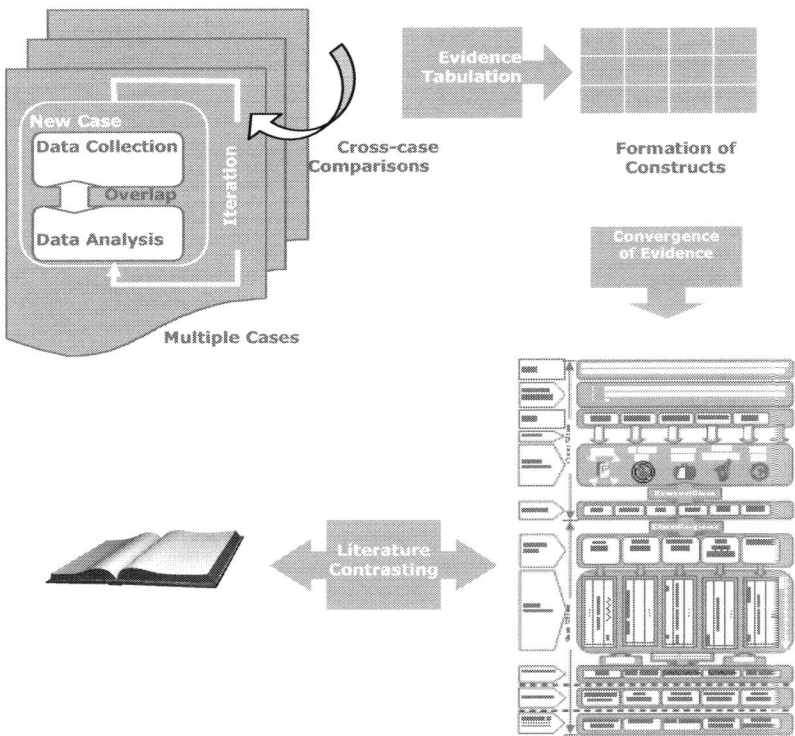

Figure 14: Overview of my research methodology

I did not set in advance the number of cases to consult. I added new cases whenever I was in doubt about some construct or component in the framework. I kept adding cases until the addition of a new case produced minimal effect on the emergent framework. In other words, I stopped adding cases once I witnessed convergence of evidence. I tried to balance the intensity of data collection of the case studies. Too much data collection and variation could have led to a complex framework. Inadequate volume of data or sparse variation on the other hand might have failed to capture the whole picture in its entirety. I was a ware of these potential risks and worked to avoid them.

To counteract the effects of initial impressions on data collected I searched for cross-case patterns. I used a mesh of (22) cells for each group of data to generate accurate and reliable constructs. To have a better understanding during comparison analysis I fell back on lens or keyhole comparisons (Walk, 1998). This comparison methodology has produced new perspectives. It allowed me to gather quality data. This wasn't easy, however. I had to do keyhole comparisons not between two cases but rather among (22).

Despite the argument about necessity to using qualitative methodologies, I used some quantitative analysis. I collected some quantitative data to measure precisely some constructs. For example, to determine the rankings of the top strategic objectives, I employed some regression analysis to come up with a representative graph (see Chapter 4). This raised the validity of the emergent framework. It should be noted here that despite considering constructs with higher replicability I did not ignore any of the ones with no repetitions. I listed them all in the tables introduced throughout this dissertation. They maybe used as variable to check in a future research (see Section 9.4).

To validate each construct in the sought framework I tabulated evidence (data) from which each construct has evolved (Miles & Huberman, 1984; Sutton & Callahan, 1987). The reason to follow this technique was the relative variation of evidence across cases. The technique followed made it easier to aggregate qualitative evidence.

Components and layout of the framework have converged from accumulative evidence (qualitative data). Gradually, a generic framework began to emerge. I compared systematically the emergent framework with evidence collected from the multiple cases one at a time. I continued this iterative process until the data corroborated well the evolving framework.

As we shall see throughout the dissertation, I was always contrasting evidence with available and relevant literature. I examined similar research focus. In particular, I was looking for agreement or contradiction. This allowed producing a more rational framework. In addition, this comparison with literature has naturally broadened my thinking. I availed from external ideas.

During my research, I came across different challenges. One major challenge was getting information from official sources. Even with the most advanced countries in e-government, getting information past the published ones was extremely difficult. For example, the majority of emails I sent for soliciting general information have received no attention although I was always explaining why the information is needed and how the information will be used. This is strange since the addresses I used for communication were explicitly placed online by government themselves to address further enquiries.

Another challenge I had to face was the different languages used for publishing official information. Many of the documentations reviewed were not in English. I had to deal with documents written in at least eight languages. Since I only know a few of them, I had to seek assistance from international students to translate the content into English. I was also using online translation services extensively. Different governments used different terminologies to describe the same construct. Since I was exploring all the possible constructs in this relatively new field, I had to pay extra attention for the accuracy of translation.

The last challenge was the relative scarcity of relevant research in the problem scope as mentioned Section 1.4. Some important previous publications were not accessible free of charge or through agreement with the VUB. I had to pay fees to get some of these articles. There were also no teams working on similar projects. Yet I managed to liaise with researchers and professionals from academia and practice during conferences, workshops and through online social networking to exchange ideas and information.

Despite all these challenges, I managed to collect all the information needed in order to produce scientifically sound findings.

Before delving into the analysis, I would like to furnish the reader with a sense of the complexity of e-government. The following chapter discusses the different challenges that face the development of e-government.

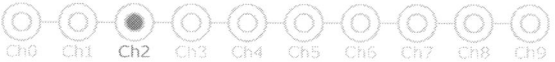
CHAPTER 2:   CHALLENGES FACING E-GOVERNMENT DEVELOPMENT

2.1   Introduction

Development of e-government is not a straightforward process. Many challenges have to be overcome during the different phases of development. Challenges start at the planning phase. Choosing the right strategies to engage in e-government cannot be trivial as every decision made has its consequences during implementation. Normally, an e-government strategy has a long time validity extending over many years. It is a national plan that depicts what the country will be doing in the next few years. Upon finishing the plan implementation and realisation, another one may begin. The point here is e-government strategy is barely changing once endorsed. Therefore, careful planning is obviously crucial and many things have to be taken into consideration. Implementation phase is where most of failures sprout and disappointments arise. Many barriers have to be overcome.

Challenges of all kinds have to be envisaged and accounted for. Otherwise, risk of failure will be grave. In this chapter, I will attempt to provide a descriptive review of the major challenges that are likely to face e-government development. The aim of this brief review is to furnish the reader with a real-life taste of predicaments in e-government development.

Breaking the Barriers to eGovernment study (BBeGov, 2007) has identified seven key categories of barriers impeding e-government development. This three-year EC-funded project was aimed at investigating the legal, organisational, technological and other barriers impeding effective e-government services. The identified barriers were:

- Leadership failures resulting from poor understanding of e-government or biased prioritisation of initiatives towards achieving short term tangible public services (e.g. in health education…etc) for constituency competition.

- Financial inhibitors, which include cost of hardware, software, training, consultation…etc.

- Digital divides and choices in terms of wealth, age, gender, disability, language, culture, geographical location, size of business…etc. All these differences should be considered in order to achieve the "no-citizen-left-behind" principle.

- Poor coordination across agencies

- Workplace and organisational inflexibility which is synonymous with *resistance to change*

- Lack of trust which fuels the controversy between data collection of individuals (which is necessary for offering services) and protecting their privacy at the same time

- Poor technical design of e-government systems (e.g. inappropriate user interfaces, usability issues, interoperability issues…etc.

2.2   Sample Cases of Challenges from Practice

Countries, despite being different in many aspects, face similar challenges in tackling e-government. Yet the severity of each individual challenge is variable across countries. This depends on local situations. For example, a richer country is likely to face less financial challenges than and a Less Developed Country (LDC). Similarly, a country with a high literacy rate should arguably face milder digital divide or lack of human skills. I have reviewed official governmental documentation of a number of countries in order to identify and understand the different challenges from a practical point of view.

Starting with the USA (OMB, 2002), the e-government programme had at one point, faced a number of barriers. These barriers included agency culture. Agencies are mostly concerned with the functional performance of their IT systems. Basic principles like 'meeting users' need' were not yet assimilated within the culture of these agencies. In addition, disparate systems were still abundant. These systems were initially installed to automate the processes. This has created islands of automation. This stage has found its way through the agency culture creating a strong resistance to change in the perception of the value of IT systems. Other barriers included lack of federal architecture of e-government, lack of trust, scarcity of adequate funding for investment in e-government, and shareholders' apathy.

In Denmark (Project e-Government, 2004; MSTI, 2004), bureaucracy was still traditionally an issue. Like in the US, islands of automation were also heavily present. Silo-oriented solutions and rigid processes were considered common impediments. In addition, there was a lack in proper knowledge in the vision and strategy of e-government on the administrative level. Moreover, the culture prevailing did not encourage inter-agency cooperation in operation. This was probably due to the perception that benefits induced might be harvested by peer organisation(s). In general, there was a lack of managerial skills and commitment. Finally, the organisational aspects were usually overlooked in favour of the technical ones.

Malaysia (8MP, 2001; 9MP, 2006) faced shortages in IT skills, information management skills, statewide management plans for IT, integrated infrastructures, and clear-cut policies related to human resources. In addition, varying computing standards across agencies, stiff laws, and lack of communities' readiness technically and culturally added up to the challenges facing e-government development in the country.

Challenges facing Brazil (Comitê Executivo do Governo Eletrônico, 2002) started at the political level. The vision of e-government was still insufficiently assimilated within many levels of the Brazilian government. e-Government was still being perceived as mere computerisation and automation of processes. On the cultural and motivational levels, there were still no mechanisms and instruments that encouraged innovation in e-government. IT units were not sufficiently motivated to apply e-government principles in accordance with the vision. There were also deficiencies in the technological infrastructure. Technical public platforms were substandard. Brazil faced difficulties in building capable intranets among agencies due to the lack of basic standards. As a result, advanced electronic communications among public servants were not widespread.

Germany (BundOnline, 2005) had basically three challenges to encounter: organisational, technical and financial. On the organisational level, the challenges included the shortages in suitable staff on the local level. In addition, there was a difficulty in shifting the traditional mentality of IT projects into the bigger context of services delivery through e-government. The technical challenges concerned basically the timely provision of basic technical components by the central government. Long delays may result in heterogeneous systems being developed by the local authorities. Lastly, financial factors needed to be taken into consideration. The fact that returns on investments are realised only later on, has made justification of investments harder. In addition, cost calculation was not always accurate and could result in wrong funding assessments. As always, implementation of new online services is associated with additional burden in terms of personnel and funding.

In Austria (ICT Strategy Unit, 2007), the challenges varied. They included integrating the fragmented IT systems, overcoming boundaries across agencies, enforcing more cooperation among them, building high quality infrastructure, and bridging the digital divide. Additionally, changes and adjustments to legislations were vital for better adaption of e-government. Businesses needed also to adapt their new systems with the new common public systems such as the new electronic identity card. There was also a need to debut more online services and to take the varying skills of employees and citizens into account when designing these services.

Australia saw harnessing ICT meticulously to achieve better and more efficient governance as a big challenge (Australian Government Information Management Office, 2006). Additionally, application of ICT has been ad-hoc at times without the necessary coordination. Bridging the disparate systems was quite a challenge.

Understanding customers' needs and insufficient resources constituted a challenge for New Zealand in its quest for developing e-government (State Services Commission, 2006). Cross-agency collaboration was no less challenging. In addition, resistance to the new paradigm of operation was taken seriously as a challenge.

Egypt had its own set of challenges. While remote authentication mechanisms and security and privacy issues comprise legal and regulatory challenges, lack of unified standards, multiple service providers, isolated communication islands (agencies) made up the major technological challenges (EISI, 2004). Cultural and economic factors were also part of the challenges the Egyptian government had to face. These included the inexistence of suitable e-payment systems and the poor penetration of credit cards. This limits the government's ambitions to offer services where citizens would pay for online. Besides, computer illiteracy and low Internet and PC penetration did not help either. On the organisational level, reluctance to modify workflow and mistrust for automation (for the fear of being illegal) were real impediments. There were also multiple auditing plus overlapping authorities among agencies. Another unique organisational challenge for Egypt was the reluctance to new philosophies and practices of modern management.

Other challenges included lack of information sharing, ownership, copyright issues and lack of unified data dictionary and definitions.

The government of Jordan came across issues related to resistance to change, inexplicably long procurement procedure, and limited financial resources and human skills (e-Government Programme, 2007). In addition, there were technical and legal challenges (including data ownership...etc).

The UK government considered itself as *not* being doing enough to maximise the use of its online services (Cabinet Office, 2000). Addressing the crucial role of the private and voluntary sectors in innovating service delivery, the government may have been insufficiently open to these sectors. There could also be an absence of the necessary incentives in institutional structures to drive service delivery forward.

In Finland (Information Society Programme, 2006; Teonsana Oy, 2008), there was still a continuation of fragmented activities creating inability to reform structures and operation. There was also a relative lack of skills and slowness in reacting to global changes. In general, there was a feeling of the need to do more to face the challenges of competition on the global level.

From the discussion above one can see that the blessing of e-government does not come without snags. The battle must be fought on a number of levels. Each level poses unique challenges. These levels can be generally divided into political, social, legal, organisational, economic and technical. The following sections discuss each of these dimensions in more details.

2.2.1 Political Challenges

Realisation of e-Government must first address political challenges. This is where the whole project starts. If political will and support do not exist, such a large-scale project will never see the light or will be patchy at best. e-Government programmes face many glitches on the road of implementation. Political support is vital at every step. Governments with rigorous e-government vision and enthusiasm (e.g. Canada, Singapore, USA) have excelled. The lack of political commitment can fail the project at the earliest stages.

However, political enthusiasm must be translated into seamless planning and dedication of all kinds of resources (monetary, skills, time, efforts, empowerment, training, education...etc). It is not enough to have political will and a strategic vision although these are the primary elements for success. Politicians' apathy to address fundamental changes or issues because of their lack of interest or inclined priorities can hinder proper e-government development. Similarly, conflicting political goals (e.g. transparency vs. privacy, participatory vs. representative democracy...etc.) are major obstacles. Likewise, conflicting interests between federal and local governments have their toll on prioritisation of e-government initiatives.

2.2.2 Social Challenges

Social adoption of e-government can be one of the characteristics of success of an e-government programme (Kumar et al, 2007; Becker et al, 2004). Each group of users has certain needs and requirements. It is necessary to understand the diversity of users' needs. The government must devise the tools and methodologies to measure users' satisfaction. A government should demonstrate to its citizens that their privacy is conserved. Laws must be modernised to assimilate the new advancements in ICT. Privacy laws should be secluded by the constitution. LDCs have fallen behind in this regard. Privacy and security must be a core component of e-Government implementation. They must not be added later on. They should be well thought out from the beginning. Furthermore, they must be reviewed constantly. Digitalised processes must incorporate security measures and be privacy-sensitive. If not taken into consideration, private information is at stake. Manipulation of voting results, for example, is possible in the absence of unblemished measures. This ushers disastrous consequences.

Hacker attacks must be taken extremely seriously. Dedicated secure intranets protected by multiple levels firewall security are normally used in e-government systems. The open Internet should never be used to carry out G2E or G2G transactions.

In addition to citizens' privacy and security, proper service continuity plans must be prepared and simulated. This guarantees continuous availability of services in severe social conditions.

With the advent of e-government, identity theft became even more catastrophic. Stolen credit card numbers is already a big issue in e-commerce with billions of dollars stolen each year. Nevertheless, the losses are mostly financial. In e-government, the term "Identity Theft" will be literally possible if no careful measures are applied especially at the level of authentication. Transactions carried out at a government's portal are completely different from that of a shopping website. They involve sensitive documents like passports, identity cards, birth certificates…etc. Some of the top sensitive processes (e.g. changing names) must be verified the traditional way.

Social challenges are different for developed and developing countries. People in developed countries are more familiar with technology compared to those of the developing countries. Leapfrogging to advanced technological solutions might cause a technological shock to many people in LDCs. If technology becomes readily available and yet the masses are incapable of using it then nothing really has been achieved. The whole project is considered a failure because it would fail to achieve its goal. An assessment of public readiness for e-government within a country must be made. This assessment should contrast the status quo and appropriateness of the technological infrastructure with current market offerings. Computer literacy surveys should be carried out to assess the severity of the digital divide and plan accordingly.

A very noticeable socio-technical concern is the digital divide. It exists in all societies but it is more severe between the north and the south on the global level. Differenced in access, skills, political participation and economic opportunities lead to *Virtual Inequality*

(Mossberger et al, 2003). The digital divide is multi-dimensional (Norris, 2001). It encompasses three aspects: global, social and democratic inequalities. Global divide refers to the gap to access the Internet between the industrialised and the developing countries. Social divide on the other hand, captures the gap between those who can afford access and those who cannot within a nation or country. Finally, democratic divide is about those who can and those who cannot engage in public life within the online community across nations or countries.

Compaine (2007) defines the digital divide as *"the perceived gap between those who have access to the latest information technologies and those who do not"*. He further illustrates through evidence that such divide exists along racial, ethnic, economic and education lines. While Hoffman & Novak (1998) demonstrate the impact of race on computer access and Internet use, other researchers (e.g. Attewell, 2001; Mossberger et al, 2003) believe that disparities in access are driven more by income, educational and age inequalities rather than by race.

The issue of whether the digital divide is closing or widening has been controversial. For example, Compaine (2007) argues that the gap between those who have and those who have-nots is closing. On the other hand, Van Dijk (2005), Mossberger et al (2003), Attewell (2001)...etc provide evidence that the gap is widening in most parts of the world.

Some researchers believe that relying heavily on technology will widen the gap. Whether or not the digital divide is a remnant of old inequalities is debatable. Yet the digital divide itself can aggravate the old social inequalities (Van Dijk, 2005). Thus, the mere presence of the Internet and the related online services does not solve the problem (Warschauwer, 2003). For example, the availability of older media such as television and radio was not proven to have bridged the information inequality.

Many researchers have suggested ways to overcome or at least mitigate the digital divide. Governments need to employ policy instruments to curb the problem. Principally, governments need to perceive the digital divide a comprehensive social problem and not just an individual misfortune (Van Dijk, 2005; Mossberger et al, 2003). In addition, it is particularly important to measure the digital divide in order to provide proper solutions depredating on the situation (Mossberger et al, 2003). Therefore, it is important to measure disparities in skills, economic opportunities and democratic inclusion across the three dimensions mentioned above. This helps the government focus its efforts and resources much better. Awareness programmes in local languages are necessary to motivate usage and access of the digital means (Best & Maclay, 2002). Van Dijk (2007) suggested that policies and measures should target four primary objectives: motivation, usage, skills building and infrastructure and resources provision. In many cases, governments who sought to provide people in LDCs with cheap computers to bring about social, economic and educational benefits have failed. Such initiatives as the $100 Laptop and others were severely lacking the appropriate infrastructure and economic conditions (Malakooty, 2007).

Another challenge is to provide access to *people with disabilities*. It is the government's responsibility to configure their online services in such a way that they are accessible by the blind, the deaf and people with other kinds of disabilities. In many cases, special hardware and software may have to be procured and made available.

Finally, as with all new inventions, e-government can be misused. Corrupt politicians in non-democratic societies can potentially use e-government in a bad way. All information including transactions is captured on government's servers. If not planned transparently, it can be possible, at least in theory, to find out to which party or candidate, a certain individual has given his or her vote. It can even be worse if the votes are manipulated electronically. This is a great threat to democracy. Therefore, legislations alone are not a deterrent. They must be backed by practical solutions for such problems.

2.2.3 Legal Challenges

Government processes follow delicate legal constraints. In fact, legal constraints come first in the planning of government processes. After all, government is supposed to enforce law and order. Failure to do so ushers corruption and even chaos. Corruption in a government has a bigger impact on the population than in a business. Governments - especially democratic ones- make sure that they abide by the law. Corruption and lack of transparency has severe political and social consequences. With this ugly formula, there is no way to address accountability. Furthermore, persecution and bias can become so widespread.

When developing technical solutions in the course of e-Government implementation, legal issues are often taken strictly into account. Despite the ability of governments to change the laws, they do not enjoy the same level of flexibility as businesses do. This is fundamentally because governments traditionally exercise control whereas businesses seek profit. In the process, a review of current laws and regulations can be modernised in light of the new advancements in operation and technology. Retarding laws can be examined for alteration or update to achieve more efficiency. Integration of legislations and regulations across agencies is as necessary for interoperability as technical standards and policies.

Full development of e-Justice faces a number of challenges. Given the nature of the Judicial system, makes it more difficult to effect new changes on laws and procedures. In addition, the complexity of the sector where there are different types of courts ranging from supreme court, electoral courts, small claim courts and many state courts, military courts... etc and the different ministries on the federal and local levels will impede integration (Thomas & Walport, 2008).

The Internet-related crime is another challenge that faces e-police. Internet has resulted in the appearance of the "cyber crime". Since the Internet spans across countries, an international cooperation is needed to counteract cyber crimes (Cuellar et al, 2001; O'Brien & Marakas, 2008). This has lead the police in many countries to fail to take appropriate actions. Therefore, cooperation between the police enforcement and the industry sector was inevitable in order to combat these types of crimes by increasing awareness among companies and citizens (EC, 2008).

One particular challenge is the fact that e-police cannot be accessed in emergencies. Many implementations reviewed reflect this limitation. For example, I have reviewed the Belgian initiative "Police-on-Web" (ePractice.eu, 2008b). The main page clearly states the site should only be used for non-urgent complaints or declarations.

Finally, governments should decree new laws and regulations. Legislations and regulations for such things as e-signatures, digital certificates, online trading, e-procurement…etc are becoming indispensable for the new era.

2.2.4   Organisational Challenges

With the distribution of power, different local strategies, cultures, structures, processes, and mindsets can develop in the different agencies. These differences pose organisational challenges that need to be dealt with for a seamless e-government implementation. They can be sources of incompatibilities during integration. Besides, identity management across all these agencies is demanding. Building trust among the different agencies with all these differences and convincing them to work together to offer shared services can sometimes be daunting. Resolving issues related to responsibilities and authority is equally cumbersome. Change management helps mitigate the failures in the individual agencies and across agencies that result from resistance to change. Finally, we have seen from the discussion of the case studies above that perception of the role of IT systems have to change in order to offer client-centric shared service delivery.

2.2.5   Economic Challenges

Government budget is finite. No matter how rich a country happens to be, financial resources are always limited. Governments are responsible for spending the 'tax-payers' money in the wisest possible way. Demonstrating the benefits of e-government for decision makers can be crucial to motivate them. Special attention must be taken in assessing how much funding is needed and how long a project will need for completion. Bottom-up cost estimation was followed in Germany to achieve more accurate assessments. Rigorous plans to draw investments have to be prepared. Public–private partnership (PPP) can probably relieve the government from many sources of cost. With special agreements, the private sector can provide public services under government surveillance and monitoring.

2.2.6   Technical Challenges

Technical hitches and glitches are countless. Building technical solutions is very much likely to bump into challenges, hindrances or even failures. Some governments choose to employ tested solutions but may discover later that they were ill suited for their needs. In some other cases technical problems might be so challenging that they halt the whole project's progress. Research and Development (R&D) is usually setup to work on such problems. Therefore, R&D must be an integral part of e-Government implementation.

The government should avoid being locked in to a certain technology provider. Most governments call for open source and open standards. For smoother implementation, governments can consider scalability and simplicity for system development.

A major technical challenge that faces e-government development is integration. This challenge is particularly high up when bridging disparate systems. Basically, there are three levels of interoperability: technical, semantic and organisational. The dissertation presents the federated model of e-government, which addresses this particular challenge.

Finally security and privacy will always be a concern when developing technical solutions. The government should make systems sufficiently secure to allow safe operation and transactions. In addition, the government should demonstrate to its constituents that their privacy receives high attention through laws and legislations. This is necessary for trust building. The higher the level of trust, the more the citizens and businesses are likely to utilise the services offered though e-government.

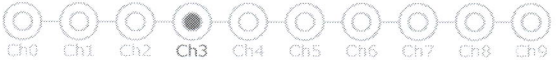
CHAPTER 3:   LITERATURE REVIEW

3.1   What is e-Government?

In today's world, Internet and the World Wide Web have become the norm of our daily lives. It is no longer acceptable to people of today to interact with government departments and services the way they used to fifteen or twenty years ago. We are living in a cyber world within the real one. In the cyber world, data are stored, transferred and processed electronically. Speed and accuracy are the standard. e-Business, e-learning, e-commerce, e-government …etc, are thriving and are at the tips of peoples' tongues.

During the last decade, most world governments have been intensively involved in establishing their own online electronic services and creating new ones to keep up with the de facto advancements in Information Technology (IT). Some governments were quite successful; others have bungled for plenty of reasons.

e-Government is not just a technical problem (Wimmer, 2002; Sharma & Gupta, 2003; Heeks, 2006a...etc). It is also a managerial one. In effect, the framework and the milieu where the technical solutions are introduced and implemented give rise to most disappointments and failures for e-government initiatives. But *what is exactly an e-government?*

According to Gartner, e-Government is '*the continuous optimisation of service delivery, constituency participation and governance by transforming internal and external relationships trough technology, the internet and new media*". From this elucidation, one could sniff out that it requires control and measurement because as the definition says it is a "*continuous optimisation* '; otherwise the whole venture will be prone to failures.

Other definitions from some high-ranking institutions include:

United Nations (UN)

> *E-government is defined as utilizing the Internet and the world-wide-web for delivering government information and services to citizens.*

World Bank

> *E-Government refers to the use by government agencies of information technologies (such as Wide Area Networks, the Internet, and mobile computing) that have the ability to transform relations with citizens, businesses, and other arms of government.*

Global Business Dialogue on Electronic Commerce

> *Electronic government refers to a situation in which administrative, legislative and judicial agencies (including both central and local*

---

governments) digitize their internal and external operations and utilize networked systems efficiently to realize better quality in the provision of public services.

Grant & Chau (2006) have reviewed the different definitions of e-government from the available literature. Based on their findings, they have suggested several characteristics that should be taken into consideration when defining e-government. The following table (Table 3) summarises these characteristics:

Characteristic	Meaning
Strong Service Delivery and Information Component	• Electronic services and information provision provides the chief mode of interaction • Transaction and feedback effected via services and information provision components
E-Government as a Transformational Endeavour	• Represents multiple levels of engagement • Cuts across functional and organisational boundaries • Digital age public sector reform • Demands new forms of interaction between citizens and government
Diverse Number of Solutions and Contexts of Application	• Country-specific • Implementation differs and patterns across contexts of application (political, OMB, 2001; OMB, social, economic) • Multiple patterns of development prevail
Electronic Government, Information, and IT	• IS/IT infrastructure essential in deploying an e-government programme • Leverages IS/IT capabilities to deliver systems and services • Overlapping functionality and knowledge • Added complexities from public sector context • IS/IT knowledge insufficient to explain and predict future trends
Integration, Service Sophistication, and Maturity	• Extends beyond service automation and efficiencies to integrated service offering • Integrative efforts and requirements increasing with added functionality and citizen-centric design • Increasing complexity and functionality requires commensurate development of understanding and knowledge of relationships among e-government and other functional areas and organisational concepts, including IS/IT contributions • Asymptoting towards higher levels of service interaction and maturity
International Phenomenon	• Diversity of e-government realisations • Crosses geographic boundaries • Adaptable to country-specific requirements • Growing number of implementations and developments worldwide

Table 3: Characteristics of different definitions of e-government from literature (adapted from Grant & Chau (2005)

These characteristic have led Grant and Chau (2006) to identifying the following functional applications of e-government:

- Interactive Services

- Service Automation & Information Provision

- Infrastructure consolidation & Standardisation

- CRM Development

- e-Democracy & e-Participation
- Collaboration & Partnership Programmes
- Marketing E-Government
- Global Business Development

However, the definitions of e-government in Grant and Chau (2006) do not represent the official governments' understanding of e-government. Since the domain of e-government is relatively new with no well-established literature yet as alluded to previously, I had to do my own assessment of *how* world governments perceive e-government. A primary concern was the lack of official documentation of this very important piece of information. Luckily, many of the national strategies I reviewed in my study have produced their own definition of e-government. The following table summarises the findings. It incorporates a list of each government's own definition of "e-government". The definitions are taken from the e-government strategies and other official documentations of the respective countries.

Country	Perception
Belgium	E-Government is a way to enhance the quality of public services offered to citizens and businesses by utilising the opportunities of modern technologies, the Internet, and the new modes of communications (ICT)
EU	E-Government is the use of Information & Communication Technologies (ICTs) to make public administrations more efficient and effective, promoting growth by cutting red tape. This is something which anyone who has spent hours waiting in line in a government building can appreciate.
France	The use of ICTs, and particularly the Internet, as a tool to achieve better government State must take a stance as guarantor (of individual freedoms, the authenticity and enforceability of dematerialised procedures and actions, the security of actions carried out by public servants, etc.) and the Government wishes to confirm this position clearly both in the formulation of the decisions taken and in their methods of application.
Germany	The IT-based overhaul of public administrations and expansion to incorporate IT-based communications
Korea	Transformation of functions and organisations of the government to improve the way the government works, and to innovate its business processes and to achieve clear and transparent administration
Singapore	Transformation of the concept of service delivery as a result of the convergence of Information Technology and Telecommunication. Infocomm technologies have the potential to transform the way government agencies work amongst themselves, the way governments deliver services to our customers, and the way governments engage the citizens and businesses. In conclusion, e-Government is about "government", not "e".
Egypt	The use of ICTs, and particularly the Internet, as a tool offer distinguished governmental services which results in better policies and services and better participation of the citizen
UK	E-Government, is not a conventional IT strategy which proposes technical solutions to a set of business needs. E-government sets a strategic direction for the way the public sector will transform itself by implementing business models which exploit the possibilities of new technology.
New Zealand	E-Government is an all-of-government approach to transforming how agencies use technology to deliver services, provide information, and interact with people, as they work to achieve the outcomes sought by government
The Netherlands	Utilisation of opportunities offered by Information and Communications Technology (ICT) to improve the standard of service to the business community and the general public.
Japan	Japan thinks of e-government as part an overall society development and that e-Government is about electronic administration and offering eServices

Country	Perception
Austria	The use of information and communication technologies in public administration combined with organisational change and new skills in order to improve public services and democratic processes and strengthen support to public policies. E-government is offered as an alternative, not as a replacement
India	e-government or electronic government refers to the use of ICTs by government agencies for any or all of the following reasons: • Exchange of information with citizens, businesses or other government departments • Speedier and more efficient delivery of public services • Improving internal efficiency • Reducing costs or increasing revenue • Re-structuring of administrative processes

Table 4: Governments' definitions and perceptions of "e-government" (Compiled from national e-government strategies)

Definitions in the table above can be simplified for the purposes of comparing the definitions against each other. Table 5 below emphasises the main theme of each of the above definitions:

Belgium:	**Use of ICT** to enhance **quality of services**
EU:	**Use of ICT** for **efficiency** and **growth** through cutting the red tape
France:	**Use of ICT** to achieve **better governance**
Germany:	**Use of ICT** for **better communication**
Korea:	**Organisational** and **functional transformation** to improve **operation, processes** and **transparency**
Singapore:	**Use of ICT** for **Service transformation** and **people engagement**
Egypt:	**USE of ICT** for **better services, policies** and **participation**
UK:	**Use of ICT** and **business models** to **transform government**
New Zealand:	**Use of ICT** to cause a **Holistic transformation** (service and information delivery and interaction with people)
The Netherlands:	**Use of ICT** to improve **service delivery**
Japan:	**Electronic administration** and **electronic service delivery**
Austria:	**Use of ICT** + **organisational change** + **new skills** =better **service delivery, democracy** and **policy support**
India:	**Use of ICT** for better **service delivery** and **efficiency**

Table 5: Figuration of governments' definitions of e-government

Most of the above definitions refer to e-government as the utilisation of *ICT* to *enhance* one or more of the following:

- Service delivery
- Internal efficiencies
- Participation
- Governance
- Democracy
- Policies support
- Growth

In some instances (particularly the UK and Austria, Korea and EU), the use of ICT is accompanied by one or more of the following:

- Organisational changes

- Functional changes

- New Skills

- New Business models

- Processes reengineering

A government willing to transform itself needs to become more flexible. New changes in operation and legislation must be accompanied by organisational changes. These changes will certainly concern many employees across the breadth and width of the government. They will no longer be able to continue to perform the daily tasks they used to. Many of these tasks will be either automated or even replaced partially or completely.

Without an impeccable change management, which involves educating, and training them, these employees will portray a strong resistance to these organisational and functional changes and may put the whole project in jeopardy. They need to acquire new skills, but *what exactly are these skills?* The British government has estimated that the following new skills are needed in order to develop e-government properly (Central IT Unit, 2000):

Leadership skills
- *Strategic understanding*
- *E-commerce principles*
- *Governing of programmes and projects*
- *Mainstreaming project management*
- *Wider markets opportunities*
- *Role of innovation*
- *Change management*

Business systems development skills
- *e-business process design*
- *Project and programme management*
- *Business case development*
- *Communications with stakeholders*
- *Risk management*
- *Benefits management*

Acquisition skills
- *Procurement*
- *Channel set-up and management*
- *Service and performance management*
- *Deal making and negotiation*
- *Relationship management/partnering*
- *Supply chain management*
- *Financial instruments*
- *Managing consultants*

End-user skills
- *Policy administrator information skills*
- *Policy administrator IT practical skills*
- *Operational systems data management skills*
- *Operational systems IT skills*

IT professionalism skills
- *Project/delivery management*
- *Programme management*
- *Business and systems analysis*
- *Consulting and customer relations*
- *Technology inc Internet*
- *Systems Integration*
- *Systems Operation*
- *Service management*

Specialist user skills
- *Communications*
- *Statistics*
- *Economics*
- *Research and analysis*
- *Operational research*
- *Finance and personnel*

Information professionalism skills
- *Information science*
- *Librarianship*
- *Systems management (inc web development)*
- *Records and archiving*

In fact, the above skills are required for developing any e-government initiative. Another point raised in the discussion of the definitions above is that for some governments new business models are needed as a premise for implementing e-government. According to the Danish strategy of e-government (Project e-Government, 2004),

> *"a business model describes what the public sector must deliver in a given business area, and how the public sector's organisation of processes should support these deliveries. A business model seeks to establish how these goals may be achieved on the basis of an analysis of business goals derived from service and efficiency requirements, It answers questions like:*

> - *What makes the area interesting, what is the "burning platform" for change? Which measurable goals can be drawn up for a new business model?*
> - *What is the vision/mission for the area?*
> - *Which business objectives describe the area, and how are these aims prioritised?*
> - *Which players perform the tasks, and how is this done today?*
> - *Where are the biggest problems, and how can they remedied? What projects should be set in motion?*

- *Which investment scenarios exist? What will be the consequences for ongoing and planned activities?*
- *What will be the organisational and structural consequences? Are there working procedures, which will have to be altered, eliminated or undertaken by others? Are there rules that should be simplified or abolished altogether?*
- *Which skills are necessary to support the business aims? Are they present, and if not; how can they be acquired?*
- *Does the new business model encompass new incentives towards citizens and/or businesses, or between public sector institutions?*
- *How can an IT architecture be designed that optimally supports the business goals? What are the critical architectural problems, when, for example, older systems are required to serve a new business model?*
- *What architecture and which solutions should be selected in order for new systems to optimally support the business development? Where can common public sector solutions and standards be utilised?*

3.2   Governments' Perception of "e-Government"

From Table 5 in the previous section, one can classify the perception of e-government as being any of the following:

- **Exploitation of ICT** and others to achieve better government
- **Government transformation** (organisational and functional)
- **Paradigm shift** (internal and external)

The following diagram (Figure 15) summarises the above findings in addition to those of the previous section. It reflects on governments' perception of what e-government is all about.

Figure 15: Governments' perception of "e-Government"

Figure 15 shows that e-government seeks to achieve certain output (mainly enhanced service deliver and internal efficiency) based on some input (mainly ICT). The perception of e-government according to Figure 15 may simply be the exploitation of ICT. This is for the majority of governments based on their definition of "e-government" in their e-government strategy. For some other governments (e.g. the UK) it means much more

---

than this. It means a whole strategic paradigm shift of how the government should be practicing governance.

3.3   e-Government's Relationship with Other Initiatives in the Digital Era

Technology attempts to abstract real-life objects for simpler and more accurate designs. Figure 16 abstracts the relation between society, businesses and government. The advent of the new ICT technologies including the Internet has opened new opportunities to do things in a completely new way in each of these sectors. The seamless connection and easy flow of information has allowed for more, efficiency, convenience and satisfaction. Many sectors wanted to take advantage of what ICT has to offer. Businesses were at the forefront of ICT utilisation. Buying and selling products and services across the internet was referred to as e-commerce (Laudon, 2006).

Undeniably, e-commerce plays an important role in development. It increases efficiency of the commercial transactions. The added convenience of conducting business online gives a strong boost for commercial activities of small and big business. Such an environment is obviously attractive to investors. The business sector as a result will grow. For this reason, e-Japan "the Japanese e-Government initiative" (IT Strategy Headquarters, 2001) has set e-commerce the next priority after the establishment of an ultrahigh-speed network infrastructure. According to e-Japan, e-Commerce is not just the digitisation of paper-based transactions but rather a creation of new modes of transactions that are never thought of before. In fact, e-government brings about efficiencies and cost reductions not only for internal government operation but also for businesses. They both become more responsive. In other words, the benefits are mutual.

As we have seen in the previous chapter, one major government responsibility is to try to reduce the digital divide. Reducing the digital divide means that knowledge becomes more and more ubiquitous which impacts all sectors in a society. Knowledge is very much needed for every society. LDCs in particular experience severe lack of professional knowledge and know-how. Governments should utilise ICT to promote good living of the society. A government should perceive itself as an enabler to other sectors like business. Public partnership with the private sector is vital. Each government must provide facilitation for building a solid ICT infrastructure. This should be part of their national strategy. Governments themselves should engage in digitizing their operation internally and externally as part of their e-government programme. This has great benefits. e-Government has a profound impact on e-commerce.. Although some people suggest that, a more ICT-centric government will increase the digital divide, yet a more efficient and responsive government will certainly furnish its citizens with convenience and satisfaction whether they receive services traditionally or electronically.

ICT can also be utilised to promote good living for the society as a whole. Many governments are taking big strides to turn their societies into "knowledge-based" societies (e.g. Japan, Finland, Korea, and Malaysia). These efforts are generally conducted under the umbrella of e-society. The Japanese and Finnish initiatives are the most elaborated. A knowledge-based society is very much likely to be more responsive and reactive to both e-commerce and e-government. Figure 16 below depicts the interaction between society government and business through e-society, e-government and e-business.

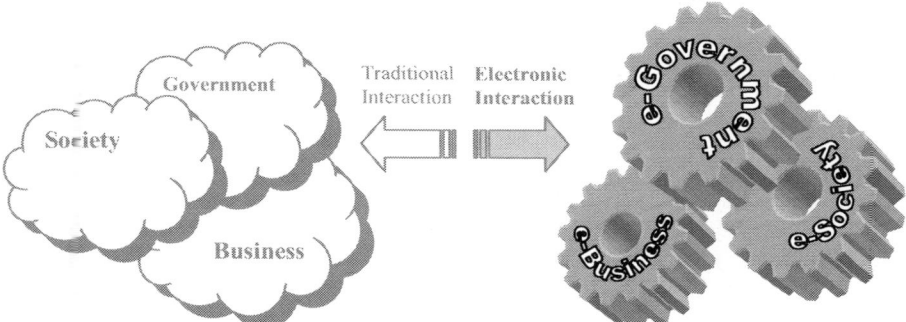

Figure 6: Abstraction of Society, government and business

From this discussion, we can see where e-government lies in relation to its environment. Understanding the interactions between e-government and the environment is vital for a comprehensive development of the nation.

3.4   e-Government Research Agenda

There has been a shift from e-government towards e-governance (Finger & Pécoud, 2003; Dawes, 2008). Some researchers call for a holistic approach to e-government rather than narrowly defined fields (Dawes, 2008). Dawes (2008) perceives e-government as a dynamic open socio-technical system. This system has six dimensions: purpose and role of government, societal trends; changing technologies; information management; human elements; and interaction and complexity. He presents this framework as a baseline for future research in e-government. Many other researchers (e.g. Evangelidis, 2004; Sorrentino & Virili, 2004) share the same vision of e-government as being a socio-technical system albeit with different perspectives.

An international study reported the results of a recent survey of future research themes in e-government. The survey recorded the responses of (383) expert in the field from (54) countries. This international survey has reviewed State-of-Play (Bicking et al, 2007) in which current topics of e-government are being researched. Regional workshops resulted in scenario building (Janssens et al, 2007) where technology was merely considered as just one factor out of many (social and environmental). Twenty-nine scenarios emerged. This was followed by gap analysis to discover missing scenarios (Pucihar et al, 2007).

The fourth step was the consolidation of these scenarios into themes (Wimmer et al, 2007). These themes were the result of extensive workshops held in the USA, Europe and Australia. These themes were then organised into (13) areas. In turn, these areas of research were categorised into four categories. To validate these themes, an international online survey was conducted. Figure 17 below depicts the results of this survey.

RELEVANCE	Confidence
• Assessing value of government investments in ICT • Mission-oriented goals and performance management	• Trust in e-government • Data privacy and personal identity • Information quality
INTEROPERABILITY	INNOVATION
• Semantic and cultural interoperability of public services • Cyber-infrastructures for e-government • Ontologies and intelligent information and knowledge management	• E-participation, citizen engagement and democratic processes • Governance of public-private-civic sector relationships • Government's role in virtual world • e-Government in the context of socio-demographic change

Figure 17: Future directions of e-government as reported by the international survey (Bicking et al, 2007)

Löfstedt (2005) mapped out current research in e-government on five axes (management and organisation; e-services; e-security; e-democracy; and interactions). She consulted the literature to figure out these axes. She stated that most of current research efforts are focused on the national level and that little attention has been give to local government level.

Lenk and Traunmüller (2000), on the other hand, have suggested four perspectives of e-government. These are citizen, processes, cooperation, and knowledge perspectives. Future research accordingly should be focus on them.

A call has been passed by some researchers and practitioners to bridge the gap between research and practice (e.g. Huberman, 1990; Mohrman et al, 2002; Peterson, 2005; Yin & Moore, 1985). This connection is particularly encouraged in e-government (Dawes & Helbig, 2007). Dawes & Helbig (2007) introduced a research-practice partnership framework. They argued that such partnership offers significant advantages as opposed to traditional contract research methods. From one hand, interests and needs of governments are the driver of these studies and findings enrich the academic knowledge in the other. Both researchers and practitioners will have a better understanding of the research question and context. Government employees are officially introduced to the aims of the study. Thus, not only will they be more responsive, but also their responses are more consistent to questionnaires for example. In addition, researchers have access to more information transparently, which helps them structure their studies better. In the end, this partnership enhances rigor and adds practical value.

Millard et al (2006) conducted a study aiming at identifying the research themes from a global perspective. They followed bottom-up and conceptually driven processes to evaluate recent research in e-government. They adopted multi-method quantitative and qualitative data collection and analysis. A wide range of instruments were used: desk research, content analysis of published research, EC supported research projects, questionnaires to 200 stakeholders involved in e-government research, a series of interviews, and active participation in a large number of workshops and conferences. This study has surfaced seventeen themes divided into three groups as followed:

Group 1

- Back-office, themes
- Interface between the back- and front-office themes
- Front-office, themes
- Cross-cutting themes

Group 2

Themes examining the impact and measurement of group 1 on the public sector and/or e-government users (citizens and businesses)

Group 3

Theme that examines the implication of group 2 impacts for wider public value and high level policy goals.

Figure 18 and Figure 19 show respectively the "as is" situation and the "to be" situation of e-government research.

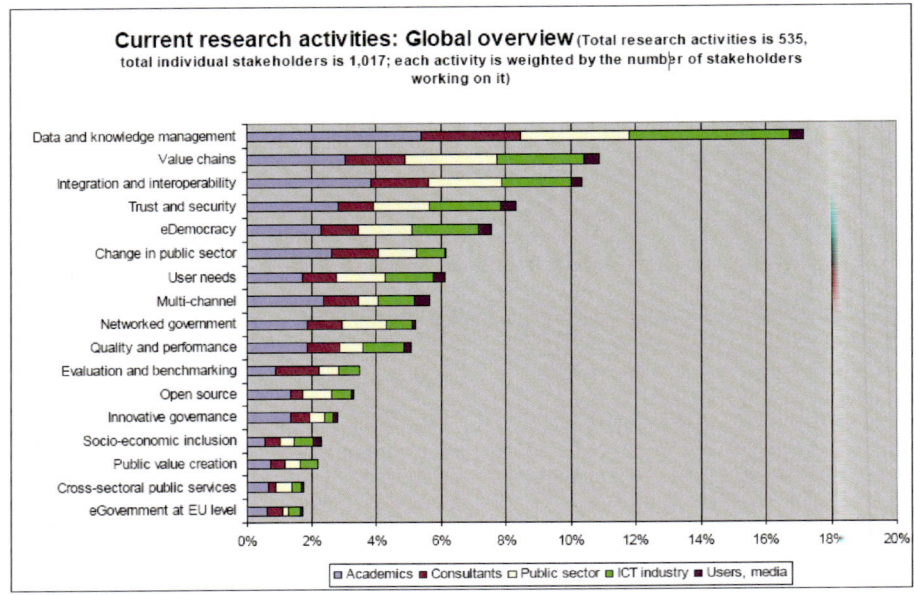

Source: Joint Research Center, European Commission (2006)

Figure 18: Current research activities: a global view

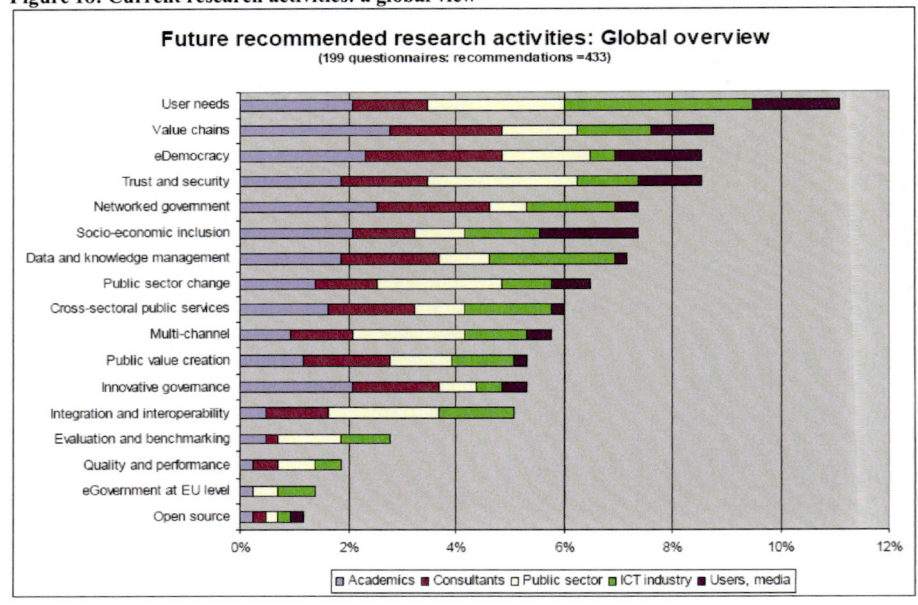

Figure 19: Recommended future research activities from a global perspective

Figure 20 shows the recommended future research themes. It manifests a clear shift from data and knowledge management, and integration and interoperability towards user needs, value chains for developing services and content, and networked multi-level services. There is a general shift from back office research into front office themes like service design, use and delivery.

Figure 20: Trends in e-government research

As Figure 20 shows, recent research of e-government focuses primarily on the technical and organisational aspects. This is in line with Grönlund's (2005) review of e-government research in which he mentioned that current research mostly focuses on informatisation and organisation.

In a bigger context, the eGovRTD2020 project was funded by the European Commission under the Sixth Framework Programme (FP6). While they are comparative in size and resources there are differences in the federations of both Unions. The EU is a federation of independent states where is the US is one country. This has its toll on funding, decision-making, priorities…etc. Table 6 shows the reflected differences between them in tackling e-government research.

e-Government research in the EU is controlled by a number of thematic priorities that meet goals related to economic and social development at the union's level. According to the Sixth Framework Programme (FP6), this control is aimed at strengthening the scientific and technological bases of industry and encouraging its international competitiveness while promoting research activities in support of other EU policies. Any research project must comply with these themes to get funding. Funding is provided mostly by the European Commission. Research focus is shifted towards ICT and its implementation at the national level. By contrast, e-government research in the USA is multidisciplinary which is not focused on ICT. This methodology fits better the concept of e-government. It requires theory-practice partnership. Government agencies cooperate with academicians to work on projects. Funding is not only provided by the federal government through the National Science Foundation (NSF) but also from other federal agencies and state governments as well as some industry support. There is a higher degree of freedom vis-à-vis the researcher to choose the methodologies than in the EU. While the US has a unified vision of e-government, the EU member states have different visions. This lack of focus can adversely affect the e-government research in the EU.

Comparison	EU	USA
Criterion of Major source of support	European Commission Community Research & Development Information Service (CORDIS)	The US National Science Foundation (NSF)
Project participants (related to major source of support)	Ministries, Universities, Research centres Private consulting companies Special agencies	University-based researchers Non-profit professional associations
Additional sources of support	Pure e-government research is mainly funded at the EU level National governments fund mainly implementation projects	Federal agencies
Conditions of success for projects	Meet programme thematic Priorities Different types of organisations International Consortium of EU Member States	Multidisciplinary approaches Partnerships with government agencies (theory and practice)
Funded projects range in size from	Total of € 3 625 million for funding Information Society Technologies over the duration of FP6	Less than € 14 840 to large projects that exceed € 1 400 000
Length of funding	A few months to up to 5 years	Typically 1 to 3 years
Characteristic of research agenda	Not directive, i.e. it does not specify questions, methods, or outcomes	Not directive, but there are specific principles to follow for the allocation of grants

Table 6: Comparison of e-government research: EU vs. US (Source: RTD2020 Project)

3.5 New Disciplines within e-Government

E-Government has witnessed major advancements during the last decade. New breakthroughs in wireless communications, satellite industry and Geographical Information Systems (GIS) have brought about new opportunities for innovative e-government applications. The applications were significant enough to become new disciplines within the context of e-government. Mobile Government (m-Government), Geographical (GIS/GPS) Government (g-Government), and Ubiquitous Government (u-Government) will be introduced immediately. Figure 21 shows these extensions of e-government. We shall explore the potential of these advanced and ubiquitous technologies. They have direct impact on the daily life of citizens/businesses, as they make possible exalted services on the go.

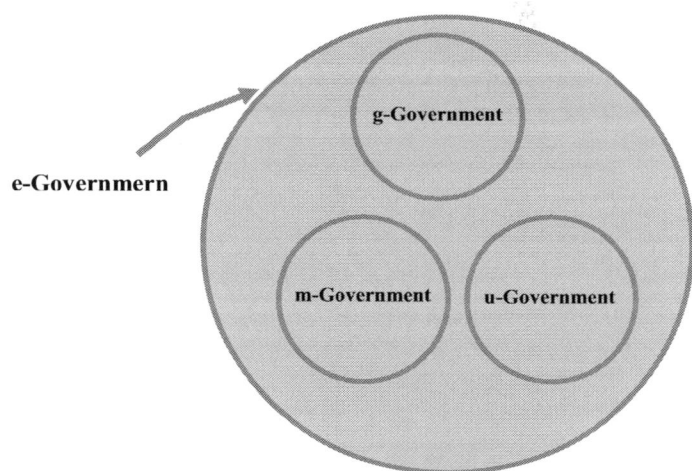

e-Governmern

Figure 2 : Extensions to e-government

3.5.1 M-Government

Cellular networks and handheld devices have achieved high penetration rates worldwide. Mobile operators have been investing in new markets worldwide. According to Gartner, revenue from mobile services will peak at almost $55 billion in 2008. GSM, GPRS and EDGE alone will account for $24.6 billion. In the Middle East and Africa, revenue from sales of mobile network infrastructure grows annually at a rate of 12% for 2005 to 2010, bringing the annual total to $8.5 billion. This constitutes a large portion of their economies. With the availability of such an advanced infrastructure, related services and economies will tag on. Installing and updating cellular networks is faster and easier than traditional landline networks. They can span large distances in remote areas.

Around 991 million mobile units were sold globally in 2006, a 21% increase over 2005. In the Eastern Europe, Middle East and Africa 52.4 million units were sold in the 4th quarter of 2006. This was 13% higher than that of 2005 of the same period. There is currently a high demand for refurbished mobile phones in emerging markets. By 2008, ultra-low-cost handsets will account for about half of all basic phones sold in regions with emerging economies.

Functionality of current mobile devices has been expanded. An MP3 player, a digital still and video camera, a GPS navigator, an FM radio, a TV and a computer processor can all be crammed into one palm-sized device today. Such devices are typically equipped with diverse communication channels. In addition to regular cellular communication, they can be hooked up with other devices through Bluetooth, WiFi, WiMAX, 3G, HSDPA, IR...etc. Adding their capacity to house software applications makes these devices superior pocket tools. They can access the Web in different ways and through any communication channel. They have their own operating systems. They can be used to do e-commerce easily. Such converged devices have been given different nomenclatures. Smartphones, PDA phones, PocketPCs, or recently Computer Phones (Cellular UMPCs).

The differences in naming conventions can be confusing but they are certainly powerful mobile gadgets. On the global level, Smartphone and PDA shipments grew ≈2.7% in 2006 compared with 2005 (Gartner Dataquest, 2007). Their sales are expected to continue to grow through 2010.

This remarkable penetration rate of handheld devices together with the expansion of wireless networks have ushered the beginning of Mobile Government (m-Government). Mobile Government (m-government)

> *strategy and its implementation by the government to provide information, deliver services, engage citizens and improve efficiency through mobile devices*

(Sang et al, 2006).

This makes it an extension of e-government to mobile platforms. In other words, it is about delivering government services and information through wireless communication networks to end users who use mobile media like mobile phones, smartphones, PDAs, Laptop computers, UMPCs...etc. This will practically allow access to government services anytime and anywhere. m-Government leverages the convenience and flexibility to a new level. It furnishes citizens and businesses with a fairly practical way to access government services. In addition, the government would be able to reach out to a larger number of people through mobile devices. An example is sending short text messages (SMS) to the masses in case of Tsunami or similar threats. Despite the obvious advantages, there are some issues to be addressed. Among these is security Mobile devices can be easily stolen or tapped into especially with the abundance of insecure WiFi networks. This puts private information at risk. Another challenge for the m-government is to customise their services for mobile phones' tiny screens, limited memory, small keypads and underpowered processing capabilities. This means re-designing their portals or employ rendering techniques. Finally, digital divide is again an issue here. Such advanced services will only be available for those who can afford and are competent to use the technology.

3.5.2 G-Government

With GIS, soliciting data becomes more efficient. Governments can design their websites to allow for spatial data search. An example is searching for the nearest governmental services. The way search results are displayed makes it quite convenient for citizens, businesses and other government units. Instead of having the results displayed in tabular form, they are layered on maps (mashups). A citizen for instance can easily look for garbage collection facilities in his/her area. Businesses can discover the local industrial or commercial sites, real estate agents, transportations facilities...etc. On the government-to-government level, g-Government can lead to more efficient cross-agency cooperation. Examples include cross-jurisdiction activities like fire-fighting, crime investigation...etc. All of these services are offered 24/7. As these services are carried out via Web applications, governments can save costs by reducing the number of staff in call centres. The city of Sacramento in the United States reported to have saved an estimate of $1.8

million per year by offering GIS-enabled Web services. Up to 500 people were serviced by their website daily.

Combining g-Government with m-Government can bring e-Government to a whole new level. About 12.7 million in-vehicle GPS navigation systems were made in 2005, and the figure for 2010 will be 30 million (Gartner Dataquest, 2006). By the end of 2010, almost 40% of handsets will support GPS. As in the case of location-based commercial services, governments can offer their services for individuals, businesses and government employees on the move. A citizen for example, can be automatically put through to the closest police station to his current location to report a crime or an accident. In the United States, mobile phone manufacturers will be obliged to include a GPS module for a better 911 service (emergency service).

3.5.3　U-Government

The rapid advances in wireless communications, feature-rich and Omni-connected handheld devices, nanotechnology, interoperability…etc will all bring us closer and closer to Ubiquitous Government (u-Government). u-Government is the ultimate form of e-Government. In u-government, services offered are really accessible anywhere anytime in plenty of ways never thought before. Ubiquitous government stems from Ubiquitous Computing. The latter describes a paradigm shift where many computational devices and systems collaborate to carry out ordinary tasks without overall systems knowledge of such tasks. Smart devices (e.g. smartphones, smart cards…etc) are becoming widely used. Nanotechnology might bring us cheaper, intelligent and ever connected inventions that make government service delivery unrestricted by time, place or means. This is sometimes referred to as *Ambient Intelligence*. With time, technologies become more advanced, efficient, faster, smarter and cheaper. Transmission of information would be seamless, timely and cheap and in various forms never thought possible.

Today, there are some examples of u-Government. Many governments have developed digital Identity cards and passports. They make it more efficient and convenient to update personal information. Digital passports are anticipated to increase efficiency and security at airports. Many cell phones are capable of accessing websites anywhere anytime using broadband wireless connections. This, though, is only the beginning to offering full u-Government services.

Such technologies bring new challenges. Privacy is traditionally an issue here. There should be rigorous regulations to make sure of safe usage of such advanced technologies. Security also becomes more challenging. These two challenges have been and will always be persistent with any new technology.

CHAPTER 4:   STRUCTURING THE STRATEGIC FRAMEWORK OF E-GOVERNMENT

4.1   Introduction

As mentioned in Chapter 0, a core objective of this dissertation was to originate a generic and best practice strategic framework of e-government. In the process and in line with the research methodology described in Section 1.6 a detailed investigation of the nature of the e-government strategy was needed. The reasoning behind this step is because the e-government strategy is a logical placeholder of such a strategic framework.

In this chapter, different versions of e-government strategies from different countries are put under scrutiny. The ambition is to try to conceptualise the components of these strategies in an effort to produce a structured generic strategy. The need to study numerous cases was basically to allow unbiased and representative concepts to emerge.

Before embarking on the analysis one needs to know what an e-government strategy really means. An e-Government strategy is a 'plan for e-government systems and their supporting infrastructure which maximises the ability of management to achieve organisational objectives' (Heeks, 2006). This plan addresses strategic directions, objectives, components, principles and implementation guidelines. It sets forth the right policies, standards and frameworks from the start. The strategy is where e-government initiatives start officially. It assures that e-government planning and implementation is always on the right track. It provides a common framework for transformation across the public sector in a country. Because of this, a high-level strategy is a top-down initiative. It is prepared by the federal government and is propagated to local authorities. Local authorities might have their own strategies but they must comply with the principles, objectives, standards, and policies of the federal government's strategy. Without this, it would be difficult to have a connected interoperable government. In a similar sense and at a higher level, EU member states take into consideration the EU's i2010 strategy (Commission of the European Communities, 2006) when devising their new national strategies of e-government.

Because of its utmost importance, the e-government strategy should be clearly understandable without any ambiguity. It was mentioned earlier (Section 1.1) that (21) countries in addition to that of the EU have been considered for analysis. Table 7 below shows that these countries together with their e-Gov Readiness Index.

Rank	Country	e-Gov Readiness Index
1	EU	NA
2	Denmark	0.91
4	US	0.86
5	Netherlands	0.86
6	Korea	0.83
7	Canada	0.82
8	Australia	0.81
9	France	0.80

Rank	Country	e-Gov Readiness Index
10	UK	0.79
11	Japan	0.77
15	Finland	0.75
16	Austria	0.74
18	New Zealand	0.74
22	Germany	0.71
23	Singapore	0.70
24	Belgium	0.68
34	Malaysia	0.61
45	Brazil	0.57
50	Jordan	0.55
54	India	0.48
79	Egypt	0.48
	Palestine	NA

Table 7: e-Government readiness index for sample countries (Source: UN E-Government Survey, 2008)

As mentioned earlier, e-government strategy is referred to repeatedly. Although, the context in most strategies was clear and easy to understand, it is always better to have a visual representation of the strategy. Having a quick look at a diagram can reveal instantly the relationships among basic elements of the e-government strategy. This chapter introduces the concept of a Strategic Framework of e-Government. This diagrammatical representation is to be considered the most abstract visualisation of an e-Government strategy.

The ultimate purpose of this chapter is to originate a generic abstraction of a best-practice strategic framework of e-government.

4.2   Best-Practice Based Methodology

The following subsections describe briefly the basic principles adopted to draw out a generic strategic framework for e-government development.

This study takes into consideration diverse nations in many respects. Trying to build a generalised framework was first thought to be challenging. It seemed that one-size would not fit all. There are many differences across the different governments. Countries differ in one or more of the following characteristics:

- Political system
- Legal system
- Economic situation
- Available technological infrastructure
- Internet and PC penetration
- Availability of skills and human resources
- Literacy rate

- Computer literacy
- Level of poverty
- Leadership
- Ethnic diversities in terms of norms, languages…etc
- Training capacity
- etc…

Other contextual differences include nationally specific benchmarks such as e-readiness, legal restrictions and the existence (or otherwise) of a nationwide e-government strategy (Becker et al, 2004). With these differences, it is impossible to copy a good example of implementation from one country for another. Yet despite all the differences, there are commonalities too. Governments face similar challenges in planning and implementing e-government. Infrastructure solutions are very much the same. In general, e-government principles are similar. In fact, I found much in common.

During this study, the focus was on commonalities and best practice. I immediately came into the dilemma of *what best practice was. What counts as best practice?* In contrast, *what would be a bad practice?* Some researchers have provided general guidelines for best practice in e-government. For example, Undheim (2008) mentions the steps necessary to create a best practice solution as follows:

- *Start with a visionary idea*
- *Design your solution as simply as possible*
- *Gain top leadership buy-in*
- *Adjust to circumstances*
- *Track stakeholder needs*
- *Understand the policy context*
- *Gain momentum*
- *Withstand criticism*
- *Ensure sustainability*

Literature related to "best practice" in the context of e-government stresses standards, which form criteria that are necessary to identify best practice cases (Kaylora et al, 2001). My attempts to find a universally adopted definition of best practice in e-government yielded no results. I reviewed a number of definitions of best practice in different contexts outside e-government. In the end, I settled on a workable definition that fits my research intention. Most of the definitions mention the fact that best practice is the best or optimal solution for a problem. BusinessDictionary.com, for example, defines "best practice" as '*Methods and techniques that have consistently shown results superior than [sic] those achieved with other means, and which are used as benchmarks to strive for. There is, however, no practice that is best for everyone or in every situation, and no best practice remains best for very long as people keep on finding better ways of doing things'.* Since there is no established literature yet in e-government, best practice has to be based on experience from practice. As mentioned earlier, best practice yields from the critical learning of successful case studies (Sharma, 2007). I needed to find a workable definition of best practice in the context of the current research problem. I define best practice as a "concept, technique, methodology, or solution that has proven to be reliable in achieving a desired objective, through experience, research and best available knowledge or technology *and that has proven to be effective through replication*". Through this definition, I am not trying to suggest a new perception of what best practice is, as a concept. As mentioned above, there is still no agreed upon definition of best practice among practitioners of e-government. This subject is still largely debatable. I am only setting a criterion for *myself* to abide by throughout my research. With this definition in mind, my interest has been on common visions, strategic objectives, priorities, components and applications. Commonality can generally indicate repetitive successes. This is particularly true if witnessed for lengthy periods. Indeed, I have consulted data that date back to the late nineties of the past century to future plans that target the late twenties of the current century. I considered replication across this period. Constructs with more replication records were given higher attention. Throughout this chapter, evidence was sorted based on this criterion.

4.3   Structure and Contents of e-Government Strategies

Analysing e-government strategies was the first step in structuring the framework. This analysis has set a rough delimiter of framework. It was necessary at this point to have a general idea about the components of the framework. This analysis has actually given me the opportunity to form an impression on the common elements in the national strategies.

In the research methodology (Section 1.6), I mentioned that it was necessary for me to start with no preconceptions. This, I believe, was necessary for letting data collection guide me through the process of compiling evidence. Preconceptions may have limited my focus. I wanted to start from the most abstract form of the e-government strategies. Thus, I began by studying the major components of the e-government strategies. These components have provided me with an initial guidance of what to look for during my quest. It was only logical to start from here.

Furthermore, I suggested earlier that the proposed framework should reflect the e-government strategy it stems from. The proposed framework should somehow summarise the e-government strategy. I studied the most prominent contents of numerous e-government strategies of my sample countries. It turned out that the following components were present and accentuated in all strategies:

- Vision
- Strategic Objectives
- Guiding Principles
- Focus Areas
- Building Blocks of e-Government (mostly infrastructural)

- Major Initiatives
- Implementation Plan

I found that the common practice to write the strategy was as Figure 22 suggests (see below). The figure shows both the common contents as well as the sequence of appearance in the national e-government strategy. Everything starts from a strategic vision. The vision is translated into strategic objectives. e-Government principles are devised to reflect on the whole of the e-government. They show the government emphasis and provide general guidance on the implementation of e-government. It is then essential to specify the preponderant areas of action (focus areas). The chosen areas are the ones to consider in satisfying the strategic objectives.

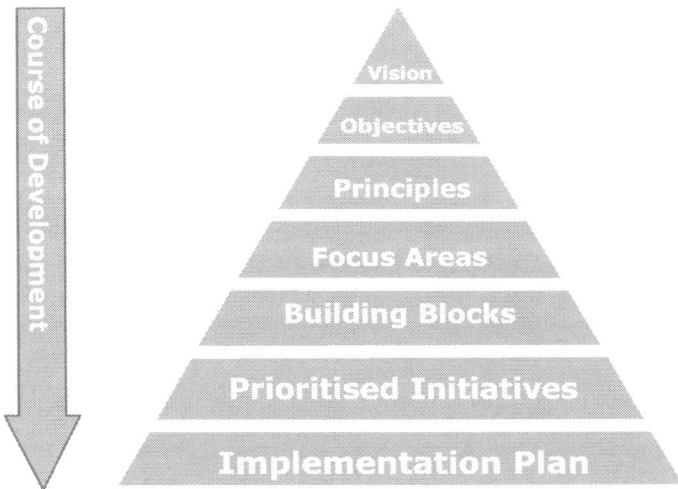

Figure 22: e-Government strategy development based on my finings

Having highlighted the focus areas, the e-government strategy describes the basic building block to construct e-government. Building blocks were found to be very similar across countries. These components are mostly infrastructure-related. I will show these common basic building blocks in a later section. All reviewed e-government strategies highlight the basic building blocks. The strategies then present the prioritised projects (initiatives) and the basis on which they were prioritised. Finally, either a full or a brief implementation plan is presented at the end of the e-government strategy.

Some researchers have strategic planning of e-government. Heeks (2006a), for example, had proposed the following steps for e-government strategic planning:

- Create the steering committee and relevant structures
- Assess current information systems and get guidance from the organisational strategy
- Set e-government objectives

- Set e-government principles
- Determine organisational and technical structures
- Disseminate the e-government plan
- Manage, evolve and review e-government strategy

Figure 22 above gives us already some hints about the layering of the proposed framework. Since the above components were found to be present in all strategies then they should be basic constructs of the sought framework.

I studied each of these components in detail in an effort to structure the strategic framework of e-government. I was particularly motivated to know the basic constructs of each of these components as well as the relationship among them. It must be said, at this point, that my research was not limited to the components found in Figure 22 above. These components, however, have provided a starting point of what to look for next. The following sections present the findings.

4.4 Vision

All e-government strategies reviewed have included a vision right at the beginning. Vision and political will are absolutely indispensable to launch the e-government project. Vision is necessary, as it will be always the motto of the e-government committee, which is normally responsible for planning and spearheading implementation (Heeks, 2006a). It will always be referred to during implementation later on. The vision is important because it reflects the policy of the government. From this vision, the committee is held accountable to lay out the mission statement, which is normally more expressive than the vision and contains further details. During analysis, there were only two instances (UK and Jordan) where mission statement was mentioned together with the vision in the e-government strategy. In most cases, only the vision was included. Therefore, I did not study the mission statement as I was only seeking commonalities and repetitions.

An e-government vision is driven by the unique setting of social, political, and economic factors and requirements (Park, 2008). One should note that the vision might change for the same country upon the introduction of a new e-government strategy. The following table lists all available visions of e-government of the countries reviewed:

Country	Vision
Australia	*Responsive Government: A New Service Agenda*
Belgium	improve public service delivery for citizens and businesses by making it faster, more convenient, less constraining and more open through:
	• to organise service delivery around the users' needs (intention-based services), regardless of the actual administrative structure;
	• to eEnable full administrative procedures, including if several administrations are involved;
	• for the administration to avoid requesting several times the same data from users ('unique data collection' principle);
	• to simplify administrative procedures and reduce the burden of

Country	Vision
	bureaucracy for citizens and businesses; and • to share and exchange data and information across government.
Denmark	Digitalisation must contribute to the creation of an efficient and coherent public sector with a high quality of service, with citizens and businesses in the centre.
Austria	Citizens and businesses of today expect from the public administration a rapid execution of their official procedures. In the era of e-mail, Internet and digital signatures; long waiting times, costly paperwork, and bureaucratic authorities will be a thing of the past. The e-Government strategy ensures efficient implementation of electronic government services.
Japan	**2001** World's most advanced UT nation within (5) years **2006** To make Japan the most advanced ICT nation with the world's highest infrastructure, ability to use ICT, and technical environment.
Finland	Good Life In Information Society: The reformation of Finland into an internationally attractive, human-centric and competitive knowledge and service society.
France	Rendering the public administration more efficient, closer, more transparent, and more accessible by the masses
Canada	To make the Canadian government the world's most connected to its citizens, with Canadians able to access all government information and services on-line at the time and place of their choosing.
Germany	A connected E-Government through: • Reliable and secure communication • Individual identification • Full accessibility to government services
Korea	The ways of working in the public sector will be improved and its processes reformed... we need to achieve smooth changes in the function and organisation of the government ... as well as actively promote transparency in public administration through e-governance.
Palestine	Ensuring every community or a village has easy access to information and no one is excluded from accessing information.
Singapore	**2006-2015** To delight customers and connect citizens through infocomm **2000-2006** To be a leading e-Government to better serve the nation in the digital economy
Jordan	e-Government in Jordan is dedicated to delivering services to people across society, irrespective of location, economic status, education or ICT ability. With its commitment to a customer-centric approach, e-Government will transform government and contribute to the Kingdom's economic and social development.

Country	Vision
Egypt	By the year 2007 the Egyptian government will be able to deliver high quality government services to the public where they are and in the format that suits them.
UK	**2001** A modernised, efficient government, alive to the latest developments in e-business, and meeting the needs of citizens and businesses **2000** Electronic commerce and the Internet are transforming economies and societies across the world. The Government is committed to giving every individual, business and community in the UK the opportunity to participate fully in the benefits flowing from these changes – in short, to getting the UK online.
India	Make all Government services accessible to the common man in his locality, through common service delivery outlets and ensure efficiency, transparency & reliability of such services at affordable costs to realise the basic needs of the common man
New Zealand	New Zealand will be a world leader in using information and technology to realise its economic, social, environmental, and cultural goals, to the benefit of all its people.
USA	The President's vision for reforming government emphasises that "government needs to reform its operations—how it goes about its business and how it treats the people it serves."
Malaysia	**Eighth Malaysian Plan** to ensure an efficient and effective government administrative machinery for continued economic development. **Ninth Malaysian Plan** to improve the public service delivery system to further enhance the quality of life of Malaysians, reduce the cost of doing business, encourage private investment and positively influence investor perceptions about Malaysia as a preferred destination for trade and investment.
The Netherlands	A Different Government
EU	e-Government as an enabler for better government, an intrinsic political objective encompassing a series of democratic, economic, social, environment and governance objectives. These objectives can be articulated around two major axes: pursuing cost-effectiveness and efficiency, and the creation of public value.

Table 8: List of e-government visions per country as taken from the national e-government strategies

As we will see later, each e-government vision mentioned above conveys a message. For a better coherence and presentation of findings, I will go through the analysis of these main message or "ultimate goals" in a later section. For the moment, I will introduce the common strategic objectives of e-government. This is the subject of the following section.

4.5   Strategic Objectives

Each government sought to achieve certain objectives from the development of its e-government programme. These objectives are extremely important. They justify the huge resources often dedicated to e-government initiatives.

As indicated earlier, unlike businesses, governments must make sure that money is spent extremely wisely. In a democratic system, the government needs to get approval of the national parliament for the budget. Government's decisions and priorities affect a wider population than businesses. It is the whole people of the country including businesses. In addition, e-government is considered just a tiny part of the overall government spending. In other words, the government has many pressing issues to account for (e.g. health, education, development...etc). Therefore, governments seek to balance spending carefully. Businesses on the other hand, generally invest in IT for competitive reasons. They have more tendencies to take on risk.

People responsible for the inception and the development of e-government must work hard to convince decision makers about the necessity for e-government. Without support from the side of leadership, e-government is doomed for failure as many studies suggested (e.g. OECD, 2003; United Nations, 2003; BBeGov, 2007). Later in the chapter (Section 4.5.2), I will present my findings about the drivers that can *push* decision makers to develop e-government.

Justification is absolutely critical for the success of e-government initiatives. The strategic objectives of e-government play an important role in this justification. Thus, a greater care must be put to devise them in a coherent manner. They should provide a complete package for what the government is going to achieve. They must not be totally unrelated or completely disconnected. For a viable implementation, the government must provide some sort of a universal focus that reflects a general direction behind the initiative. For example, some strategic objectives are focussed around providing more citizen satisfaction (e.g. Singapore). Others seek to achieve more citizen participation or democracy (e.g. Korea, Egypt...etc.) and so on. This focus might come in response to existing deficiencies or shortcomings.

Because of the absolute importance of the strategic objectives behind e-government implementation, they are highlighted in the national e-government strategy. They are referred to them as *strategic* here because they stem from the e-government strategy. They also show a long term and high impact intent. They guide an important investment. It is a transparency imperative for these objectives to be always a coherent part of any e-government initiative.

Normally, strategic objectives constitute an elaboration on the vision. Vision and objectives appear at the very first part of any e-government strategy. This predilection reflects their importance. This antecedent positioning immediately shows the directions the government is taking.

I analysed and compared the strategic objectives found in each of the e-government strategies of the countries listed above. I also studied the perception of each of the individual governments of what e-government meant to them. Finally, I examined the drivers behind the development of e-government.

My interim purpose was to introduce a model that helps classify the strategic objectives of e-government based on the maturity level of these objectives. I based my finding on real-life cases of the (21) countries in addition to the EU. I also consulted the relevant work of other researchers.

To see exactly what strategic objectives the majority of governments sought after, I studied all e-government strategies of this group of countries. The following radar plot (Figure 23) shows strategic objectives based on their popularity among countries.

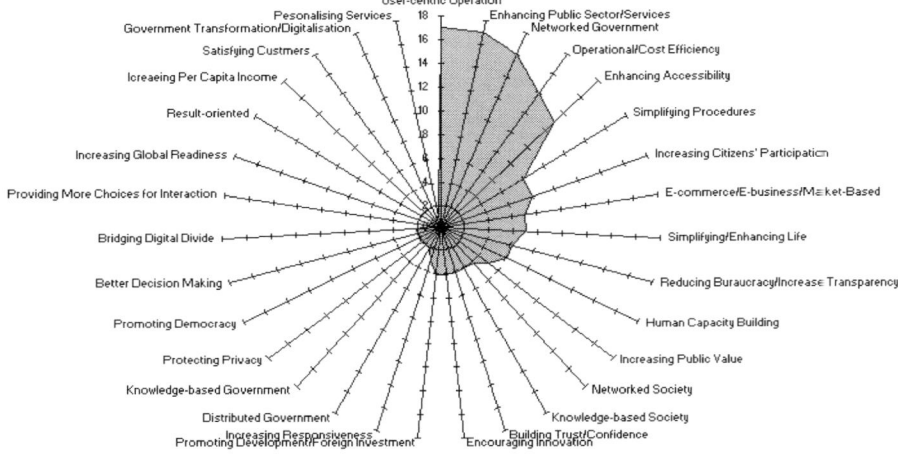

Figure 23: Popularity of strategic objectives as evidenced in the e-government strategies of the sample countries

I started by tabulating each country's vision and strategic objectives. I studied each objective to find out what meanings it held. I panned through the mesh of objectives looking for similarities. Afterwards, I was able to introduce a list of objectives that can fairly precisely represent each of the original individual objectives. This way, 31 representative strategic objectives were identified. The objectives were then examined collectively for commonality.

For each common objective, I counted the number of countries that adopt a similar one. For instance user-centric operation/orientation scored (17). In other words, out of (22) countries (17) of them that declared in their e-government strategy that user centricity is a strategic objective. The same methodology was applied to each common objective

This study revealed that the number one strategic objective sought after by governments was "user-orientation". In fact, some studies have accentuated the importance of client-centricity (e.g. CcGov, 2007, Dutil et al, 2007, ECOTEC, 2008). Practically, to achieve cost-effective, relevant and personalised services e-government needs to be client-centric as revealed by a new study (CceGov, 2007). The study also concluded that customer focus and addressing customers' changing needs enhances democratic dialog.

Enhancement of public sector capacity for better services, networked government, efficiency, simpler procedures, boast citizen's participation, business facilitation, simplification of life, increasing public value and human capacity building are respectively among the most prominent strategic objectives that appeared in the e-government strategies.

These objectives have affected the design of the strategic framework of e-government. For example, the developed framework has manifested client-centric design. This was because client centricity was found to be the number one strategic objective. The other strategic objectives have at times forced a particular layout of some relevant parts of the framework.

4.5.1 The Ultimate Goal of e-Government

There is a main message behind each e-government strategy. This is due the fact that the vision manifests a strong focus on one or two ultimate goal(s) (Park, 2008). In practice, such message is more pronounced in the vision. I looked at these messages in a similar way to that I followed upon analysing the strategic objectives (see previous section for details). The messages from the e-government strategies can be considered as "ultimate goals". They form the aspiration of the government from the development of e-government. Researching them was absolutely necessary to classify the strategic objectives presented in the previous section.

Ultimate Goal	Adopting Countries
Leadership in e-Government	Austria, Singapore, Canada, Korea, New Zealand, Japan, Australia, UK, Finland
Government Transformation	UK, New Zealand, Malaysia, Jordan
Better services, better government	Australia, Belgium
Promotion of Citizenship/Democracy	Brazil, Korea
Move government online	Canada, UK
Modern and efficient administration	Austria, USA
Better connection with citizens	Canada, Singapore
Public administration	France
Delight/Satisfy citizens	Singapore
E-Business/E-Commerce - based	UK
Responsive government	Australia
Whole of government	Canada
Smarter and faster services at a reduced cost	Canada
Virtual public administration	Belgium
Digitalisation of public sector	Denmark
Achieve economic and social progress	Egypt
Create knowledge-emergent society	Japan
Cooperative administration structure	Austria

Ultimate Goal	Adopting Countries
Ubiquitous government	Japan
More efficient federal administration	Germany
Many agencies but one government	Singapore
Making government work for its customers	New Zealand
Different government	Netherlands
Achieve attractive, humane and competitive service society	Finland
A tool for better government in its broadest sense.	EU

Table 9: Ultimate goals of e-government

Table 9 above lists the ultimate goals behind each government behind their e-government initiative. The table is sorted based on popularity of the ultimate goals of e-government in a descending order. One can immediately see that seeking leadership in e-government, promotion of citizenship/democracy, better services, better government, moving government online, and government transformation are common ultimate goals for e-government. Seeking leadership may explain partially why governments dedicate ample resources to implement e-government projects. Other countries simply do not want to be left behind what has become a global phenomenon.

Millard & Horlings (2008) suggested that governments seek to achieve three objectives: efficiency; effectiveness; and governance. In achieving *efficiency,* the constituent is seen as a tax-payer. When the government seeks to achieve *effectiveness,* the constituent is considered a consumer. In seeking *governance,* the relationship with the constituent is citizenship. Looking back at Table 9 above reveals that ultimate goals of e-government can generally be categorised into four domains:

1. Achieving internal efficiencies: These set of goals are intended to streamline internal operation. Processes are reengineered and resources (time, effort, cost...etc.) are rationalised to offer more for less. Here, we have efficient utilisation of ICT to reduce time, cost, and duplicated efforts. Figure 23 shows a number of strategic objectives that belong to this domain:

- Networked government
- Simplifying procedure
- Distributed government
- Better decision making
- Result-oriented government
- Government transformation/digitalisation

2. Achieving external efficiencies: This domain incorporates all the objectives that increase efficiencies in the relationship between government on the one hand and constituents and society on the other. These objectives are actually focused around providing a better experience and increasing value for citizens. The top strategic goal in

Figure 23 "user-centricity" lies in this category. Other strategic objectives that belong to this category are:

- Enhancing public services
- Enhancing Accessibility
- E-commerce/e-business/market based government
- Simplifying/enhancing life
- Increasing public value
- Building trust/confidence
- Increasing responsiveness
- Encouraging innovation
- Providing more choices for interaction
- Satisfying customers
- Personalising services

We witnessed a shift towards this domain. In contrast, older versions of e-government strategies concentrated on the first domain.

3. Better Governance: This domain comprises the kinds of strategic objectives that bring about social benefits. Examples of such objectives from Figure 23 are:

- Increasing citizens' participation
- Reducing bureaucracy/increasing transparency
- Building human capacity
- Creating a networked society
- Creating a knowledge-based society
- Promoting development/attract foreign investment
- Protecting privacy
- Promoting democracy
- Bridging the digital divide
- Increasing global readiness
- Increasing the per capita income

Thus, rather than concentrating on the constituent, these strategic objectives target the society at large.

4. Leadership aspirations: For some government it seems that self-esteem and aspirations for global leadership can justify huge investments in some domain. Some governments

find early successes in their e-government programme a driving force to pioneer. Such successes are a source of national pride (Bhatnagar, 2004). These aspirations are not just applicable to developed countries. Some countries have developed pioneering project unsurpassed by many developed countries (e.g. Brazil's voting system, Malaysian myKad multipurpose card...etc.). Seeking pride has been witnessed throughout history. A prominent example is President Kennedy's promise to Americans to be the first to go to the moon. In my research, I found a number of governments that chose to excel in e-government. The following is a list of countries with leadership messages from their e-government strategies:

- Austria: Achieving a place in the EU's top 5 e-government leaders

- Singapore: To be #1 in the world in harnessing infocomm to add value to the economy and society

- Canada: To make the Canadian government the world's most connected to its citizens

- Korea: To become the world's best open e-government

- New Zealand: New Zealand will be a world leader in using information and technology to realise its economic, social, environmental, and cultural goals, to the benefit of all its people

- Japan: To become the world's most advanced IT nation within five years

- Australia: To maintain Australia's position as a leading information economy

- United Kingdom: To insure the UK's place as a leader in the global economy

- Finland: Finland claims to have been recognised as the global leader in the use of public electronic services

The above goals of leadership have appeared as part of the vision of the cited countries.

Figure 24 below shows my maturity model of strategic objectives. It summarises the above domains of strategic e-government objectives. In addition, it shows the maturity level of these domains. This model can be used to classify maturity of strategic objectives of any e-government programme. For example, if the declared strategic objectives of e-government are oriented towards operational proficiency then the government exhibits maturity Level 1. If the objectives are mostly about adding value to clients then it exhibits maturity Level 2 and so on.

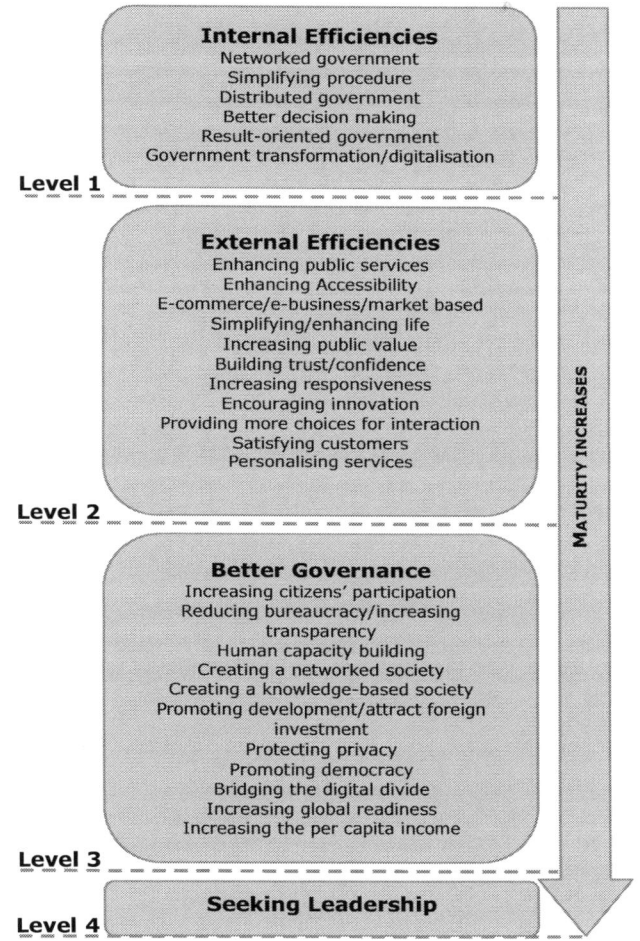

Figure 24: Maturity model of strategic objectives of e-government

Level 1 – Internal Efficiencies

A government exhibits Level 1 maturity if its set of objectives seeks to induce internal efficiencies. This includes the rationalisation of resources. With these kinds of objectives, the beneficiary will be the government itself. Constituents, however, will avail indirectly from the resulting efficiencies. Brazil, for example, is among the rationalising countries in our study.

The Level 1 is a minimal requirement towards e-government. The logical earliest step in achieving constituents' efficiencies and benefits is to achieve internal efficiencies first. This primary level with its associated internal efficiencies is important as it captures the e-government's pay off at an early stage. This encourages decision makers to move on to higher levels of strategic objectives.

Level 2 – External Efficiencies

At this level, all objectives converge into constituent satisfaction. This level directs much of the attention to clients' needs. The government strives to offer higher quality services. One aim is also to provide constituents with enhanced accessibility, more responsiveness, and a sense of trust and security. Some governments had even taken constituent satisfaction into a whole new level. One particular example in our study is the case of Singapore. Their vision was not only to satisfy constituents but also to "delight" them. The USA and the UK have devised e-government strategies that had met better the needs of businesses. This is aimed at making these countries more attractive for investments by being more business-aware.

The Canadian government has drawn its vision of being the most connected government to its citizens. It has moved more than (135) of the most commonly used services online. The government of Japan has moved from e-government to u-government. It's framework of *ubiquitous government* promises access anywhere, anytime, by anyone through anything. This vision seems to be more attainable than ever before because of the immerging advancements in mobile technologies (see Section 3.5.1 for more details). Among the Japanese targets for the year 2010, is to have 100% of the population connected to the Internet through high speed or ultra high-speed connections. It also sets the target to have 80% of the population to feel comfortable with ICT. Finland has started the "Ubiquitous Information Society Programme" to support the development of Finland's information society. All these efforts furnish the users with elevated levels of convenience.

Level 3 – Better Governance

This maturity level of strategic objectives addresses the needs of the society as a whole. The aim is to achieve better governance. As mentioned earlier, there is a shift from e-government towards e-governance. This probably makes more sense. The basic role of a government is to practise governance. In fact, some countries (e.g. India) use "e-Governance" instead of e-government to refer to their programme. e-Governance entails a wider prospect than e-government. It also stresses the socio-technical nature of the relationship between government and society in the information age. Riley (2003) defines governance as 'a way of describing the links between government and its broader environment - political, social and administrative'. In contrast, e-government is mostly concerned with utilising ICT tools to provide government services. While citizens are thought of as recipients of government services in e-government, they are seen as participants in e-governance.

Promoting democracy, accountability, transparency, inclusion and protecting privacy are just some examples of strategic objectives in this context. Some governments (e.g. Egypt and India) believe that e-government which leads to reform is a tool for development.

This is quite comprehensible. More transparency, democracy, participation, bridging digital divide...etc. will assure more foreign investment.

Level 4 – Seeking Leadership

This is naturally the most challenging and ambitious objective of e-government. This goal is prestigious. Huge resources have to be implemented and managed carefully to achieve this goal. Canada, Singapore, Korea, Japan and others have always competed for leadership in e-government.

It is worthy to note that leadership is not something that is leapfrogged at. It requires an incremental approach in which targets are scheduled over a reasonable period of time. After completion of a certain phase, another-with new targets- may begin.

Normally, a government that chooses to develop its e-government programme progresses across the four maturity levels. My model is structured in a logically sequential manner. I recommend that governments know their status quo maturity level and then devise their strategic objectives to pursue to the next level. Skipping through maturity levels is not advised. For example, it is not wise to think about adding value to citizens (Level 2) before achieving internal efficiencies (Level 1) first.

The setting of objectives of e-government depends on a number of factors. Perceived importance of e-government is a key delimiter of the target level. The more the government values its e-government endeavour, the higher the maturity of their objective will be. A government seeking leadership in e-government certainly considers it to be of great importance.

Elevated government aspirations can drive up strategic objectives to a higher level. It can be the case where e-government is considered important but there is a lack of aspiration towards realising it. This aspiration can sometimes stem from competition especially at the level of local governments (Coursey & Killingsworth, 2005). For this aspiration to become a reality there needs to be basically two premises: political support and resources. Many studies have confirmed the need for political support (e.g. Signore et al, 2005). It counts as a key factor for success of e-government initiatives. This is particularly true as such initiatives usually span a lengthy period of time in which ruling parties can change. On the other hand, any such large-scale project as e-government must be carefully, considered. Needed resources have to be accounted for meticulously. These resources range from financial, managerial skills, technical skills...and so on.

Another important factor for devising objectives for e-government strategies is current achievements and status quo. This is why there are different versions of e-government strategies. The objectives change as progress is made. New goals build on the achieved ones.

Finally, government's view of its constituents decides the objectives of e-government. As discussed above, there are three perceptions of the relationship with constituents. Each of these perceptions entails a dedicated level of service from the government side. For example, if a government perceives it constituents as consumers then it must set them at the centre of its operation. It must also offer higher quality services. The government must as well employ modern CRM tools. It should customise, personalise and bundle services. Constituent satisfaction here is very important.

Other factors affecting the maturity level of the strategic objectives are the drivers that push e-government development including the internal deficiencies. We wil explore these drivers in the next subsection.

4.5.2   Drivers of e-Government

In the preceding section, we have seen that governments have certain objectives for implementing e-government. These objectives describe *what* they are after. This section tries to answer the question of *why* governments choose to go after these objectives in the first place. In other words, *what drives governments to initiate e-government programmes?*

Drivers behind e-government start from the context. Context is the environment in which the government operates. Flak et al (2005) for example conducted a survey in an effort to highlight the drivers for implementing e-government initiatives in some municipalities in Norway. They found two distinct motivations for developing e-government in the Norwegian context. The first one was improving efficiency and the other included the expansion of services.

Gáspár (2008) summarised the potential drivers for e-government across EU member states to be public administration reform, globalisation challenges, the increased availability and efficient use of resources from local -especially structural- funds and the changing user's need and demand. On the other hand, Centeno et al (2004) assessed that the drivers could be clustered around the modernisation and reforms in the public administration and the development of the Information Society. Finally, Tassabehji & Elliman (2006) related the main drivers of e-government to exemplar of the private sector's implementation and use of e-commerce and e-business.

In this study, basic drivers are drawn right from the findings evidenced in the e-government strategies and other government documentations. I basically used the declared drivers rather than guessing them. I claim that this methodology is a better way to go. In addition, this study has an international dimension since the cases reviewed are not limited to one particular country or region. This makes the findings more generic in comparison to previous studies.

Politicians have the power to overrule the decisions made by the administration (Flak et al, 2005). Thus, they can influence e-government adoption. The legitimate question is, *why don't they drive e-government development promptly?* Flak et al (2005) answered this question with another, *why should they?* They argued that politicians need to be *pushed* in order to drive e-government development. Therefore, they constitute an intermediate driver for e-government. The real driver would be the constituents. In a democratic society, constituents' calls for development of e-government can be heard but they need to be educated first about the benefits that come out from e-government implementation (BBeGov, 2007). This is actually a typical role of civic organisations. In many instances, governments themselves have carried out this role in order to urge citizens to use their online services. A prominent example is the Canadian awareness programme (Government On-Line, 2004; Government On-Line, 2005; Government On-Line, 2006; Public Works and Government Services Canada, 2005) which was set for this kind of purpose. One of the reasons for Canada's continued success in e-government was its leadership in customer service and its efforts to inform and educate citizens about its offerings (Cole & Vivienne, 2005). Other examples from Belgium include the Agence Wallonne des Télécommunications (AWT). The AWT produced short films to raise awareness about ICT and digital public services. These films were broadcast in the local TV stations.

Some governments have taken several actions to promote more usage of their services. An example is the UK's strategy (Cabinet Office, 2000), which addressed issues of accessibility. They have assigned services to channels that encourage their use. This means that the UK's government prioritises its channels, unlike Belgium, for instance, which treats all channels equally and considers the online channel to be just a new channel (Accenture, 2003). The government knows that many people either do not have access to technologies or do not possess the skills to use them. The government understands that some people are not aware of the existence of some of its services or do not know how to access them. Some others who know about these services might find them very difficult to use. Therefore, the government of the UK has pledged to make its service easy to find and use. They also created trusted services to encourage using online services.

I compared the drivers of e-government that were declared in the strategies or other government documentations. I tabulated the results based on replication as usual. Then I clustered them into appropriate domains.

Table 10 lists the countries bound by common drivers of e-government. The table is sorted based on the citation of drivers in the national e-government strategies from the most common to the least common.

Driver of e-Government	Declaring Countries
New user expectations	France, USA, Finland, Korea, The Netherlands, , Jordan, Brazil, Austria, New Zealand, EU, Australia, Denmark, Canada, Singapore
Limited resources/ performance issues	France, USA, Finland, Korea, The Netherlands, Brazil, New Zealand, Denmark, Singapore
Need for economic growth/development	India, Finland, Malaysia, Egypt, Brazil, Belgium, Denmark
Accessibility issues	UK, Japan, Egypt, Brazil, Austria, New Zealand
Urge for quality/convenient services	USA, Korea, Jordan, Austria, New Zealand, Belgium
Global competition	Finland, Malaysia, Egypt, Demark, Singapore
Need for cost reduction	USA, Austria, New Zealand
Transparency	India, Austria, Denmark
New opportunities of ICT	UK, The Netherlands, Denmark
Leadership aspirations	UK, Korea, Australia

Driver of e-Government	Declaring Countries
Social issues (poverty, aging population...etc)	Japan, Brazil, Denmark
Enable teamwork among employees	USA, EU, New Zealand
Demand for more democracy	India, Egypt
Urge for good governance	India, EU
Modernisation of the state	France, UK
Digital divide/inclusion	Malaysia, Brazil
Fulfilment of policies or directives	New Zealand, Malaysia
Urge to enhance quality of life	Malaysia
Added value	USA
Urge to achieve more equality	Brazil
Online access becoming cannel of choice	Singapore

Table 10: Drivers of e-government (Compiled from national e-government strategies)

Table 11 below shows the same drivers of Table 10 above but this time clustered into the domains that stimulate each driver. All drivers fit nicely in one or more of these domains.

Domain	Driver
Social	New user expectations
Economic/organisational	Limited resources/ performance issues
Economic	Need for economic growth/development
Organisational	Accessibility issues
Social	Urge for quality/convenient services
Economic	Global competition
Economic	Need for cost reduction
Social	Transparency
Economic/organisational	New opportunities of ICT
Political	Leadership aspirations
Social	Social issues (poverty, aging population...etc)
Organisational	Enable teamwork among employees
Social	Demand for more democracy
Social/organisational	Urge for good governance
Organisational	Modernisation of the state
Social	Digital divide/inclusion
Political	Fulfilment of policies or directives
Social/political	Urge to enhance quality of life
Economic	Added value
Social	Urge to achieve more equality
Social	Online access becoming channel of choice

Table 11: Domains of e-government drivers

The findings in Table 11 above reveal that drivers of e-government can be generally classified into organisational, social, economic and political. These domains show where the pressure for e-government development comes from. A government would find itself under pressure to develop e-government when it is under organisational, social, economic or political pressures. The lesser these pressures are the more reluctant the government would be to embrace e-government. Yet as mentioned before, there must be enough resources and political leadership to implement e-government.

The differential amount of pressure from each domain can affect the direction of implementation of e-government. For example, more social pressure can result in more client-centric operation while more organisational pressure may result in more internal efficiencies.

The following diagram depicts the pressure domains that push the government to develop e-government.

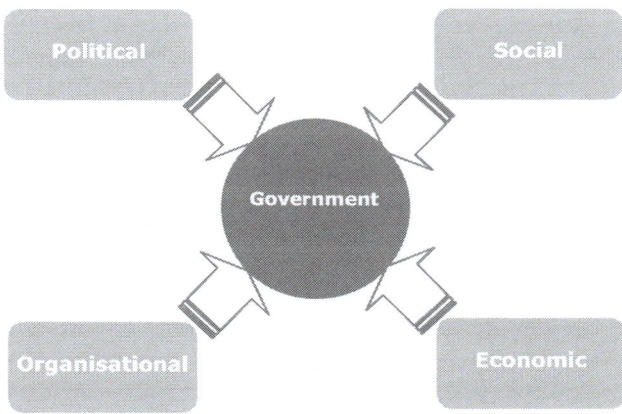

Figure 25: The government is under political, organisational, social and economic pressures that push for development of e-government

The strongest domain of pressure according to Table 11 above is the social domain. It houses the strongest driver of e-government. This piece of finding supports my previous argument about the necessity to educate the society of the benefits associated with e-government. To push the government to develop e-government initiatives, there has to be a strong social pressure.

4.6 Guiding Principles - Trends

In this study, the common guiding principles of e-government were explored. These principles define the general themes of e-government projects. I managed to capture the trend in these guiding principles from a global perspective. These trends show *where* world governments are heading in their e-government programmes. The findings tell us about *what qualities* can be expected from e-government in the coming few years. Common trends in e-government strategies play an important role in designing the strategic framework. They delimit the possible constraints. In addition, they provide focus and control over design and implementation.

I collected the guiding principles through delving into the strategies at hand of the (21) countries. Table 12 below lists these principles sorted in terms of adoption by the different countries in a descending order.

Guiding Principle	Adopting Countries
Efficiency/capacity	India, Jordan, The Netherlands, Egypt, Australia, New Zealand, Finland, Austria
Participatory government/Considerate administration	Korea, The Netherlands, Egypt, Brazil, New Zealand, UK, Finland, Austria, Denmark
Universal Accessibility	India, Japan, Brazil, UK, Austria, New Zealand
User-oriented	Japan, Egypt, Australia, UK, Denmark
Convenience/Satisfaction	India, The Netherlands, New Zealand, Austria
Interoperability	Finland, France, Denmark, Austria
Knowledge-based government	Korea, Finland, Brazil, UK, Belgium, Germany
Transparency	India, The Netherlands, Austria
Reliability	India, The Netherlands, Jordan
Trust	Finland, The Netherlands, New Zealand
Networked/integrated government	Korea, Brazil, New Zealand
Quality	The Netherlands, Jordan, Denmark
Open source/standards	Brazil, France, Austria
Redundancy Control	Jordan, The Netherlands
Flexibility	Jordan, Denmark
User-friendliness	Japan, Austria
Orchestration/standardisation	Palestine, Brazil
Rationalisation of resources	Brazil, Denmark
Shared services	Australia, Denmark, New Zealand, Korea
Mutualism & Cooperation	France, Austria
Privacy	The Netherlands, Austria
Channel of choice	The Netherlands
Personalisation	The Netherlands
Accountability	The Netherlands
Balanced Social development	Finland
One-stop-shop	India, Korea, Austria
Responsiveness	The Netherlands
Build on previous accomplishments	Palestine
Resources are essential	Palestine
Value for money	Australia
Security	Jordan
Scalability	Jordan
Manageability	Jordan
Continuity	Jordan
Creativity	Japan
In conjunction with the European Commission	France
Shared software development	France
Competitiveness	Finland
Sustainability	Austria
One-time information entry	Australia

Guiding Principle	Adopting Countries
No wrong door	New Zealand, Australia
Service packaging	New Zealand
Attract employees	New Zealand

Table 12: Common guiding principles of e-government by country (Developed from national e-government strategies)

The most recurring guiding principle is to always consider efficiency while devising solutions. As we have seen previously, this is a requirement for Level 1 maturity "Internal Efficiencies". As you may recall, this was a basic objective of e-government. This part of our study has just shown that the basic guiding principle is set to guide that basic objective.

The second guiding principle is to design e-government in such away to allow greater participation from the side of the constituents. Clearly, this is a social requirement that also calls for the government to become more responsive and considerate vis-à-vis its constituents. A responsive government is aimed at offering better services. To achieve this, it needs to achieve internal efficiency.

The third most important guiding principle for e-government is to achieve universal access. Throughout my quest, I have seen that accessibility is given amplified attention. This is actually, quite logical. There is no point in designing state-of-the-art services (online or otherwise) at high costs without them being accessible to everyone. Services should be accessible to all regardless of their financial abilities, language, geographical location...etc.

User-centricity was found earlier to be the most sought after strategic objective. Appearing here at position number four, has surprised me. This means that governments do not give it the necessary attention. I expected a guiding principle that enforces client centricity on the design of every system or service. This is especially because I have used the same group of countries to generate both the common guiding principles and the common strategic objectives. Still though, it is in an advanced position among the guiding principles.

User-orientation, universal accessibility, considerate administration, convenience and satisfaction, transparency, reliability, trust, quality, user-friendliness, shared services and privacy are all controls aimed at service delivery domain of e-government. On the other hand, public efficiency and capacity, redundancy control, flexibility and rationalisation of resources target internal efficiencies. Finally, interoperability, knowledge-based government, networked/integrated government, open-source/standards, orchestration/standardisation and mutualism and cooperation are controls to insure a connected government.

The fact that each government in this study has created a portal means that they made a great step forward towards one-stop shop. Still, not all of them have explicitly adopted the one-stop service delivery model. The portal per se does not guarantee a one-stop-shop. It requires designing all the e-government systems to be *connected* in such a way that no matter where the user starts his or her quest, he or she will always be pointed to the right service. This clearly needs collaboration among all government units. Therefore, this guiding principle should receive more attention for a better user experience.

The proposed framework should incorporate the major guiding principles listed above. They affect the general layout of the framework, particularly the relationships among the components.

The common guiding principles of Table 12 above were found to target three areas of e-government: service delivery, internal efficiencies and government networking. These three areas were found to capture most attention of world governments, as we shall see in the next section.

4.7   Focus Areas of e-Government

In the previous section, it was mentioned that there are three main areas targeted basically by certain guiding principles. These areas were service delivery, internal efficiencies and government networking. I wanted to certify this fact by measuring another construct.

To do this, I looked at the key areas targeted by e-government strategies. I relied on the focus areas declared by governments themselves in the strategies. Similar to the methodologies described before, I tabulated the findings in Table 13 below. The left column lists the common focus areas sorted by replicaility. The right column squeezes in for each focus area the countries as articulated in their national e-government strategies as well as probably other official documents. Again, the findings are sorted top-down based on the number of countries.

Focus Area	Countries
Service Delivery	India, Egypt, Canada, Germany, Austria, The Netherlands, Denmark
Internal Efficiency	India, Brazil, UK, The Netherlands, Denmark, Egypt
Government Networking	Germany, Finland, Denmark, Austria, Brazil, Belgium
Infrastructure Development	Palestine, India, Japan, Egypt, Brazil, Germany
Accessibility/Interface	India, Canada, UK, Finland
Administrative Reform	Korea, Finland, The Netherlands, Belgium
Knowledge/Information Management	Korea, India, Brazil, Germany
Legislation/Regulations	Palestine, India, Egypt, UK
HR Development	Palestine, India, Japan
e-Commerce/business adaptation	Japan, Egypt, UK
Cooperation	Austria, Belgium
PPP	Austria, UK
Simplifying procedures	The Netherlands, Belgium
Engagement of people	Austria, Finland
Building confidence/trust in online services	Canada
Standardisation	Germany

Table 13: Focus areas of e-government (developed from national e-government strategies)

From Table 13 above, one can see that the number one focus area is service delivery. We have seen a similar aspiration during analysis perception of e-government in Section 3.2. This piece of finding shows that the majority of governments pay the greatest attention to service delivery, which was found to be a main aim of e-government in the alluded section. A government service can be either informational, interactive or transactional (United Nations, 2001). Governments seek better service delivery. Nevertheless, *what does better service delivery mean? What governments need to do in order to achieve better services?*

France has explicitly stated in its strategy (ADAE, 2004) that better services are attained when they posses certain characteristics. First, they should be user-centric. The service should be designed from the user's perspective. Services should *not* be designed per government's satisfaction and agenda but rather according to user's satisfaction and related needs. Secondly, the services must be personalised. Just like medical subscriptions, government services should be customised based on the profile of each user. Personalisation should not compromise accessibility. Services must be accessible to all. This includes people with disabilities, foreigners...etc. Better services correspond to usability and simplicity. For example, users should not be bothered by having to enter the same information repeatedly for the different forms. This goes hand-in-hand with process re-engineering efforts ad adaptation of laws. No complexities must be sustained by the users. These complexities must be transferred to the back office. Finally, the complexities should not affect government's performance. The government should be responsive according to user's expectations. All of these contribute to better service delivery in France's view.

I have mentioned above that complexities must be moved to the back office in order to achieve better services. Of course, front office and back office should be well integrated. Yet this should not mean mixing up all the efforts between the two. It is necessary to achieve a clear understanding of the functions and capacities of each of them. Focus areas of Table 13 can be split between the two major domains. Table 14 below clusters the focus areas into two domains: front office and back office.

Front Office	Back Office
Service Delivery	Collaboration/Coordination/Integration/Cooperation
Accessibility	Infrastructure
Building Trust	Operational Efficiency
PPP	Administrative Reform
Building Trust	HR Development
e-Inclusion	Knowledge/Information Management
	Common Standards
	Regulations
	e-Commerce Adaptation

Table 14: Focus areas split into back office and front office domains

However, intensities of efforts in these focus areas are not equal. The list in Table 13 is sorted according to the intensity of work from top to bottom. The number of countries indicates the intensity of work carried out in the respective area. The table reflects the priorities of action for governments. The top four focus areas of e-government now are Service delivery, internal efficiency, government networking and infrastructure development. Yet work on infrastructure will not continue to be a major action area of e-government for two reasons:

- Government investments in infrastructure are not as eager as that of business
- This domain is absolutely important at the starting phase of e-government. Yet many governments have already achieved mature IT infrastructures.

This leaves us with three major areas of action: Service delivery, internal efficiency and government networking.

Figure 26 shows the major action areas of e-government. As the figure indicates, these three areas have mutual interactions and effects (The Danish government, Local Government Denmark (LGDK) and Danish Regions, 2007). For example, internal efficiency caused by the simplification of procedures ad regulations will result in more convenient and efficient service delivery. Likewise, a networked government will offer shared services and will stimulate efficient operation.

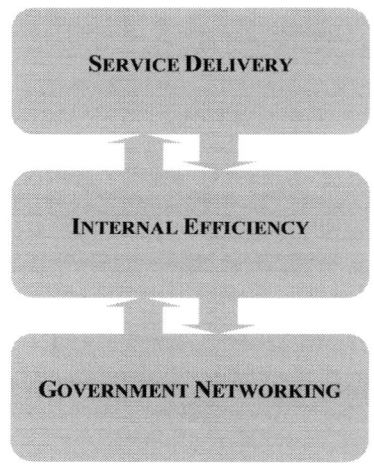

Figure 26: Major focus areas of e-government

Front office is basically concerned with service delivery. Back office, in contrast, has to do with the introduction of internal efficiencies and internal government networking. These two domains have been identified clearly in my strategic framework of e-government. It is worth mentioning at this point that governments' efforts are disproportionally focused between these two domains. For example, while Belgium, Austria and France focus more on back office systems, other countries like Canada and the UK focus their efforts on service delivery. The objective of the latter countries was obvious in their strategies. They declared that they seek to move most of their services on line during a set time frame. This reflects partly the prioritisation of channels. Belgium, for example, treats all the channels equally as mentioned before. Concentrating on back office would serve not only online users but also traditional users who use other channels such as in-person, post, telephone…etc. The philosophy of countries who concentrate more on front office is that the online channel has readily become the channel of choice for the conveniences it introduces.

In the previous section, I presented my findings regarding the common guiding principles of e-government. This section has channeled in evidence for clustering focus areas down to three. Guiding principles and focus areas are found to be connected. This is due to the fact that guiding principles are designed to control planning and implementation in a certain area. Thus, everything is connected in the findings. Throughout this study, I always sought to find the connection within the findings. For example, I have classified the guiding principles based on the three focus areas described previously. Figure 27 below attaches a number of guiding principles for each of focus area. I must say that not all the guiding principles identified in the previous section are limited to these three focus areas but most of them are.

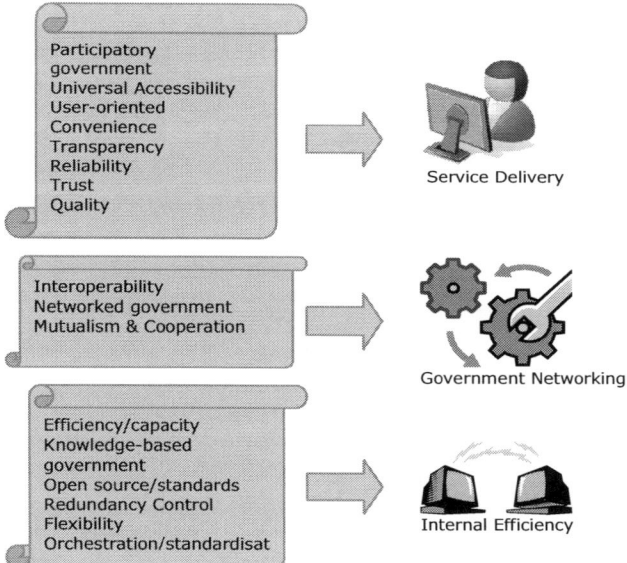

Figure 27: Guiding principles for each focus area of e-government

Figure 27 above gives us a very important insight about what the major focus areas of e-government are and what the guiding principles are, from a best practice perspective. This is particularly beneficial for countries where e-government is not developed yet. It readily gives those hints on where to start and what principles to adopt. The figure also gives insights to all governments -regardless of their maturity in e-government- about what other governments are doing and in what spirits.

4.8   Building Blocks of e-Government

A similar approach was followed in order to discern the common basic building blocks of e-government. Not all governments have explicitly stated the building blocks in their strategies. For such cases in particular, I had to look at the major projects carried out during implementation of e-government. This allowed me to figure out the basic blocks implicitly.

Through comparative analysis, it was possible to structure a list of common elements that serve as strategic building blocks.

The following table (Table 15) classifies the basic strategic blocks of e-government into three categories: technical, organisational, and functional:

Technical Components	Portals Intra-governmental Secure Network Databases / Authentic sources E-Identification Interoperability tools and framework Knowledge Management infrastructure Form Server E-Procurement infrastructure E-Payment Systems E-Archiving Channel Integration Platform …
Organisational Components	Organisational Framework Legal Framework Technical Framework Implementation Framework Security Framework …
Policies & Standards Guidelines	Interoperability Standards Reusability Legal Standards E-Signature Legislation Semantic Interoperability …

Table 15: Basic components of e-government

Technical Components -Infrastructure

Technical components were found to be given greater importance in the studied e-government strategies. This prioritisation is natural since they form the underlying technical infrastructure that enables building service on top. Without these components, e-government will simply fail to function.

Portals

The national government portal provides the one-stop shop for online services. Presumably, all government services whether local or federal are accessible from the portal. Normally the government portal displays links to content drawn from local sources. Management of just these links can prove to be challenging. I could identify a number of best practice cases in government portal management. The case below is one of the most interesting ones.

Case Study 1 – Swiss Portal Management

Switzerland is a federation of originally 26 states. These states are currently referred to as cantons. Each canton has its own constitution, parliament, government and courts (ICA Country Report 2004). Cantons, in turn, are divided into communes. Currently, there are 2842 communes country-wide in total. Some one-fifth of these communes have even a parliament of their own (ICA Country Report 2004).

Regulation and standards are set forth locally which means that communes have a high level of autonomy. These communes maintain population register and civil protection. In addition, their authorities spread over to education, social affairs, energy supply, road building, local planning, and taxation as well as other areas. To this, there is no one unified regulatory authority to enforce common standards among communes of different cantons. On top of that, these communes speak four different languages (German, French, Italian and Rhaeto-Romanic). This makes the country highly heterogenic in terms of culture, language, regulations, terminologies and laws.

That said; it was hard to come up with a single system that is administered centrally down to the granular details. In 2003 the Swiss Government has decided to offer online services to its citizens like many other countries. The government has faced the huge variations alluded above. It soon realised that no one state-run authority can provide online services to the whole population because of the autonomous status of both cantons and the subsidiary communes. Each commune must then provide online services to its population. This could have led to a huge number of local portals should this be done individually. It would have also made transformation of information almost impossible because of the legacy systems already in place that underlie the IT infrastructures of the different communes not to mention language differences. This would have limited citizens from browsing services and information offered by communes other than the ones they belong to because of the differences in language and terminologies as said before. Luckily the Swiss government has had a good IT strategy. They have wanted to develop a single large-scale portal (www.ch.ch) that draws its information and services from the local communes. The idea was to distribute the underlying system of the portal among the local communes. Hyperlinks and online resources are maintained locally by the each commune. When a resource's URL is changed it is reflected in the portal and the complexity of just managing the huge number of hyperlinks of the 2842 communes was resolved. The portal was a success attributed to the Swiss government. It has been

---

working seamlessly since 2003 and it lived up to its promises of providing one-stop governmental portal to Swiss citizens and foreign nationals.

Intra-governmental Secure Network

Intra-governmental secure network is referred to in different nomenclatures. The essence however, is to provide a network to interconnect local federal authorities together in order to exchange information in a secure, fast and reliable manner. For example, in Belgium such a network is referred to as FEDMAN (Federal Metropolitan Area Network). In Canada, it is named the (SC) Secure Channel whereas in Germany the network is called Governikus and in the UK, it is the (GSI) Government Secure Intranet and so on.

Databases

The same holds true for the public databases. The government needs to store information about citizens, business and other entities. A trend way as we so earlier was to store information only once and access several times. Therefore, the information stored should be unique with no chance for duplication to avoid inconsistency (except potentially for some cases to provide speedier access). In Belgium, there are sources of authentic information thus the term used to describe these databases is "Authentic Sources". Similar databases are used in other countries albeit with different terminologies. In the case of the Netherlands for example, they refer to these databases as "National Registries".

Electronic Identification

The forth most basic technical component is Electronic Identification. It crucial for a government to identify each of its users in an uncompromising way. Identity theft on the government level can have severe consequences. As described in Section 2.2.2, Identity Theft can become a serious problem if not accounted for properly.

Knowledge Management

Many governments have adopted the knowledge-based principle for implementing their e-government programme (e.g. Korea, Finland, Brazil, UK, Belgium and Germany). Knowledge has become an important resource in the information era. Today's economies are also knowledge-based. Knowledge has become a key factor in the production process in the new global environment (Delanghe et al, 2004). An example from Belgium is the economies of the northern and southern parts. Knowledge based economy in the northern part has surpassed that industrial-based in the south (Statistics Belgium).

Yet transferring knowledge management concepts from the business sector to the public sector is not sufficient (Wimmer & Traunmüller, 2003). In the public sector, complexities include goal structure, multi-level legislation complexities, legal interpretation, and complex operation across authorities (Bellamy & Taylor, 1998; Lenk & Traunmüller, 1999). Knowledge management in the public sector has to account for extra requirements not present in business including legal retrieval systems, policy formulation, citizen cards, certain marks in citizen information, privacy (Wimmer & Traunmüller, 2003). In fact, cross-agency processes might involve different terminologies, documents' writing languages, and interpretations. This is particularly true for countries with multiple levels of governance (e.g. Belgium, Switzerland...etc). Klischewski & Jeenicke (2004) have suggested the use of Semantic web technologies, which they argue, would address these challenges. Semantic Web refers to information intended for machine use rather than human comprehension (Berners-Lee et al, 2001).

Ontologies and standardisation are basic requirements for interoperability in e-government systems. Without interoperability, it will not be possible to provide shared services efficiently. Interoperability tools and standards are used to provide a common language for all systems to exchange information.

Forms Server

Usually a citizen has to fill in an application form upon soliciting a government service. Many services are provided with the participation of a number of departments or units. For such services, the citizen has to fill in a plethora of forms. Traditionally, he or she has to visit each of these departments individually. In many instances, many of the application forms contain pretty much the same basic data such as national number, name, address ...etc. The citizen or business is bothered by entering the same data repeatedly. A better solution is to redesign these forms for efficiency to allow the citizen to enter data only once. The entered data can then be used by the different departments.

Electronic forms server can host the different application forms of government services. Such servers are built to diminish redundancy in application forms and manage the form handling complexities. For example, the Federal Office of Administration in Germany has implemented the forms server (Cabinet Decision, 2002) to store the forms in one place (or links to local forms at times). Forms on this server are kept up-to-date. Beside forms themselves, description and use of each form are also stored. The majority of these forms, however, remain in PDF or Word format. In other words, they are not interactive forms. According to the Federal office, the server has further enhanced standards. In a similar direction, the Austrian government has enforced a "Form Style Guide" for better standardisation across government agencies.

Other Technical Components

Lesser common technical components include e-Payment systems. These systems allow users to make online transactions with the government. This can be done in cooperation with banking sector. Reliable electronic archiving can facilitate handling of all sorts of archives. It allows for faster information retrieval and efficient storage. Finally, channel integration has become a necessity to support the "channel of choice" convenience.

Organisational Components

On the organisational level, the government should incur organisational changes and introduce some important organisational elements. E-government is not just a technical challenge. E-government implementation requires careful change management (Papantoniou et al, 2001). I have seen while analysing the e-government strategies that organisational components have received lesser elaboration compared to the technical components of e-government. Most strategies, however, have included the organisational chart or the administrative framework of e-government. Fewer governments have assigned clear rules and responsibilities for each organisational entity.

e-Government vision in particular should be disseminated across all organisational level as it carries an important message. Such a message should be known and assimilated by every employee. This is necessary to educate the overall common goal of the e-government programme. This goal must be sought to be achieved by everyone.

We have seen previously (Section 3.2) during the analysis of perception of e-government that it is not just IT solutions. In fact, organisational changes are a basic input of e-government (Figure 15). The components of this domain must be devised very carefully as this can be the difference between success and failure (Papantoniou et al, 2001).

Policies and Standards Guidelines

These guidelines are designed to control the operation of the different functions (applications) within the federal and local governments. They provide guidelines and standards that make these applications interoperable. Without these components, the e-government work will be patchy and islands of automation will sprout.

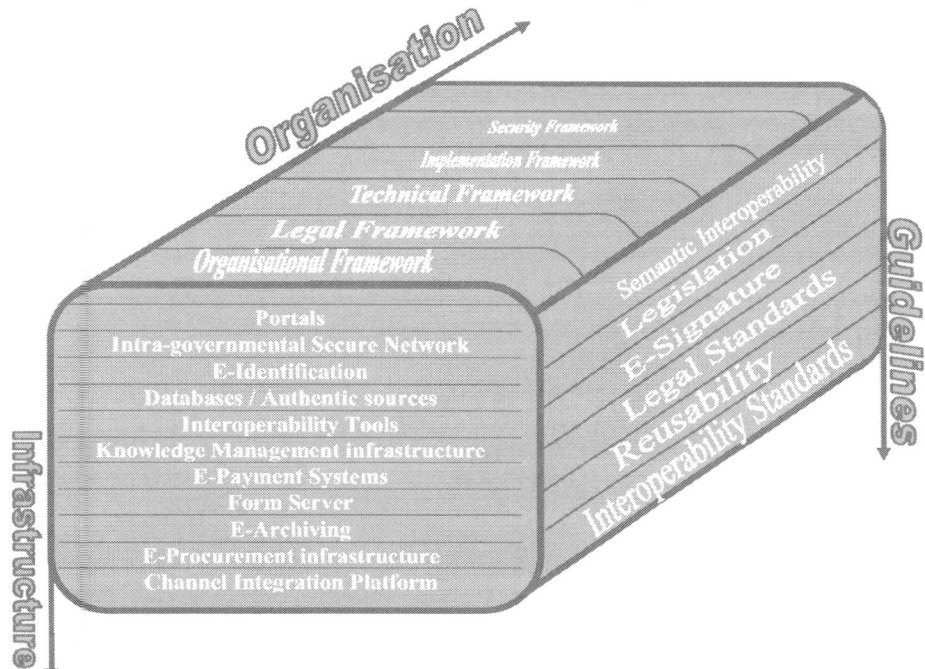

Figure 28: e-Government components cube

Figure 28 shows above the different components of e-government. This cube of basic components of e-government depicts the organisation of e-government from a practical perspective. It shows how governments visualise the components of their e-government programmes. The cube is based on commonalities in describing the building blocks as evidenced in the national strategies of e-government of the samples countries.

4.9   Modularity

As mentioned earlier, newer versions of e-government strategies are very common. This comes as a response to changes in the environment. Even some parts of the e-government strategy can be fixed, updated, or changed. The proposed strategic framework of e-government must thus exhibit a flexible design. Rigid frameworks will fail to survive in a world where technology advances rapidly. In addition, reform can result in many organisational and even possibly functional changes.

Modularity allows flexibility. Therefore, the proposed framework is modular. It is easy to add new modules to the framework. It is also convenient to update a certain module without messing up the whole framework. As such, the proposed strategic framework is fully extensible. It can be extended with all kinds of sub-frameworks and architectures.

Modularity serves another purpose set forth as one of the basic characteristics of the sought framework. It makes the framework layout less cluttered and more legible. It was also found to be one of the trends in some e-government strategies (e.g Austria, The Netherlands, Jordan…etc). These strategies have been planned to be modular. The strategic framework of e-government presented in the following chapter, is a core framework that needs local customisation.

At this point, all the bricks and mortar to structure the strategic framework of e-government are ready at hand. The next chapter introduces this framework and elaborates on its components.

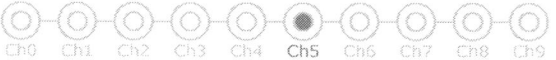

CHAPTER 5: THE STRATEGIC FRAMEWORK OF E-GOVERNMENT

5.1 Introduction

In the previous chapter, I have introduced the findings that pertain to structuring the sought strategic framework of e-government. To recap, I will briefly summarise the main points once again.

The intention was to make the strategic framework work as an abstraction or the e-government strategy. Therefore, I researched the main common parts of the e-government strategies at hand. These were found to be:

- vision;
- strategic objectives;
- guiding principles;
- building blocks;
- prioritised initiatives (applications) and
- implementation plan.

The above is a generic layout of an e-government strategy based on the keyhole comparison analysis. For each of the above components, I presented the best practice findings. The findings reflect not only the common elements but also the trends.

In addition to the above components, I also presented the merits of such a strategic framework. These merits include:

- graphical representation of the e-government;
- simplicity;
- generality;
- best-practice orientation;
- extensibility of the framework;
- flexibility;
- customisability and
- modularity.

Lastly, I have reviewed the relevant work of other researchers. This review has allowed me to form new perspectives and considerations. I sought to test either agreement or disagreement with the available literature. The review has also helped me in articulating the differences between my work and the rest. It also allowed me to state clearly my contributions to the body of knowledge.

The remaining challenge was to put together a framework that can really capture he main components and exhibit the merits stated above. As I mentioned in the research methodology, the outcome was affected by every new case I added to my study. In other words, the framework is actually a direct result of the convergence of evidence. The followed structured case approach has allowed the framework to emerge.

Figure 29 presents the proposed strategic framework of e-government. This is the generic and best practice framework I was seeking to put together.

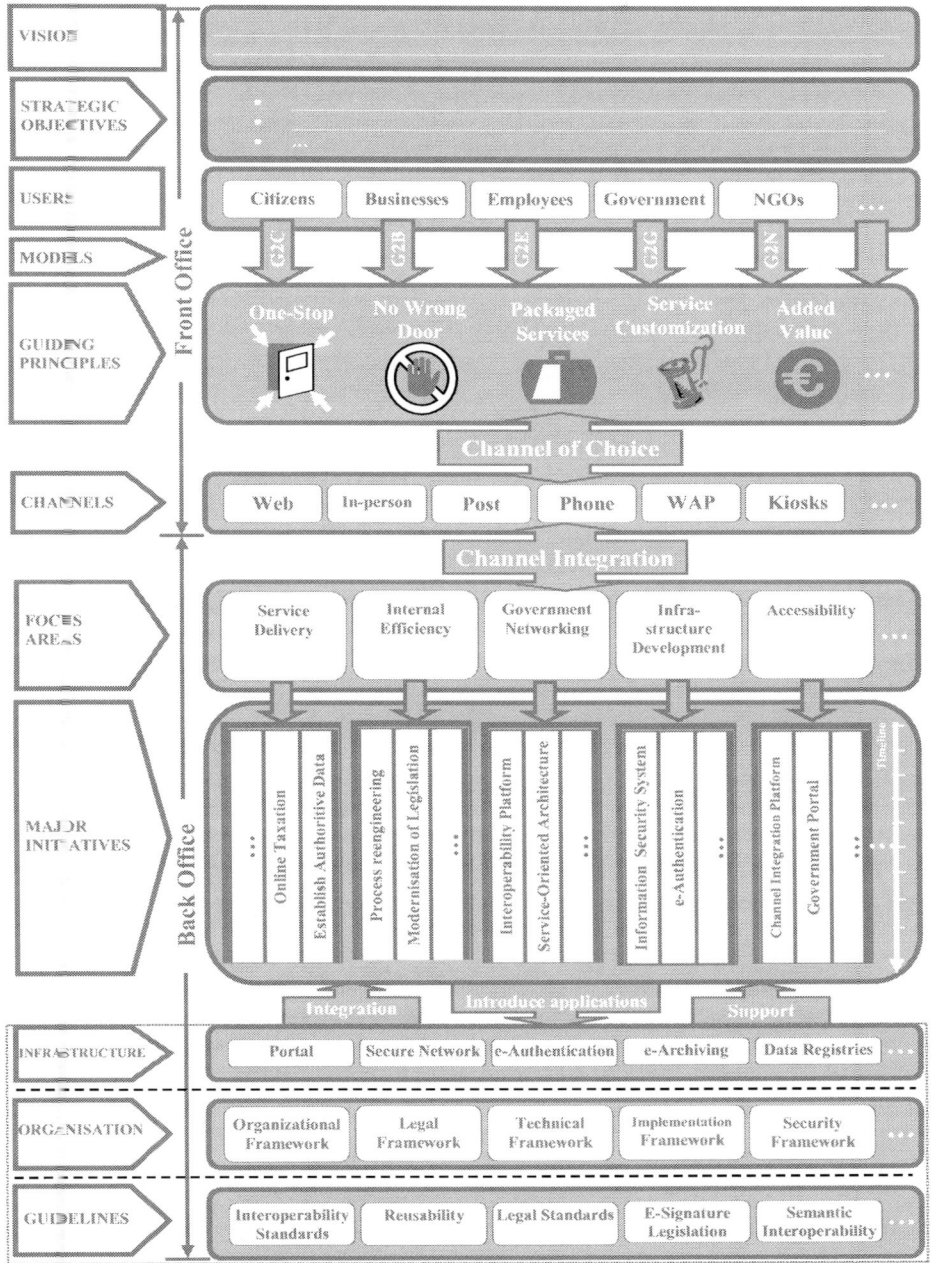

Figure 29: The proposed strategic framework of e-government

As we can see, the layering reflects the common components of the strategic frameworks of e-government reviewed. The general flow of the layout matches up roughly the general layout of e-government strategies described in the previous chapter.

The framework is obviously modularised. Each component is a module in itself. Figure 29 shows these modules and the relationship among them. One can see that there are more modules than the basic common components of the generic e-government strategy described above. The reason is this framework shows more than just the common components of an e-government strategy. I will come to this in a moment. Let me first enumerate the modules of the framework. These modules are:

- Vision
- Strategic objectives
- Users
- Delivery modes
- Guiding principles
- Channels
- Priority areas
- Major initiatives
- Infrastructure
- Organisation
- Guidelines

The framework is subdivided into two main parts: the front office pane and back office pane.

5.2   Front Office Pane

The front office pane is composed of vision, strategic objectives, users, modes of e-government service delivery, guiding principles and delivery channels.

5.2.1   Vision

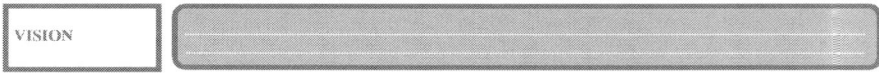

Figure 30: The vision module

Vision reflects the strategic intention of an e-government strategy. The proposed strategic framework highlights the vision by putting it at the top. As mentioned earlier, this strategic framework serves as a quick reference to an e-government strategy. It should be made available to all stakeholders. Therefore, the inclusion of the vision in the framework is extremely important. This helps rendering the vision more pronounced and memorable. Besides, vision was clearly the number one common component in the e-government strategies (see previous chapter).

As we have seen in Chapter 4, most government visions are centred on one of the following ultimate goals:

- Internal efficiencies

- External efficiencies

- Better governance

- Leadership in e-government development

5.2.2 Strategic Objectives

Figure 31: The strategic objectives module

Strategic objectives provide elaboration on the vision. They add value to the vision. It is thus equally important to include them in the framework. Strategic objectives are always a very important part of any e-government strategy. In addition, objectives decide the elements of some other modules, as we shall see later.

5.2.3 Users

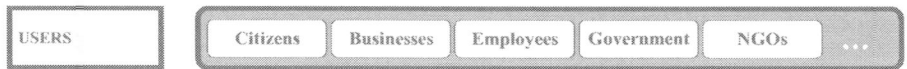

Figure 32: The users' module

As we have seen in Figure 23, client-orientation in e-government is the number one recurring strategic objective. It has become a major trend in e-government. Furthermore, many countries in the sample (e.g. Australia, France, India, Jordan, New Zealand, UK, USA...etc) have included clustering of users in their national strategies. In addition, clustering users accentuates the delivery models (see next module) and stresses personalisation of services. To address these requirements and realities the module of users has been included.

This module lists all possible users who can interact with the government and avail from its services. The framework incorporates only the traditional clusters of users. Other users (e.g. banks) can be added to the module as desired. This depends on how elaborate the government wants to make its clustering of users.

5.2.4   Models

Figure 33: The models module

e-Government models describe the relationship between the groups of users and service delivery module. Examples of these models are Government-to-Citizen (G2C), Government-to-Business (G2B), Government-to-Government (G2G)...etc.

5.2.5   Guiding Principles

Figure 34: The guiding principles of e-government module

This module lists some trendy guiding principles as found in our study. These principles are mostly service-related. One-stop access; no wrong door; packaged services; service customisation and added value are some of these trendy examples. A government can update this module with any of its own guiding principles.

5.2.6   Access Channels

Figure 35: The access channels module

This module comprises the list of delivery channels adopted by the majority of governments to deliver services. Some of the channels are traditional (e.g. face-to-face, post, fax...etc) while others are electronic (e.g. Web, e-mail, WAP, kiosks, SMS. .etc). It is worthy to note that some governments prioritise channels (e.g. Canada) while others simply give equal attention to all channels (e.g. Belgium). The module allows channel prioritisation. Later on (Chapter 6), we will see how this prioritisation can be done through an example.

Channel of choice and channel integration were found to be an obvious trend in e-government. Channel of choice means that the government empowers its users to choose whichever channel they prefer. Channel integration assures that no matter what channel is used to access government services it will be treated with the same efficiency at the back office level. The two notions are depicted clearly in our framework as connectors.

5.3   Back Office Pane

Complexities of back office operation are sought to be hidden from the users' view. The proposed framework makes a clear distinction between the two views. This view slots in focus areas in e-government realisation; major initiatives to meet priorities; basic infrastructure to provide seamless operation of e-government; organisation elements and policies and standards guidelines.

5.3.1   Focus Areas

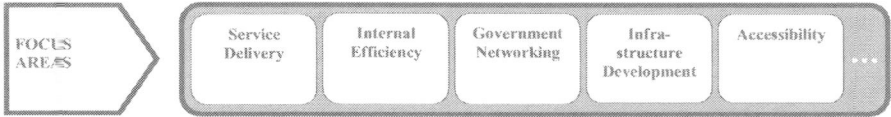

Figure 36: The focus areas module

I found out that focus areas occupy a sizable portion of most e-government strategies. With each new version of the strategy, new priorities can be added or even replace the old ones. This could be the case upon completion of a certain phase in the e-government programme. I included in the module the most common areas of action. In case of a new strategy debuting, the module can be updated easily without affecting the whole framework. The update should propagate to only one related module "Major Initiatives".

5.3.2   Major Initiatives

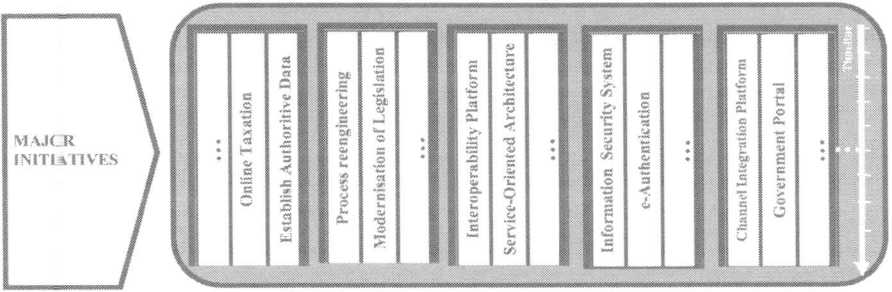

Figure 37: The major initiatives module

Major initiatives are actually strategic projects carried out to fulfill the priorities of e-government (focus areas). They are clustered within the module in relation to the focus area(s). Initiatives can overlap for more than one focus area. In this case, a project or a group of projects fulfills more than one focus area. It is easy to reflect such an overlap within the module. The following is a real example from New Zealand. This example shows a project called "establishment of Authoritive Data" overlapping two focus areas

"Service Delivery" and "Internal Efficiency". This means that this project addresses both "Service Deliver" and "Internal Efficiency".

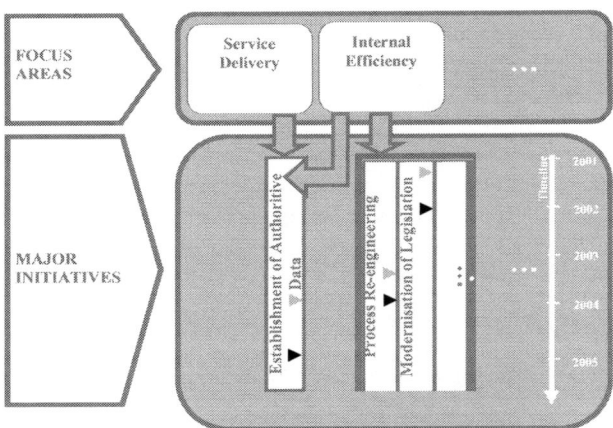

Figure 38: A customised view of the focus areas and Major initiatives modules

Furthermore, this module can also show a rough implementation timeline. Each project has a start date and a finish date. These are indicated by the gray and black arrows respectively. In the example above (Figure 38) the start date of the "Establishment of Authoritive Data" initiative is roughly the beginning of 2004 ad the finish date is roughly the beginning 2005. This should be treated as an optional addition to the framework. It is better removed should it clutter the framework. Finally, the initiatives in this module can decide which applications are needed to be built. Applications are chosen based on their necessity and the prioritised initiatives they support.

5.3.3 Infrastructure

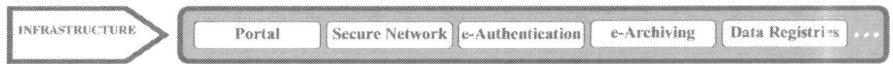

Figure 39: The infrastructure module

This module fits in components of the basic technical infrastructure. The included components in the module are the ones found to be common through the gap analysis of the e-government strategies-the subject of this study. As mentioned in the previous chapter, they are mainly the portal, which is the one-stop gateway to e-government services, a secure intra-governmental network, e-Payment system, e-Archiving system and data registries (referred to in some texts as authentic sources). There is room for any other strategic component within the module. This module supports the applications of the previous one.

5.3.4   Organisation

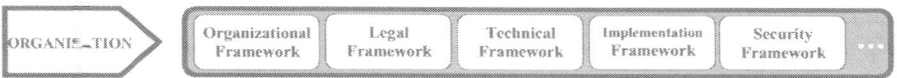

Figure 40   The governance module

A number of sub-frameworks belong to this module. Examples include organisational framework, legal framework, technical framework, security framework…etc. One merit mentioned for the proposed framework is its extensibility. This particular module and the next one, demonstrate that this core framework can be augmented with references to all kinds of frameworks and architectures.

5.3.5   Policies and Standards

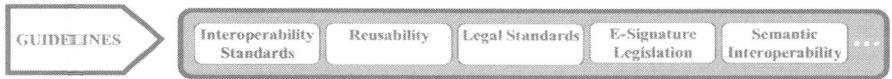

Figure 41 The policies and standards module

Naturally, any strategic framework provides a description of policies and standards of e-government. Policies and standards must be clearly defined to achieve such objectives inter alia as interoperability, collaboration, sharing, reusability, and replication. I found such objectives to be very common in the e-government strategies reviewed. Therefore, and because of their importance, I provided a module to incorporate the different standards and policy initiative. To have a successful implementation; thoughtful consideration must be given to all kinds of standards and policies well in advance.

5.4   Applicability of the Framework

The strategic framework of e-government provides a prototype for e-government strategies that has been developed in a scientific way. The framework has the potential to guide the development of e-government strategies. The framework is independent of specific characteristics of one country or another. It is rather designed to be generic. As mentioned earlier, it is populated with elements that were found to be most commonly used by sample countries. Although it needs local customisations by the individual countries, it has a structure that is necessary for any e-government strategy. This structure, as we have seen, is based on best practice. The question now is: *is this framework applicable?* To answer this question, I will present the Palestinian e-government framework.

Case Study 2 – The Palestinian e-Government Framework

I was personally involved in laying out the strategy in my developing home country and we had to do first some research in order to figure out a baseline for an e-government framework. If the strategic framework of e-government had been available, it would have saved us duplications of efforts. It would have also allowed us to focus efforts on our strategic objectives rather than wasting a lot of time wandering about where to go or what methodology to adopt or even worse what case to follow. It simply would have served as an initial guide for planning our own e-government strategy.

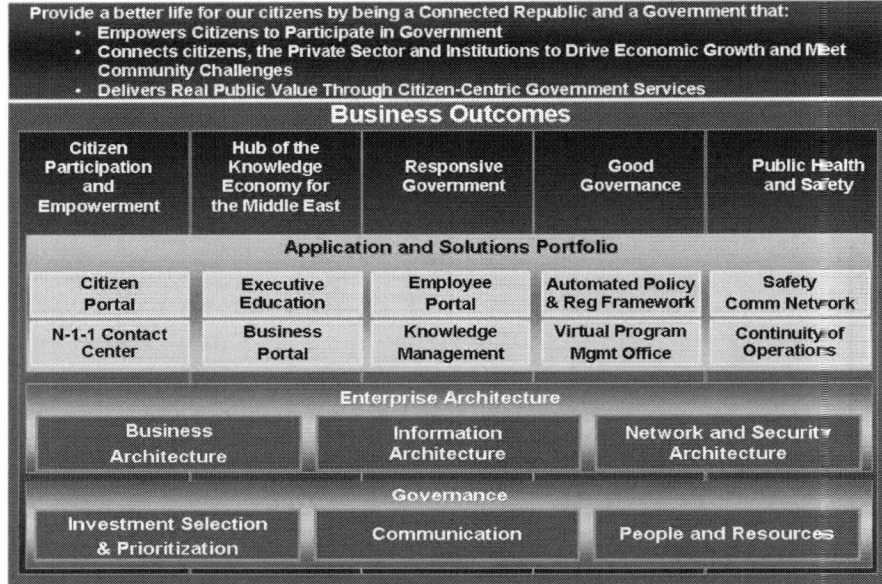

Figure x: The Palestinian framework of e-government (Source: e-Gov Coordination Mission, 2006)

Figure x above shows the Palestinian e-government framework. As we can see, it states the vision at the top and presents right after a set of five strategic objectives which is in agreement with the developed strategic framework of e-government. These objectives are referred to in Figure x as 'Business Outcomes'. However, the ultimate goal behind these objectives is not well focused. First off, they cover a number of domains each with its own challenges that clearly require extensive work and ample resources and skills which were not sufficiently available. This creates the impression that these objectives are utopic. Furthermore, according to the maturity model of strategic objectives they fall in more than one domain of maturity. For example 'Responsive Government' is a Level 2 strategic objective. Whereas 'Citizen Participation and Empowerment' and 'Good Governance' are Level 3 objectives. Finally, 'Becoming Hub of the Knowledge Economy of the Middle East' is clearly a Level 4 strategic objective. The vision itself 'Being a Connected Republic' is a Level 1 strategic objective. Having research the situation in the country, I hardly believe that internal efficiencies have been realised yet (Level 1). For example, websites of ministries are still managed separately. They still manifest online presence only with no real applications with content developed locally. This makes pursuing higher levels of maturity questionable.

This is similar to trying to achieve everything in one step. In practice, governments concentrate on achieving a particular maturity level through a set of strategic objectives. Therefore, it was common among sample countries to produce several national e-government strategies with each building on the achievements made in the previous ones. In other word, whenever a new phase of e-government development is completed, a new one (with a new e-government strategy) may start. What should have been done is assessing the current maturity level of e-government in the country and planning to pursue a higher one through a set of related strategic objectives.

The Palestinian framework proceeds to set the initiatives that fulfill each strategic objective. For example, 'Safety Comm Network' and 'Continuity of Operations' are two e-government initiatives aimed at satisfying the strategic objective 'Public Health and Safety'. Yet the framework fails to incorporate initiatives or solutions that cover more than one focus are. This is just because e-government initiatives were linked to each strategic objective directly rather than to focus areas which the framework is lacking. This is lack of focus on specific areas would make the whole e-government programme difficult to achieve.

Furthermore, the framework does not reflect the client-centric vision of the government. It neither clusters customers nor shows any guidelines in this regard. Whereas, the strategic framework of e-government, even its generic form, does cluster clients and shows models of delivery for each group of clients and shows relevant guiding principles. Lacking also are basic components such as organisational, legal, operational and technical elements.

In short, the Palestinian framework of e-government is lacking basic elements that are necessary for a sound e-government framework. In this example, I have demonstrated both the applicability of the framework and the necessity of its inclusion in an e-government strategy.

5.5   Limitations

Although I considered best practice when developing the framework, yet a basic question remains. Is best practice constant over time? Newer technologies, methodologies and knowledge can produce new best practices. They can shift trends remarkably. This study, however, came after years of practice in e-government. Some governments have achieved mature levels of implementation. The framework is a product of many years of cumulative experience and observation of e-government programmes. Even though, e-government is still at large a work in progress. The term best practice has become a buzzword. The word *best* might imply an utmost solution for a particular situation. It maybe a good idea to change the term into *better* or *good* practice as this would imply continually changing practices for better performances. Yet the term best practice has stuck in literature and practice alike. This dissertation does not advocate that the word "best" indicate an absolute reality. It rather relates it to current available knowledge and expertise. In other words, it is time-specific.

I tried to make the list of countries as representative as possible. I considered countries like Canada, Singapore, USA, Japan, Korea...etc, all of which have introduced many innovations in e-government. The criteria followed for choosing the countries can be debatable but in the end of the day, I was constrained with the documentation available at hand.

The intention for the introduced framework was to make it generic enough to allow adoption by a large number of countries. Generality, though, has a price. Some countries might find it ill suited for their national strategy. Nonetheless, e-government principles are similar across countries, though individual characteristics always differ. There comes the importance of the proposed framework. It is generic enough to be adopted by any country.

5.6   Conclusions

I have introduced a generic strategic framework for e-government. This framework is very useful to incorporate in e-government strategies. It simply adds value to an e-government strategy. Not only does this graphical representation recap the basic elements of the strategy, it also visualises the relationships among the basic components within the strategy. It has been found that no such framework was present in most e-government strategies reviewed in this study. This gives rise to the importance of the proposed framework.

The proposed framework offers a comprehensive view of the e-government programme. It incorporates very important components of front office and back office views. It has been modularised for flexibility, extensibilities and customisability.

Unlike other frameworks, the proposed one is best practice based. It comes as result of a comprehensive study of e-government strategies produced by (21) in addition to the European Union. I hope that the proposed framework will help practitioners and researchers for better implementation and understanding of e-government.

One of my prominent findings in this research is the noticeable concentration on the technical components of e-government. I found out the following components labeled as "Basic Components" in the majority of strategies reviewed:

- Electronic access to government
- Electronic authentication
- Unique identification numbers for citizens and businesses
- Key registers/Authentic sources
- Electronic personal identification (chip cards)
- Electronic information exchange

- Fast connections between government organisation

Although these technical components are crucial for building the basic infrastructure, yet a holistic view of e-government must be depicted in the strategy. Since there has been a shift from e-Government to e-Governance (e.g. Marche & Macniven, 2003; Dawes, 2008) other socio-technical components must receive proper attention.

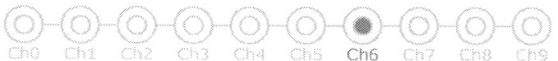
CHAPTER 6:	HOW TO USE THE STRATEGIC FRAMEWORK OF E-GOVERNMENT

6.1   Introduction

The strategic framework of e-government presented in the previous chapter enhances the e-government strategy it stems from. Thus, the domain of its application is the e-government strategy development. Heeks (2006a) in his book "Implementing and Managing e-Government: An International Text" has approached this strategic domain of e-government. In chapter 3, he discussed the development process of an e-government strategy. Heeks (2006a) stated that an e-government strategy seeks to answer three questions:

1. Where is status quo of the government?

2. Where would the government want to be?

3. How would the government get there?

He also presented the steps needed to develop an e-government strategy as I have discussed earlier in Chapter 4.

This thesis does not advocate a certain approach for developing an e-government strategy. Nor does it suggest *what* an e-government strategy should look like. It only introduces a strategic framework for e-government. This "value-adding" framework came after analyzing the commonalities in the contents of sample e-government strategies.

This chapter provides a full guide for using the developed strategic framework of e-government. In addition, it identifies the users of the framework. It clarifies how each of them can utilise the framework. Furthermore, the chapter comments on the different possible customisations of the framework. It also explores drivers and pillars of e-government. Also in the chapter is a presentation of the critical success factors of e-government. Towards the end, the chapter concludes with a number of guidelines on how to induce public value through the framework.

The next section starts by explaining the different symbols used in structuring the framework.

6.2   Key Symbols of the Framework

The strategic framework of e-government is structured using some key symbols. Each symbol represents a certain element or component. Some symbols may have different variants. Each variant supplies extra information. The following table (Table 16) describes the key symbols and their possible variants employed in the framework design:

Symbol	Description

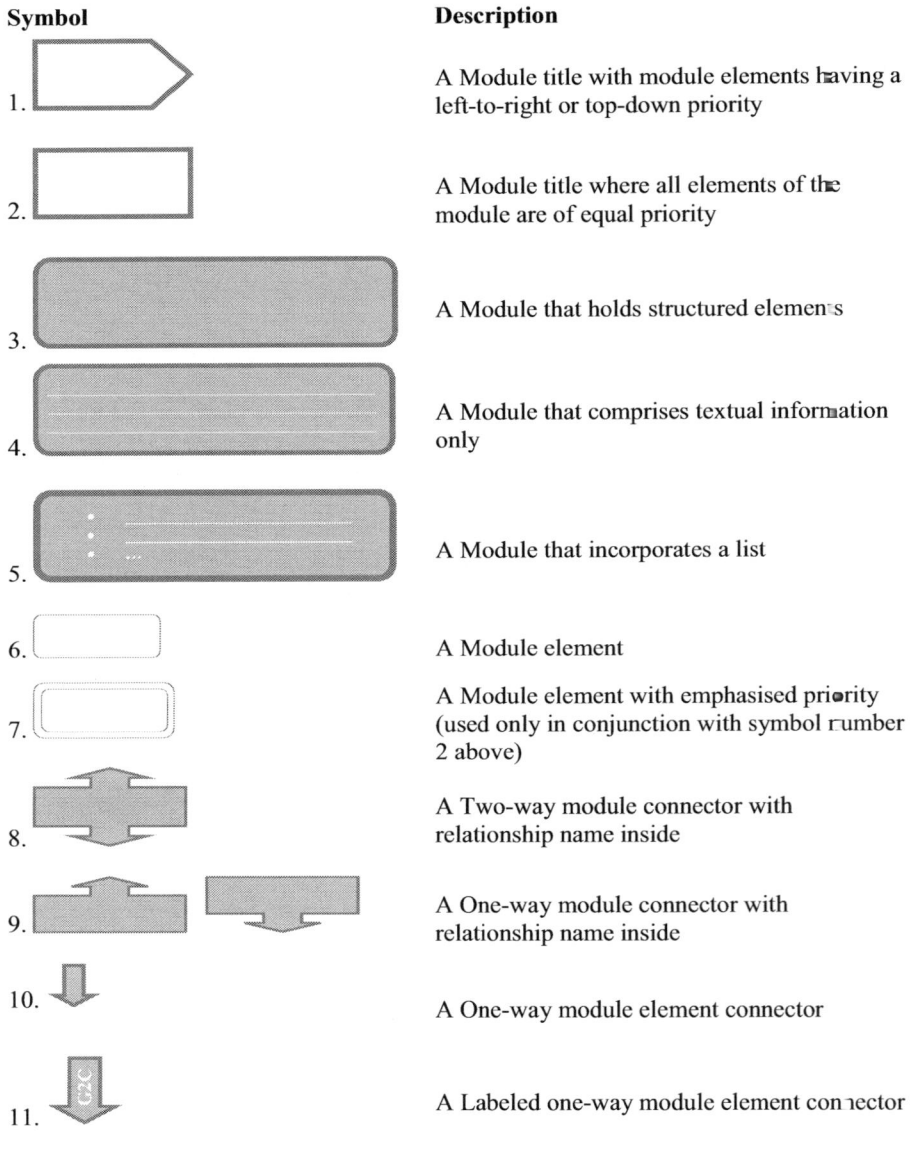

Symbol

1.

2.

3.

4.

5.

6.

7.

8.

9.

10.

11.

Description

A Module title with module elements having a left-to-right or top-down priority

A Module title where all elements of the module are of equal priority

A Module that holds structured elements

A Module that comprises textual information only

A Module that incorporates a list

A Module element

A Module element with emphasised priority (used only in conjunction with symbol number 2 above)

A Two-way module connector with relationship name inside

A One-way module connector with relationship name inside

A One-way module element connector

A Labeled one-way module element connector

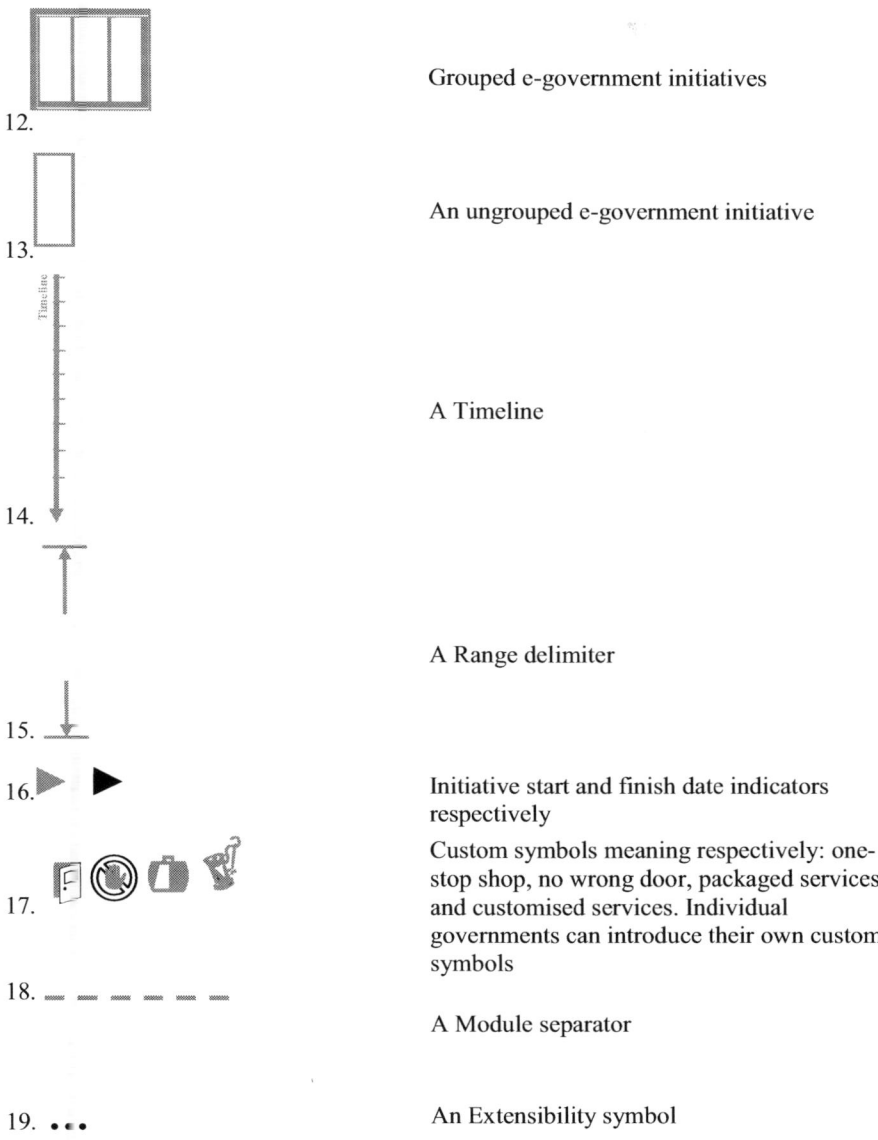

12.   Grouped e-government initiatives

13.   An ungrouped e-government initiative

14.   A Timeline

15.   A Range delimiter

16.   Initiative start and finish date indicators respectively

17.   Custom symbols meaning respectively: one-stop shop, no wrong door, packaged services and customised services. Individual governments can introduce their own custom symbols

18.   A Module separator

19.   An Extensibility symbol

Table 16: Key symbols used in the strategic framework of e-government

6.3   Using the Strategic Framework of e-Government

The first thing to understand before using this strategic framework is its generali y. It is a generic strategic framework. It does not pertain to one particular country or a group of countries with specific characteristics. As mentioned earlier, I incorporated countries from al five continents. They obviously differ in the social, economic, demographic, and political domains. The only common denominator among them is their ambition for a better e-government development. This framework represents what they all have in common towards this goal.

As it stands, the framework incorporates the basic elements of an e-government strategy. As we have seen in the previous chapters, the framework was structured around best practice and trends in e-government development. The notions, principles and components taken into consideration are the most intensively used ones. I looked for repetitiveness to rank each particular construct. This makes it a very useful learning tool for every government wishing to see where the majority of governments are go ng. It is particularly useful for countries with less developed e-government who still wander about best practices in strategic planning of e-government.

The structure and content of the strategic framework of e-government was base 1 on the best available knowledge, scientific literature and best practice. The accumulative experience during the last fifteen years has been employed to build the framework. This is not to claim that e-government has reached its maturity. Yet considerable efforts from both practice and literature has brought about some successes and enriched experiences. In my research I have learned much about these experiences which reflected on the development of the framework.

Because of its generality, the framework should not be used as is without local customisation. It should only be perceived as a skeletal framework for national e-government strategies. This was an intention since the beginning of my research. The framework was conceived to be generic enough to fit any government. By so doing, I intended to increase its value. In particular, I meant to render it a generic learning tool as well as an omni applicable framework. Each module of the framework is easily extensible and expediently customisable. In each of the modules, one notices that there are dots (symbol number 19 in Table 16) towards the edge. These dots indicate that further elements can be added as seen in the example below.

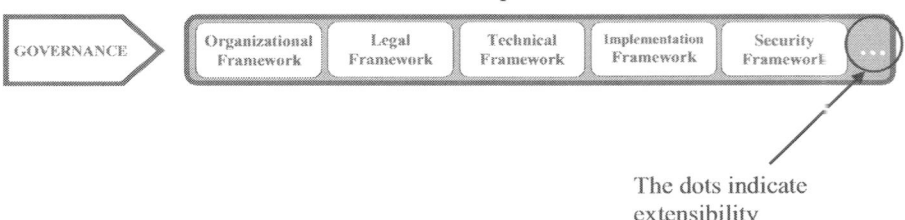

The dots indicate
extensibility

Figure 42: Extensibility in an example module

If a particular government desires to incorporate more elements than the space allows, it can simply place the framework in landscape mode or dedicate a bigger paper size like an A3 for example. This extension also applies to adding more modules either at the end or anywhere in the framework. In case a compelling need arises to introduce a new module somewhere in the framework, then the linkage with adjacent modules must be explained. Yet in its current layout and with the incorporated elements, the generic framework captures the essence of most e-government strategies.

As noticed in Figure 29 of the previous chapter, the framework is populated with some best practice elements. These elements are in place as they were found repeatedly in the e-government strategies. Their presence in the strategic framework is just indicative. They should in no way be considered as a must. We know that governments differ in their level of maturity. In fact, it could be the case for a particular government that some element(s) might have already been satisfied in some previous e-government plan. Thus, these elements must be replaced by others in a new plan.

The government is able to show its strategic intent through the vision and strategic objectives modules. These two modules are completely empty in my strategic framework. They await customisation by the individual governments. Normally, this is the first part of the framework to be customised. Every other module will normally follow the vision module. The general direction of customising the framework runs from top to bottom. This is in agreement with what has been mentioned in Chapter 4 about the development of e-government strategies. First, the vision is filled in. Strategic objectives then follow. Afterwards, individual governments cluster their users and delivery channels. This might involve new types of users with corresponding channels. Then the guiding principles are highlighted.

There is a room for channel prioritisation in the strategic framework. Prioritised channels are double outlined (Symbol number 7) as the example below illustrates (Figure 43). The example shows two channels with special attention: the online and the in-person ones. The other channels are given less weight but they all share the same priority level. This is evident through using symbol number 2 for the title of the module.

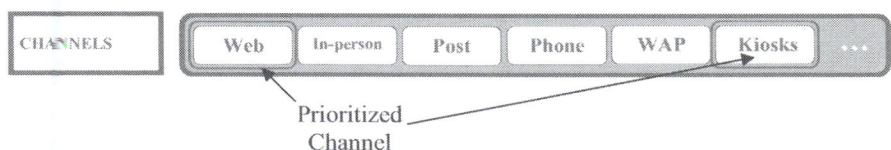

Prioritized
Channel

Figure 43: Prioritisation of delivery channels

Upon customizing the delivery channels, the next step is to highlight the focus areas. Focus areas are country-specific but the module is populated with areas of intensified efforts as evidenced in Table 13 of Chapter 4. These major areas of action have been targeted by the majority of governments for seemingly a great impact. The focus areas in the module are sorted according to their importance from left to right, as the module title is designated symbol number 1.

Finally, pictograms of symbol group number 17 appeared in Table 16 without labeling. However, these pictograms were actually labeled in the strategic framework of e-government as was shown in Figure 29 and later in Figure 34. Such pictograms are more recognisable when labeled (Namatame et al, 2007). Therefore, labeled pictograms are encouraged to use upon customising the framework with government-specific guiding principles.

6.4   Prioritisation of Projects

The framework provides room for incorporating prioritised initiatives. I found governments launching initiatives that address certain priority area(s). This is why these two modules are correlated in the strategic framework of e-government. I provided inter-module connectors between individual focus areas and their pertinent initiatives. Once the government identifies its focus areas and places them in the module, they can extend a connector(s) to the initiatives that address them. As pointed out earlier, one initiative can fulfill one or more focus areas. Refer to the previous illustration in Figure 38 for more details. The question is now, *how are e-government initiatives prioritised in practice?*

Heeks (2006a) introduced a prioritisation schema of e-government initiatives. According to this schema, high priority projects would be those with high impact/benefit and low cost/risk. I have investigated how the different governments prioritise their initiatives (projects) in practice. Some governments prioritise their e-government initiatives collaboratively across agencies (e.g. France). Others leave the prioritizing to the agency or sector involved (e.g. New Zealand). Countries like the USA have assigned the prioritisation process to the taskforce that carries out e-government development. The taskforce has taken the following steps to come up with a list of final prioritised projects:

Step 1
Taskforce conducted a questionnaire through email and interviews of government employees in the different agencies to identify projects

Step 2
Taskforce held two rounds of prioritisation to indentify initiatives that cover the projects in Step 1. Prioritisation was based on:
- value to citizens;
- potential improvement in agency efficiency and the
- likelihood of deploying within 18 to 24 months.

Step 3
Initial business cases were developed for each of the emerging initiatives, yielding estimates of benefits, costs and risks

Step 4
Using this data from the business cases, the most promising initiatives were recommended for deployment

Step 5
Other initiatives that are necessary for operation of e-government were added. e-Authentication was selected to address the authentication security needs that cut across federal e-Government initiatives

In general, the prioritisation process is based on the considerations described in Figure 44 below. Prioritised initiatives are the ones that address an absolute necessity, increase value to citizens, have greater impact (efficiency, ROI, political return...etc) and serve a strategic goal. In addition, the prioritised initiatives should exhibit less time to market, pose less risk of failure and consume lesser resources. All these factors must be put in balance when considering prioritizing e-government initiatives.

Some literature, however, call for prioritizing initiatives based on the group of users. Accenture (2003) for example calls for prioritizing initiatives targeting businesses. The reason is that the impact on businesses (profits, savings, and time saved) will be higher. Besides, businesses can avail better from government offerings, as they possess more resources, better infrastructure...etc. Although some governments as we have seen earlier in the analysis are oriented towards better business enablement (e.g. Japan, Germany, Singapore, UK, USA) this did not reflect on prioritisation of their initiatives. The e-government strategies I have reviewed did not show such inclination.

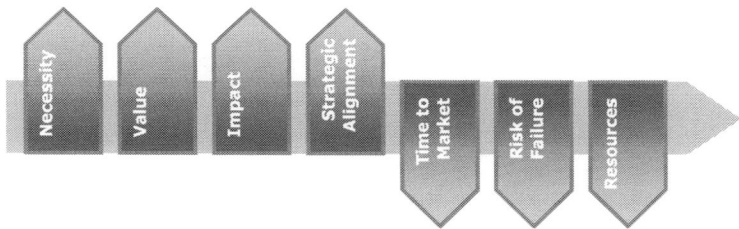

Figure 44: Prioritisation of initiatives (adapted from Heeks, 2006a and practice)

It has been mentioned in Chapter 4 that one key element in an e-government strategy was found to be the implementation plan. In many cases, such a plan was published in separate document (e.g. Austria and UK). For the majority of countries however, it was bundled with the e-government strategy albeit with lesser details. For this reason the strategic framework of e-government, demonstrates a rough implementation scheduling of e-government initiatives. This is achieved through symbols number 14 and 16 as demonstrated before (Table 16). The timeline is graduated with years. In case the space allows there could be additional markings for the month on the timeline. In this sort of implementation, I have managed to conserve clarity and provide extra valuable information at a glance.

While we are still at implementation, there are three maturity levels of e-government implementation (United Nations, 2008). The first level is building the necessary infrastructure. Infrastructure provides supports for a newly launched application. When there are a number of applications up and running the next thing to think about is integrating them so that they can input/output to each other (Figure 45). The last maturity level in implementation of e-government is total transformation. It is synonymous with "networked government".

Figure 45: Major phases of implementation as well as focus and challenge areas (adapted from United Nations (2008))

These three implementation maturity levels have replaced the previous five levels used in the e-Government Readiness Report (United Nations, 2005) for simplification reasons. The previous reasons were emerging (online presence), enhanced (dynamic content), interactive (e-mail interactions and downloadable forms), transactional (online transactions including e-payment) and networked (service integration across agencies) respectively.

Other implementation maturity levels include Layne & Lee (2001). There four-stage model starts with cataloging which is essentially posting information online. Such information includes downloadable forms but there is no interaction with the government website. The second stage involves interaction through Web forms connected to databases. The third stage exhibits vertical integration. At this stage, individual department systems are integrated but there is no cross-department integration. The final stage involves full integration across agencies at which stage the government becomes "networked".

A similar four-stage model was developed by Bhatnagar (2004). The stages are Web presence; limited interactions; transactions; and Transformation.

Not only does this strategic framework briefly describe the implementation framework but it also provides references to other sub frameworks. These sub frameworks include organisational framework, legislative framework, technical framework, security framework...etc. As mentioned previously, the strategic framework of e-government is just a core one that references the main elements and their interconnection. The idea is to educate the reader of the framework about the existence of these elements. In addition, how these elements relate to one another. This is necessary to form a top-level understanding about the e-government project as a whole. Where possible it supplies extra information provided that no clattering ensues.

The last module in the strategic framework of e-government references the different policies and standards for the overall development of e-government. Such standards may include interoperability, reusability, legislation, e-signature...etc. It is very important to work out these standards and government policies during the early days of development for three main reasons. The first reason is to control the overall development of e-government. This saves the government many troubles. They provide a basis, which can be referred to during the development process. Without guiding standards and specific policies, it is hard to write service level agreements. It would also cause disagreements about how a final solution would look like. The second reason is that standards enforce uniformity, which is necessary for interoperability and operation among diverse agencies.

The last reason is to facilitate better auditing, benchmarking and monitoring (e.g. procurement). In short, there should be standards for everything.

As an example, the following are some *legal* standards from Belgium:

- Law on the right of access to administrative documents
- Law on the Protection of Private Life
- e-Commerce Laws
- e-Communications Law
- Law on the use of Electronic Signature in Judicial and Extra-Judicial Proceedings
- Law on Electronic Signatures and Certification Services
- Royal Decree on e-Procurement
- Transposition of the EC directive

6.5   Users of the strategic framework of e-government

Typically, the committee or taskforce responsible for spearheading the development of e-government is responsible for designing the strategic framework of e-government. However, the use of the framework is not constrained to this committee or taskforce. There are other potential users of the framework. These users are mainly: administrators, IT-professionals, auditors and academicians. The following sections describe briefly how each of these users can utilise the strategic framework of e-government.

6.5.1   Administrators

It is important for the administrators to know that such a framework exists in the first place. This is quite crucial since administrators are responsible for decision-making. Local initiatives must be aligned with the general strategy of e-government. Such alignment is necessary for such reasons as interoperability, mutualism, cooperation, coordination….etc. Knowing about the existence of the framework from the side of administrators will make them take it and its requirements into consideration when launching local initiatives.

Knowing about the framework alone is *not* an end goal in itself. Administrators should work to support its implementation and enforce alignment. They should make sure that all aspects of new projects abide by its principles, policies, sub architectures, policies and standards.

As has been mentioned before, leadership involvement and commitment is key for success. Orchestration among administrators across agencies will prop up e-government development and keep it in course.

Administrator should educate professionals working in local projects about the policies, stands and constraints that underlie the framework. System analysis, database designers,

---

consultants and programmers must all consult the framework and the underlying architectures when planning or implementing projects within their organisation.

6.5.2 Professionals

Professionals are people who carry out planning, designing and implementing e-government initiatives and applications. These professionals include information, architects, information managers, database designers, application programmers, software engineers, consultant system analysis, database designers, consultants and programmers...etc. As mentioned above, these professionals must be taught to comply with guiding principles, standards and policies stemming from the strategic framework of e-government. This is essential because there are important guiding principles that this framework holds. These principle (e.g. user-centricity, shared service deliver.. etc) are meant to be met by all the initiatives under the umbrella of e-government. Each project must fit with the overall e-government through the common standards, specifications and guiding principles, the framework demonstrates.

It has been mentioned in Chapter 4 that government networking is one of three key areas of major actions (focus areas) of e-government. To assure viability, a reference framework is needed. At the very core lies the strategic framework of e-government. Professionals should always consider the strategic framework as a top-level reference. It forms the basis for shared standards. Such standards can enforce common look-an-feel, interface layout, language...etc. Other standards and specifications might be enacted for procurement basis in a similar manner as we have seen in the Belgian example. Moreover, for public-private partnership (PPP), the strategic framework with its sub frameworks should be a coherent reference that governs the contracts and agreements.

Finally, the framework can also be used for better decision-making even on the professional level.

6.5.3 Auditors

With its structure and components, the framework already provides some basic guideline for auditors. The framework per se assists auditors to assess implementation in contrast with the strategic framework. Auditors can check the strategic alignment of e-government initiatives against the strategic framework. In addition, the framework provides very important elements to take into consideration for auditing and benchmarking. For example, if one of the principles was "government networking" then auditors can investigate compliance with this principle across initiatives being audited. The same statement can be made about all other guiding principles. Auditors will also find the underlying standards, policies and specifications a valuable reference to do their job effectively.

6.5.4 Academicians

The strategic framework of e-government has an educational value. It gives researchers hands-on reference of what e-government strategies comprise and in what manner. The framework provides a conceptual understanding of e-government strategies. The structuring process of the framework has revealed important scientific findings as a bi-product. For example, this study has resulted in revealing how governments perceive e-government. The provided model in Figure 15 can help researchers in the analysis of the theoretical view of e-government in contrast with the practical view. This might provide an opportunity for future investigation of the potential paradox.

The study has also shed some light on how an e-government strategy is developed in practice. The findings included the steps followed for it development as evidenced from the 22 cases (Figure 22).

The developed Maturity Model of Strategic Objectives (Figure 24) can also furnish researchers with an analysis tool for judging government maturity based on its strategic objectives. The model can be used as testing tool in the hands of researchers in some future studies that take strategic objectives as a parameter.

The study has also revealed realistic drivers of e-government. Figure 25 provides the reader with the main domains of pressure that can cause governments to develop e-government. This might be a starting point for further research in these fields. The findings also divulged the basic components of e-government from the governments' point of view (Figure 28) which adds more perspectives to researchers in e-government.

All of these provide academic value and add to the body of knowledge as will later be discussed in more detail in Chapter 9.

A very important result of this study is that it bridges a gap in current scientific research. It has been mentioned earlier (Section 1.4) that virtually *no* research has been done to investigate the presence of a strategic framework of e-government. This neglect is not only witnessed in literature but it has also propagated to practice. It has been demonstrated through Table 1 that no one country has produced a similar framework in the way the study advocated.

Finally, the framework highlights the important concepts from hands-on data. The structured case analysis produced interesting findings concerning a number of constructs. It provides researchers with trends in e-government implementation. I addition it shows where efforts and resources are being poured.

6.6   Initial Projects to Start With

The major initial projects of e-government for many countries in each of my sample strategies have been reviewed. These projects were found to be directly related to the focus areas of the individual governments. This confirms their proper positioning in the strategic framework of e-government (Major Initiatives Module).

Some governments, however, *classify* these projects differently. For example, the USA (OME, 2002) strategy classifies them based in the model (i.e. G2C, G2B and G2G) as well as internal efficiencies and per necessity of overall operation. Denmark (Project e-Government, 2004) classifies them in two categories: internal and external (citizens and businesses). India (MCIT, 2006; MICT, 2007; MCIT, 2008), however, categorises them into federal government, local governments and integration initiatives. Some other projects belong to enabling integrated services. Belgium (Federal Planning Bureau Economic Analyses and Forecasts, 2002) has launched two groups of projects: sectoral (functional) and general.

France (ADAE, 2004) has classified the projects into two groups: service delivery and modernisation of the government. Service delivery-related projects are further clustered based on the users' group. For examples, a number of projects are grouped for citizen services; another cluster of projects is dedicated for services intended for businesses. A third cluster is dedicated for services intended for associations and so on. The modernisation group of projects is further clustered into four groups: enhancements of public services, reinforcement of security of information systems, schema director of e-government and communication tools and evaluation.

Some other countries had no special clustering or classification of their projects (e.g. Malaysia, Germany, The Netherlands and UK).

The detailed list of initial projects of e-government for the countries reviewed can be found in Appendix C.

6.7   Alignment with e-Government Strategy and Joint Projects

Each project or initiative launched under the umbrella of e-government on the local or federal levels must be in a complete agreement with the e-government strategy. This alignment is necessary because as we have seen previously, the initiatives are generally orchestrated around a number of focus areas in order to achieve the strategic objectives.

Strategic Agreement	e-Government Initiative Assessment
Vision agreement	
Objectives served	
Priorities fulfilled	
Policies and Standards abidance notes	
Users serviced	
Resources required	
Budget limitation	
Infrastructure	
Values induced	

Table 17: Strategic alignment assessment form

To facilitate this alignment when planning for a project; an assessment form can be used. Table 17 gives a simplified idea about such a form. This example is just to check strategic orientation. Only strategic components are checked for alignment. It does not qualify for nitty-gritty details (technical, organisational, or standards and policies). Appropriate detailed forms and documentations are necessary for these purposes.

In the final results of the E-awareness Survey carried out in New Zealand in 2003, there were (178) departments involved in e-government initiatives. Only 29% of the departments surveyed have *discussed* alignment with e-government strategy. 22% have not and 49% did not answer (E-awareness Survey, 2003). This clearly shows that the strategic alignment of e-government initiatives is *not* considered seriously.

In the same survey, 25% of initiatives involved more than one agency actively contributing resources. 67% of initiatives involved only one agency's resources and 8% of respondents did not answer. This again shows the lack of joint project development. Such a lack of cooperation in the development of common projects can have serious consequences on "networked government" and "shared services" ambitions. Shared services and government integration can only achieve maximum efficiency when all agencies involved have participated in developing the shared services. Cooperation, in this case, should obviously be enforced top-down. The federal government must take its responsibility in orchestrating the joint development of e-government projects.

6.8   Critical Success Factors

There have been a number of efforts to study the success factors of e-government (e.g. Bhatnagar 2004; Chowdhury et al, 2006; Becker et al, 2004; Papantoniou et al, 2001; Mahrer & Brandtweiner, 2004; Evangelidis et al, 2002; Gichoya et al, 2006; Pardo & Scholl 2002; Gil-García & Pardo, 2005; Park, 2008).

Park (2008) related the factors affecting the success of e-government to the value induced by the e-government initiatives. He developed two instruments to measure the value. The first instrument measures the means objectives in terms of public trust, information access, public accessibility, and quality of services. The other instrument measures the fundamental objectives in terms of timesavings, efficiency of service to citizen, and social awareness. The overall value is the sum of the values of the previous objectives. Each of the previous objectives is assigned a weight based on a survey of 210 users of government service users. This study, however, is oriented towards, the user's point of view. Accordingly, success of e-government is eventually, manifested through users' adoption of government services. This approach is particularly important since the world average of users' take up of e-government online services is merely 30% (Kumar et al, 2007).

Becker et al (2004) have conducted an empirical study to figure out the factors that influence success of e-government. They used internal data from 56 and external data from 70 local municipal administrations in northern Germany region of "Muensterland". Thus, the study reflects the perception of government agencies. Potential factors that do not exhibit national characteristics were taken into consideration. The study has shown that internal re-organisation is the most significant factor in the success of e-government. This includes government readiness and policies and practices (Lowery, 2001). This finding is in full agreement with my own (Figure 46 below). However, there is a generality issue in their study as data are just from one country. My approach is more generalised as I used data from 22 countries.

Another survey meant to represent success factors in the developing countries was conducted in Bangladesh (Chowdhury et al, 2006). The study found the following factors to affect the success of e-government:

- Political will

- Adequacy of the technical infrastructure

- Overall vision and strategy

- Effective project management

- Politics/self interest

- Competencies of the officials involved

- Change management

Bhatnagar (2004) has classified success factors of e-government according to the maturity level of e-government implementation. While content, awareness, aesthetics and access count as critical success factors at Web presence stage, other factors become critical at other stages. For example, leadership starts to become critical at transaction and transformation stages.

Many of the above studies have taken place in one country, which is ill suited for generalisability. In addition, these studies do not reflect the federal government's unified view of what the success factors are. I wanted to explore this domain based on a much wider and thus more representative group of countries.

I collected information from e-government strategies as well as other official documents. In these official documents, the governments have stated explicitly the critical success factors of e-government. As usual for each common success factor, I conjugated the countries. The results are then tabulated and sorted top-down based on intensity of replication. Table 18 below presents the end finding.

Success Factor	Countries
Reform (structure, processes, laws...etc.)	Finland, Australia, Denmark, Austria, Malaysia, USA, India, The Netherlands
Efficient and robust use of technology	Finland, The Netherlands, Australia, Austria, Canada, Malaysia
Collaboration	France, The Netherlands, EU, Denmark, Austria, Canada
Political leadership/ownership	The Netherlands, Denmark, Malaysia, India
Availability of skilled staff and capacity building	Germany, Austria, Finland, Malaysia
Rules and responsibilities (organisational)	Germany, The Netherlands
Need to show pay off of e-government	Germany, Denmark

Success Factor	Countries
Monetary resources	Palestine, Malaysia
Client readiness	Austria, Canada
Public-Private Partnership (PPP)	Denmark, India
Citizen-centricity	Austria, Canada
Integrated infrastructure	Denmark, USA
Robust infrastructure development	Singapore, India
Adopt successful models and best practices	Denmark, USA
Central development of basic components	Germany
Likelihood of timely completion	Germany
Capacity assessment for implementation	Denmark
Bottom-up cost calculation	Germany
Multilateral agreements for authentic sources	Netherlands
Technical Support	Palestine
Knowledge management for flexibility	EU
Prioritisation	Denmark
Open standards	Denmark
Flexible infrastructure	Denmark
e-Government as a comprehensive strategic concept	Austria
Interoperability/open interfaces	Austria
One-stop shop	Austria
Security and privacy	Canada
Ease of use	Canada
Mindset shift	Malaysia
Continuous measurement and monitoring	USA
Flexibility and adaptation to change	New Zealand
Dedicated team	India
Defined standards, policies and architectures	India
Change management	India

Table 13: Critical success factors of e-government ranked by occurrence across countries (Developed from national e-government strategies)

All of the above critical success factors are important. However, they do not all exhibit the same weight. The table is sorted based on the number of countries that consider a particular success factor critical to their case. As evident in the table, the most cited success factors are the top five in a descending order. These are respectively: reform, technology, collaboration, leadership and staff.

This important piece of finding teaches us that there are five pillars for e-government initiatives. They form the cornerstones for the success of e-government as seen by governments. The reason I called them pillars is their utmost importance. If any of these pillars fail, then the whole of e-government is likely to fail. Failure in e-government means the inability to reach the set goals (Dada, 2006). Figure 46 represents this reality.

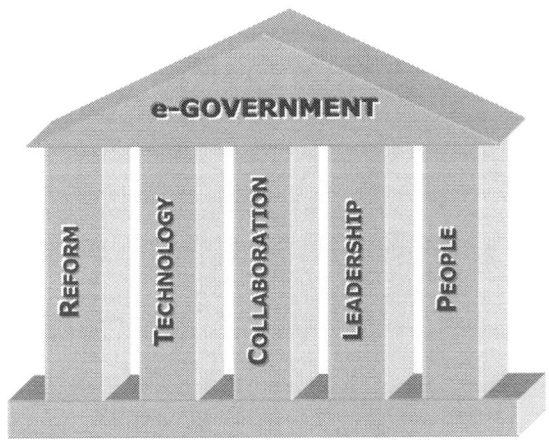

Figure 46: Pillars of e-government

Another important comment to make is that reform in the government is obviously accented and thus receives higher attention. This renders serious reform a bi-product of e-government implementation. In fact, some studies considered reform as a key driver of e-government (Centeno et all, 2005). The government's legal system, operational procedures, regulations and organisation would presumably become more efficent and convenient.

6.9 Measurement and Benchmarking of e-Government

In this section, I will discuss briefly the measurement techniques of the strategic progress of e-government. In the process, literature is discussed first followed by methodologies conducted in practice. We shall see the differences between the proposed theoretical methodologies against practical demeanor.

Benchmarking allows authorities to measure a specific policy or programme's progress and identify successes and failures during a specific period (UN, 2001). This allows making early adjustments to curb problems. Benchmarking in the context of this study is aimed at measuring implementation against strategic objectives. Benchmarking is considered as a tool in the hands of the government to assess how well it is meeting its objectives and how these objectives could be met more effectively (De la Porte & Pochet, 2001). A benchmark is defined as 'a standard or point of reference against which things may be compared or assessed' (Pearsall, 1999).

Benchmarking could be carried out either top-down or bottom-up. Top-down benchmarking is imposed from the federal government on the local governments. In contrast, bottom-up benchmarking is initiated by the local authorities. Table 19 summarises the differences for each of these two approaches (developed from Tronti, 1998; De la Porte & Pochet, 2001; practice).

Top-down	Bottom-up
Imposes uniform benchmarks	Looks for best practices
Uniform quality assurance policies agencies-wide	stimulates organisational learning
Oriented towards achieving common objectives	Might result in performance gaps across agencies
Assumption is that all agencies have the same objectives	Flexibility to choose appropriate benchmarks to meet local objectives
Can reveal hidden global patterns	
Best for assessing cross-agency challenges and progress (e.g. collaboration, shared service delivery...etc)	More accurate indicators in comparison to finding valid indicators across agencies

Table 19: Bottom-up vs. top-down benchmarking of e-government

The first legitimate question shall be then *what do we need to measure in e-government?* Heeks (2006b) has seen that there are four stages each with specific objectives to measure. These are readiness, availability, uptake and impact. These four meters are the most important performance indicators of e-government according to Heeks (2006b). Readiness measurement is assessed by awareness, infrastructure and digital divide. Availability is judged by supply adequacy and maturity stage of e-government. My proposed model (Figure 24) can be used to measure maturity of strategic objectives. Demand for government services, usage and user divide can connote uptake. Lastly, efficiency, effectiveness and equity are measures of impact.

Kearns (2004) has proposed a measurement for public value. His methodology attempts to measure three domains: service delivery, contribution of e-government to deliver outcomes and e-government contribution to public trust. Indicators of service delivery are: take-up, satisfaction, information quality offered to the public, level of choice offered, user-centricity, access equity and cost of service provision. eGEP (2006) has added three more domains of measurement of public value: efficiency (organisational value), effectiveness (user value) and democracy (political value). Each of these new domains has a number of indicators to measure as shown in Table 20 below.

Value Domain	Indicators	Sample Measures
Efficiency: Organisational Value	Financial Flows	Reduction in overhead costs Staff time saving per case handled
	Staff Empowerment	% staff with ICT skills Staff satisfaction rating
	Organisation / IT Architecture	Number of re-designed business processes Volume of authenticated digital documents exchanged
Effectiveness: User Value	Administrative Burden	Time saved per transaction for citizens Overhead cost saving for businesses (travel, postage, fees)
	User Value/Satisfaction	Time saved per transaction for citizens Overhead cost saving for businesses (travel, postage, fees)
	Inclusivity of Service	e-Government usage by disadvantaged groups Number of SMEs bidding for public tenders online

Value Domain	Indicators	Sample Measures
Democracy: Political Value	Openness	Number of policy drafts available online Response time to online queries
	Transparency and Accountability	Number of processes traceable online Number of agencies reporting budgets online
	Participation	Accessibility rating of e-government sites Number of contributions to online discussion forums

Table 20: Public value measurement of e-government (eGEP, 2006)

Gupta & Jana (2003) developed a framework for e-government measurement. The framework is split into hard measures and soft measures as follows.

Hard Measures:

- Cost benefit analysis

- Benchmarks in e-government: Grading is done from the perspective of implementation rather than perspective of "end-users"
  - IT expenses as percentage of total revenues
  - Percent of downtime (when computer is not available)
  - CPU usage (as percentage of total capacity)
  - Percent of IS projects completed on time and within budget as part of e-government projects

Soft Measures:

- Scoring method: identifies all the key performance issues with tangible and intangible benefits and assigns a weight to each of them, then the weighted average of all the attributes is calculated. The item with the highest score is judged the best service provider in comparison to similar organisations. Assessing intangible benefits is done by linking the evaluation of these benefits to the factors that are most important to organisational performance

- Stages of e-government: (I) cataloguing, (II) transaction, (III) vertical integration, and (IV) horizontal integration.

- Sociological angle: opinion survey would be useful to gauge the responses of employees' adaptability and responsiveness in the new systems.

Hierarchy of measures: 6 Levels

Level	Measured Change
Return on investment	Monetary
Total costs and revenues	Monetary
Improvement in quality of planning and control	Time required to work out plans, Cost of planning, Managerial time required for control, Degree of automation, Forewarning, Cost of control

Quality of decisions	Frequency of failures/reversal of decisions, Number of alternatives examined, Time required for decisions, Number of decisions, Availability of decision support systems, Cost of decisions.
Value of information	Usefulness (in terms of validity, accuracy, clarity, frequency, sufficiency, timeliness, reliability, relevancy, message content and cost).
System characteristics	Number of people required, equipment and facilities, response time, frequency of breakdowns, inputs, outputs, number of forms, number of operations, number of storages, sizes and quality of data bank, size and quality of model bank, flexibility, simplicity, degree of automation, scope of business components that are related by the MIS, user satisfaction, error rates, persistent problem areas, ease of maintenance and modification, unplanned-for impact on company performance, savings, cost, etc.

Figure 47: Framework of e-government measurement (Gupta & Jana, 2003)

The objective of this study is to assess strategic benchmarking of e-government. In other words *how to assess progress against the strategic objectives?* In practice, sample countries developed different approaches to benchmark e-government. For example, Figure 48 shows the framework of e-government benchmarking in New Zealand (State Services Commission, 2006). Once the strategic objectives are well defined appropriate indicators are figured out for each objective.

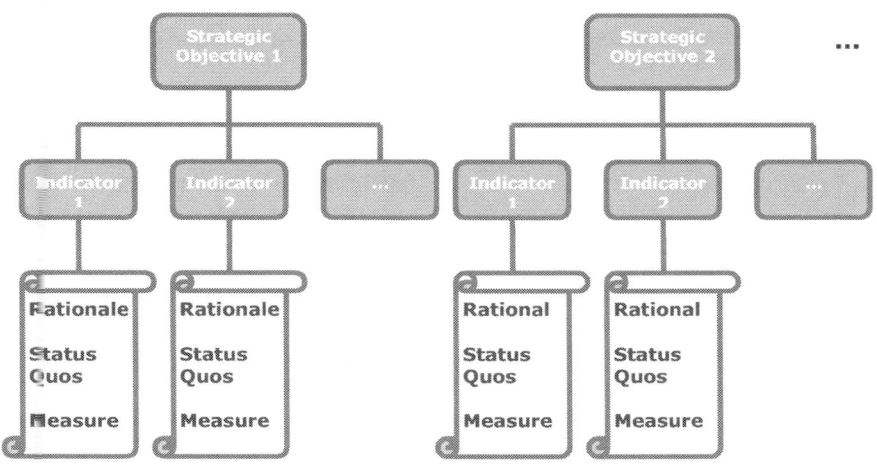

Figure 48: New Zealand's framework of e-government benchmarking (developed from State Services Commission, 2006)

The rationale for each indicator is then specified. Status quos is analyzed per each indicator. Finally, assessment measurement for the indicator is researched.

Another relevant example is the e-government benchmarking and monitoring framework of the United States (Figure 49). The framework starts by identifying the strategic objectives. For each strategic objective, requirements and measures are stipulated. Then strategic tasks to realise the objective are identified. For every task, a number of tactics or procedures are planned with set target dates, and coordinator and responsible officials.

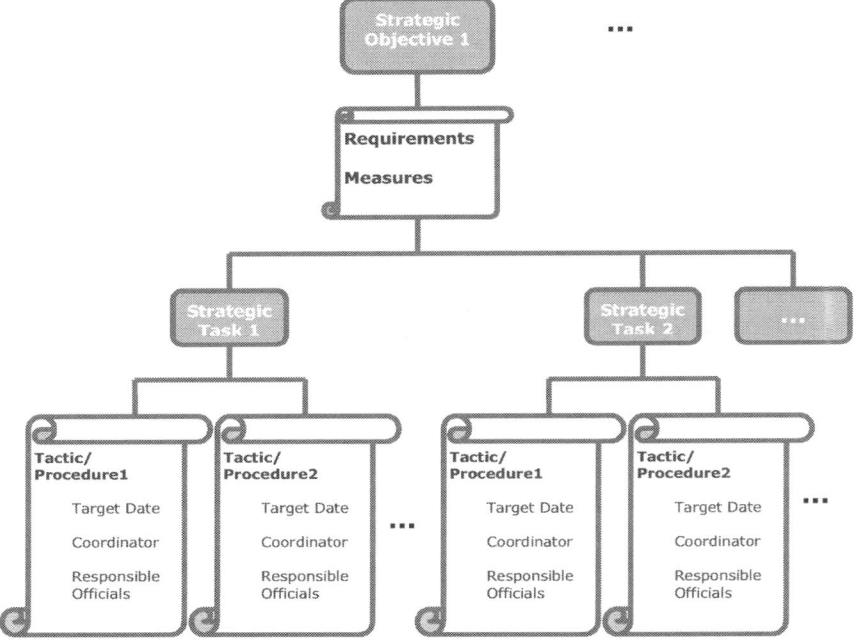

Figure 49: US monitoring and benchmarking frame work of e-government (developed from US Department of the Interior, 2007)

Canada's framework, by contrast, is a nine-stepped methodology as shown in Figure 50 (Public Works and Government Services Canada, 2005). The methodology takes a holistic approach to assess the overall of e-government in Canada. The methodology starts by literature review to look for best practice in e-government benchmarking. It incorporates cost and benefit analysis with complete case studies. Roll-up analysis examines the achievement of results across the e-government Initiatives with respect to cost-effectiveness.

Canada

Step 1: Review Literature
Step 2: Establish Cost and Benefit Categories
Step 3: Conduct Departmental Survey and Review Existing Data

Step 4: Complete Case Studies
Step 5: Identify GOL Projects/Endeavours Objectives
Step 6: Classify Programmes and Services
Step 7: Analyze Benefits
Step 8: Analyze Costs
Step 9: Conduct Roll up Analysis

Figure 50: Canada's Assessment framework of e-government (Source: Public Works and Government Services Canada, 2005)

In Denmark, the assessment strategy of e-government was less structured (Project eGovernment, 2004). It started by identifying status quos. The strategy was devised to allow for adjustments and updates to implementing e-government. It involved getting feedback from participants and shareholders. The feedback comprised obstacles faced, attitudes towards vision and projects of e-government and assessments. The strategy also involved discussions of future strategy with representatives of the public sector. It also involved gathering international experiences to avail from in strategy works where relevant. It was also meant to assess Denmark's maturity on the global level.

The German approach is less elaborated but it basically sets strategic objectives and then creates a number of tasks to achieve each one.

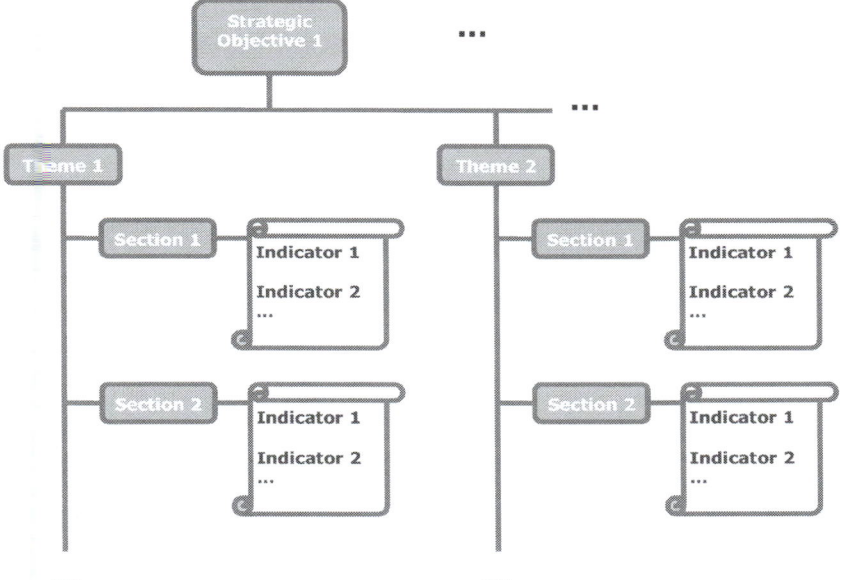

Figure 51: EU's i2010 benchmarking framework (developed from Commission of the European Communities, 2006)

Finally, the EU's i2010 Benchmarking Framework creates themes for each main objective. In turn, these themes are further partitioned into sections. For each section, one or more indicators are specified as shown in Figure 51.

The more elaborated and detailed the benchmarking is, the better the chances of success are. For example, providing requirements for each objective or specifying target date, coordinator and responsible officials for each tactic or procedure in the US framework is certainly better as it guides usage in further details. Likewise, dividing strategic objectives into themes and sections would make it more accurate to specify qualifying indicators. Furthermore, the benchmarking process should be given appropriate attention during elaboration of the strategic objectives. It must be demonstrated that such objectives are measurable. If an objective cannot be measured then it could not be managed.

6.10   Characteristics of Success

In the previous section, we have seen how governments assess performance and success or failure. But how does success look like according to these governments? In other words, *when do governments consider their e-government to be successful?*

Some researchers consider public take up of services as an indicator for success (Kumar et al, 2007; Becker et al, 2004). Yet different governments have different points of view on the issue. For example, New Zealand considers its e-government to be successful when convenience and satisfaction in government services becomes evidence from the users' perspective (State Services Commission, 2006). In addition, when there is strong internal integration and efficiency on the internal level there would be enough trust and active participation on the social level.

The United States' government considers itself successful when conducting business with the government becomes easier (OMB, 2002). In addition, success is manifested through a well-protected privacy. Provision of appropriate security is also considered as a characteristic of success. Finally, when citizens and businesses can visit one point-of-service online or by telephone, that reflects the "United States Government."

Characteristics of success for the Austrian government involve easy operation and uniform structure (ICT Strategy Unit, 2007). In addition, logical processes should make it easy to use e-government services. Everyone wishing to use the services offered by electronic administration should have the opportunity to do so, regardless of whether they do so from a home computer or from a public terminal.

In another example, Singapore has set the following achievements as indicators of success (Project Steering Committee, 2006):

Delighted Customers

- Widely-used e-Services and Satisfied Customers
- Seamless User Experience

- Easier to use Government Websites and e-Services through:
  o Unified One-Stop Government Portal
  o Web Interface Standards (WIS)
  o Enhanced ease of using online services
  o Enhanced search for online public information and services

- Extended Reach of Government e-Services

Connected Citizens

- Citizens consulted on policies

- e-Communities created

Networked Government

- Adoption of Good Infocomm Management Practices

- Development of Singapore Government Enterprise Architecture

- Effective Enabling Infrastructure to Accelerate Integrated Service Delivery Across Public Sector

- Secure Government Systems

- Sharing through Knowledge Management (KM)

Evaluation of these characteristics of success can take the form of simple questions. For example, the government of New Zealand has given some sample questions to assess success of e-government in the country. These questions were (e-Government Programme, 2008):

- Are New Zealanders able to achieve the results they need, without searching across many agencies?

- Can New Zealanders get consistent service whichever combination of channels they use to engage with government?

- Can New Zealanders provide information to government just once, or do they have to provide the same information many times to different agencies?

- Do workers in State agencies work with colleagues across the sector to put results for New Zealanders ahead of individual agency interests?

- Are they drawing on the best examples of learning and development and tools from across the government sector?

- Are mechanisms being developed for agencies to work together and share information and research?

- Are infrastructure and systems supporting collaboration and partnership?

- Are New Zealanders using the services provided by agencies, and are barriers to access being reduced?

- Are New Zealanders finding the government services intended for them?

- How much do agencies know about the experience of service users and do they use this knowledge to improve service delivery?

- Do New Zealanders have confidence in the integrity of government agencies and workers?

In short, these are actually connected to the fulfillment of the strategic objectives of e-government. It is noticeable though that this sample of countries has paid particular attention to characteristics of success across three spheres:

- Users of public services

- Government operational efficiency and

- Society

6.11 Achieving Public Value

Public value is a slippery concept but can be defined as both contributing to, and providing an enabling framework for, economic growth, jobs, competitiveness, and sustainable development, but also encompassing public governance and its many intangible public goods, such as inclusion, democracy, quality of life, citizenship, trust, continuity, stability, and universal human rights.

Millard et al (2006)

A simplistic definition of public value could be "the value created by government through services, laws, regulation and other actions." (Kelly et al 2001). Front end of service delivery is conditional to the consolidation of back-end systems and processes (UN e-government survey, 2008). Furthermore, re-engineering of the internal structures and processes of the administration are key requirements for genuine cost savings and quality improvements (Millard, 2003). In addition, it is the value induced that attracts citizens to use online government services (Park, 2008). Thus, through increasing the value of online services the government would actually be helping more adoption of their services. This leads to success the success of the whole e-government programme (Kumar et al, 2007; Becker et al, 2004). Achieve more with less is sought after by many governments based on my findings. They aim at producing high impact using the fewest resources. Value and efficiency are connected in the sense that the former is mostly conditional to the latter.

e-Government is not an end requirement in itself but rather a tool to achieve public value (Centeno, 2004). Value can have different interpretations depending on which country we are talking about. For example, Finland considers e-government as a tool to increase competency in the global arena (in response to China's, India's and Korea's phenomena). This is actually a strategic objective of Finland. In fact, value is the overall benefits resulting from the development of e-government. Yet the cited values in the e-government strategies are mostly those related to strategic objectives.

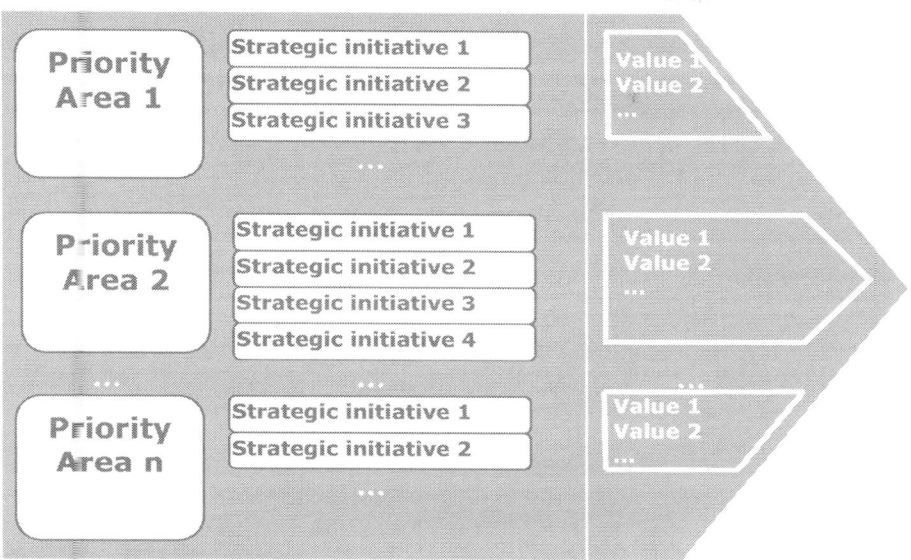

Figure 52: Achieving public value

The strategic objectives-as seen earlier-are realised through the arduous efforts in the *focus areas* of e-government. The question I attempted to answer was, *where does value creation lie in the introduced strategic framework of e-government?* I have examined the best practices as a first guidance. In general, most countries referred to the value as the direct benefits from key applications (e.g. e-taxation, e-registration of vehicles…etc) as well as other projects related to reforms (new efficient laws and regulations, process reengineering…etc). The value domain can be the government itself, citizens or the society. These parties are the ones who can avail from the induced values.

Figure 52 above shows induced values resulting from initiatives and applications. Focus areas are based on the strategic objectives. These focus areas are ultimately translated into initiatives (projects) such as simplification of procedures that have a direct value in terms of reduced costs, efforts or time or they could be translated into an application or solution such as online taxation that also have similar values. However, in order to achieve value, measurable outcomes must be identified beforehand. Value has to be measurable to be assessed.

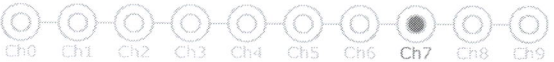
CHAPTER 7: THE UNDERLYING TECHNICAL ARCHITECTURE: THE FEDERATED MODEL OF E-GOVERNMENT

7.1 Introduction

Chapter 5 has introduced the strategic framework of e-government. That framework was built for the top strategic level of e-government. Nonetheless, it did not answer many of the pressing questions of *how to develop a sustainable e-government that is flexible, interoperable and manageable.* The next step on the agenda of my research was to figure out a proper technical model that can underpins the framework. This chapter introduces the federated model of e-government. This model was designed from the start to achieve better manageability, flexibility, sustainability, cost reduction, and security of e-government.

Numerous research efforts concentrating on technology platform integration and development have been reviewed (e.g. Tambouris, 2001; Scholl, 2005; Themistocleous & Irani 2005; Anthopoulos & Tsoukalas, 2005; Klischewski & Jeenicke, 2004; Punia & Saxena, 2004; Klischewski, 2004; Janssen & Cresswell, 2005). These contributions, however, are more rewarding and viable for governments that do not yet have an IT infrastructure and plan to establish one. Yet most governments, as we have seen in Chapter 2, have already abundant disparate systems in place. Each of these systems was built to serve and support a particular department that has distinct requirements. In most cases, there was a lack of vision of integration as decisions upon technologies were taken by the local governments.

Local Governments (LGs) in addition to municipalities in modern democracies have an elevated level of autonomy. This stems from one of the golden rules of a democratic society division of authority. Traditionally, priorities and budgeting in light with national and domestic laws direct the work of these LGs. This differs much from businesses where decisions are mostly centrally made. Resistance to change on the side of government employees can be more evident and severe than in businesses. Rebuilding of the IT infrastructure entails replacing hardware and software in addition to training employees on the new systems. The costs can be awfully far above the ground.

Research has shown that communications and information flow from departments to headquarter and vice-versa is far more frequent and seamless in businesses than LGs and central government (Scholl, 2005). This tendency to keep information private within departments and LGs renders much of integration efforts ineffective.

That said; it could be better and cheaper to adopt a different approach. *Abstraction* of e-government and *encapsulation* of LGs demands much fewer costs and can face far less resistance. Abstraction of e-government is to look at LGs as separate entities having local characteristics (regulations, data, government processes…etc). Encapsulation of LGs, on the other hand, means that there is rigorous integration among these entities and individual local characteristics are kept private. This idea has a lot in common with object-oriented methodologies that are already applied in some businesses.

The purpose of this chapter is to introduce a model that materialises the ideas of e-government *abstraction* and *encapsulation*. The chapter would touch on the technical aspects of the model, but at large the model will be conceptual.

7.2   Can business Models be Applied to Governments?

As the purpose of establishing an LG is different from that of a firm the nature of each is different and the models to be used for operation would also be different. A previous study has revealed the following discrepancies between the two (Grönlund, 2004):

- A firm aims to maximise profit but a government furnishes its citizens with services and maintains stability and well-being of the society. The latter is obviously not a clearly defined goal.

- Citizenship (relationship between a citizen and the government) is very different from consumership (relationship between the customer and the firm). The paradigm of relationship management is different for each.

- A government follows legal and policy processes while firms normally have administrative and technical ones.

- Business value drives business whereas constituents' needs drive government actions.

As a result, although businesses and government use similar technologies, implementations are different. This difference is manifested as:

- In governments, the technical orientation is focused on: e-government, e-workflow (processes), and e-democracy (e-participation and e-voting) whereas the focus is on e-commerce, e-business, outsourcing and integration for businesses.

- Interoperability and data sharing across levels and among branches faces legal, political, and social, challenges whereas technical issues are being the least (Scholl, 2005).

- Although many businesses have started to empower their employees to make their own judgments at times, decision-making in businesses is still made centrally at large. This leads to managerial, organisational, and technical problems.

While information sharing among government units or LGs improves transparency, government units are reluctant to share information as mentioned above. This has to do very much with the stiff bureaucracy in their working environment. Government units remain much like silos where cross-functional processes barely exit. Each unit maintains a sort of autonomous status and specific processes. These processes are not very well integrated among LGs. This lack of integration causes inefficiency and fails to achieve shared service delivery. It restrains transparency as well.

Nowadays, most businesses implement cross-functional processes and abandon silos style of operation. The purpose is to make a more flattened and thus flexible and efficient workflow (Laudon 2006). This methodology *cannot* be directly applied to governmental units, as the emphasis for the latter is correctness and credibility rather than speed and efficiency.

In short a government is not a firm. Borrowing successful models from business does not necessarily mean that they will also work well for governments.

Table 21 below summarises the major differences between business and government:

Criteria	Business	Government
Aim	Maximise Profit (Clearly Defined)	Well-being of Society (Stability)
Driver	Business Value	Constituents' Needs
Processes	Administrative/Technical	Legal/Political
Clients Relationship Paradigm	Consumership	Citizenship
Operation	Centralised	Decentralised/Autonomous
Emphasis	Efficiency, Profitability	Correctness, credibility

Table 21: Differences between government and business (adapted from Grönlund, 2005)

The table shows that e-government and e-business differ in many ways. Therefore, they cannot be approached the same way. If platform integration has worked well for e-business it may not work well for e-government. This is where our model fits in.

Further details on the technical realisation of the model will be introduced later in the chapter. The model meets both managerial as well as technical requirements of e-government implementation.

7.3 Structuring the Federated Model of e-Government

In the following subsections, the federated model of e-government will be introduced. Abstraction of e-government is the basis for simplification of implementation. This ideas is first discussed and then the sought qualities the model will be defined. The basic components of the model will then follow.

7.3.1 Abstraction of e-Government

With the federated model of e-government, LGs are perceived as a collection of disparate entities where there is little or no integration among them. This way, the central government can save a lot of efforts and costs in trying to integrate disparate (legacy) systems of the different LGs. In this manner the IT systems within an LG is a property of that particular LG. According to this model, there is no real need to replace incompatible systems. Furthermore, the central government should not pay attention to the way a particular system within an LG works but should rather be concerned with inputs and outputs of that system. Central government can view a system of a particular LG as an *abstract* object within its collection of systems (objects). This definition on the technical level would as well fit the organisational level. The federated model of e-government can preserve the autonomous status of LGs and the seemingly long-lasting bureaucracy.

The model is not very much concerned with the detailed workflow or processes within each object (an LG's IT system) but is rather concerned with the "interfacing" among objects (LGs). This renders the whole system platform modeling simpler, cheaper and easier to implement.

7.3.2   Qualities of the Federated Model

Because the whole platform is now partitioned into simpler objects, a government can implement its IT platform incrementally instead of all-at-once and thereby minimizing the risk of failure. In addition, this reduces complexity. The whole system is subdivided into manageable and simpler subsystems. No low-level system integration is necessary. The model fits incremental approach (usually perceived as safe implementation).

The model protects autonomy of LGs because local information and processes are kept and preserved locally. Since local information and flow of processes are not accessible from outside the LG; impact of successful hacking attempts is reduced which makes the whole system more secure as opposed to a centrally managed operations and databases. Think about terrorism, wars or natural catastrophes.

This model enables a government to implement its IT platform incrementally instead of all-at-once and thereby minimizing cost and risk of failure. Government processes play a significant role in the success of an e-government project. Unlike business processes, government processes are plagued by (Punia & Saxena 2004):

- Processes are vertical and not cross-functional: This is due to the fact stated above that government structure is hierarchical and departmental (vertical silos) which renders processes inefficient.

- Lack of ownership: It is hard to specify the responsible person(s) or unit(s) for part or all activities within a process.

- Absence of practical measurement of process performance: Bureaucracy has much to do with this problem.

Given these facts, it becomes obvious that process integration in e-Government is even harder to achieve than in businesses. This manifests another quality of the proposed model, which hides the details of each e-government process within an LG or government unit. It is only concerned with inputs and outputs of each process. It does however support the integration of bigger processes across LGs.

Change management is crucial for a successful implementation of a new large-scale project. It has to be said that employees, in general, hate to change the way they used to work for lengthy periods of time. Moving to new IT systems is often resisted by some employees because of the obligation of training on the new system and the possible change of responsibility/authority. There is also the inconvenience of adapting to the new systems. This problem can play a significant role in the failure of a project (Laudon,

2006). Government employees, in particular, are even more resistant to change. They work in bureaucratic hierarchies as opposed to business employees who work in a relatively more flexible and changing environment. They even intend sometimes to disrupt the whole project implementation process putting at risk all efforts made to make a new system a reality. The proposed model leaves much of the internal processes within an LG intact. This allows piloting and testing systems in LGs with minimal risks. This approach calls for lesser changes of roles on the side of government employees. Since no radical changes are introduced, no demanding change management is needed anymore.

On the other hand, incorporating new LGs into the system is quite simple and easy. Even with numerous new LGs joining in, poses no threats to system integrity. Besides, no there is no pressing need to replace hardware or software as long as they work properly to serve the individual departments.

7.3.3 Components of the Federated Model

In the previous section, I have described the qualities of the model. In order for the model to be coherent and to achieve the objectives set forth above, the model should include some important basic components. These components should enable the model to exhibit the necessary encapsulation and abstraction features mentioned earlier. In the following subsections, I will describe in details the basic components of the model.

Governmental Entities

Government Entities (GEs) are viewed as black box entities. Each GE represents an autonomous governmental unit that hides its internal processes and flow of information. This component can typically be an LG, a governmental unit or even a municipality. As seen in Figure 53 below, each GE has the ability to interact with one or more different entities within the model through interfaces and messages. There is no need for uniformity of processes within the different LGs. This maintains their assumed autonomy. This arrangement does not threaten the long-living bureaucracy and hierarchy of the LGs. This is owing to the use of interfaces that have built-in messaging protocols. Thus no operational neither behavioral change is needed in any of the GEs. In this way, legacy systems can remain in place. There is a need, however, to convert data format from each legacy system into a unified format. Conversion is done through "Interfaces". This is described in the following subsection.

Interfaces

Interfaces achieve the sought separation of responsibilities and distribution of authorities among GEs. Interfaces are implemented practically through contracts among the different LGs. Such contracts include information rights, process ownership, responsibilities…etc. The contracts should be implemented carefully and accurately. They control and coordinate the relationships among GEs as per regulations set forth by the government. Interfaces describe in great detail the type of information that a particular entity can provide (e.g. personal records of a citizen) as well as the set of services that this particular GE can provide (e.g. issuing a passport). Interfaces are responsible for Cross-GE process integration. Figure 54 below depicts a typical GE encapsulated by its interface. Any GE that needs to interact with another must do that only via its interface. An interface, as such, works as a shield of the LG to achieve encapsulation. This helps keep the internal operation and data of a particular LG private. Only information set to be public can accessible via the interface. The degree of openness of an Interface affects the transparency of that LG. The more open the Interface is the better transparency becomes (Figure 54). Services offered by a particular GE (e.g. a ministry) can vary greatly. Therefore, each Interface has multiple levels of interaction. Communication between GEs through their interfaces is the subject of the next subsection

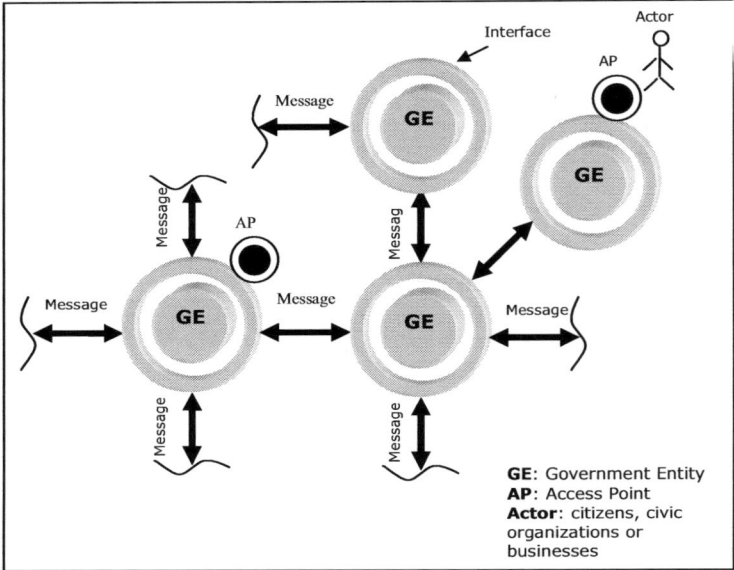

Figure 53: The federated model of e-government

Messages

It was mentioned above that interfaces in any GE should be finite and clearly defined. They represent the information and services (operations or tasks) that a particular GE can offer. As shown in Figure 53 above, a message must be sent to a concerned LG in order to request a service. These messages can originate at some GE. Each message sent must be identifiable. For example, source of the message should be known. Additionally, Message format must be standardised across the system. A message can be used to ask for a service or it can be loaded with a whole document. Proper authorisations and identifying information of the sender are incorporated in each message.

Access Points

Access points (APs) act as inputs and outputs between the system and the Actors (social bodies including citizens, businesses, and civic organisations). An AP can be a traditional help desk, a Web portal or any other access channel. As Figure 53 shows, we may have more than one AP in the model. Should a particular LG provide direct services to the public, then this LG will most likely have an associated AP. Through these APs or "portals", social bodies can request services or information. These requests may trigger consecutive messages and activities (processes) throughout the concerned GE(s). The GEs continue to interact through messaging until the requested service is fulfilled. Feedback is delivered through either the same AP or another one.

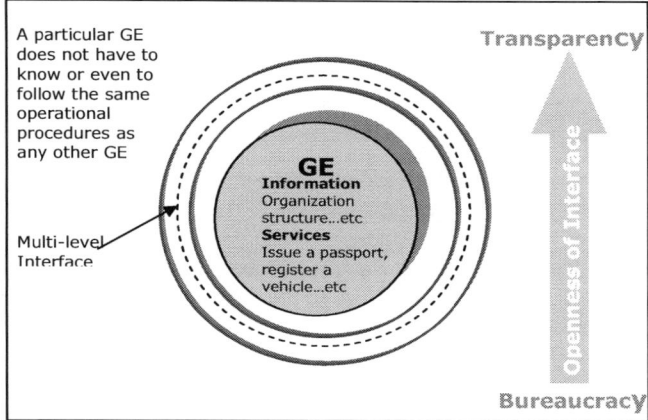

Figure 54: A detailed view a typical GE

From the description of the model one realises that it can best fit a democratic governmental system, which is based on the idea of distributing authorities, and the empowerment of autonomous GEs as mentioned earlier.

This model is *not* the very best for totalitarian regimes where decision-making is central and propagates from the top central government down to its none-autonomous branches.

Case Study 3 – The Federated Enterprise Architecture, New Zealand

In its quest for offering shared services, the government of New Zealand has built what they called "The Federated Enterprise Architecture—FEA". This networked model has been designed to achieve better interoperability. It has similar components to the Federated Model of e-Government (Figure 55 below).

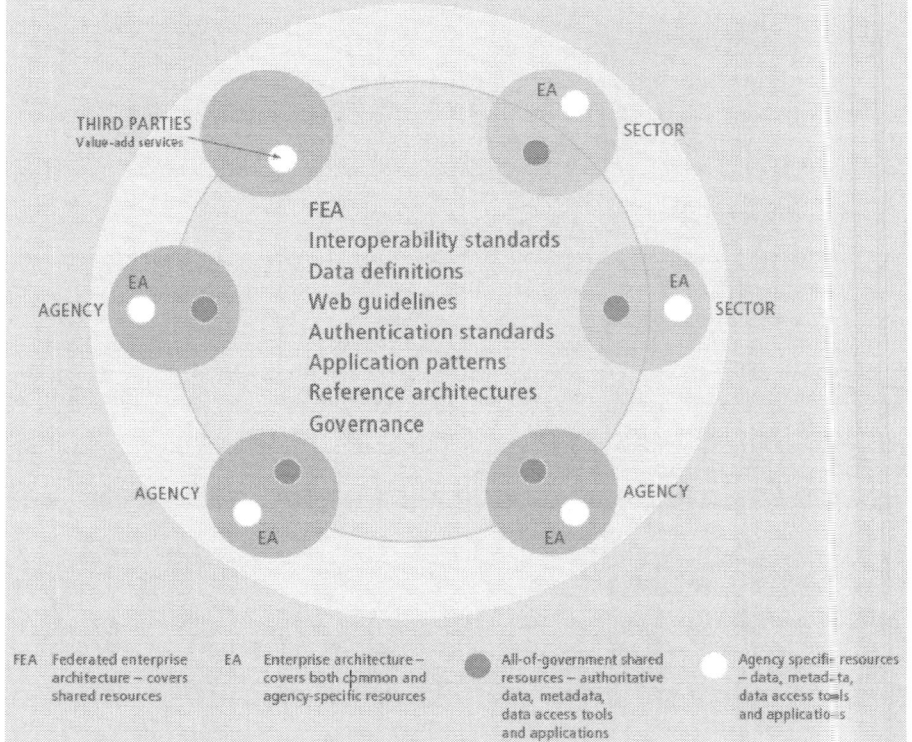

Figure 55: Federated Enterprise Model—FEA, New Zealand
Source: Strategy for e-government 2006- enabling transformation

The different agencies are represented as entities in the model. Each entity has two types of resources: internal and federal. As indicated in the Figure 55, these resources are basically data, metadata, access tools and applications. This separation between nternal and federal data stresses again the sort of abstraction promoted by my model. Agencies have connectors which correspond to interfaces in the federated model of e-government. According to the provided description of the FEA, these connectors must comply with the standards, policies and protocols needed to allow for interoperability across the different agencies.

The similarities between the federated model of e-government and New Zealand's FEA indicate that the former can be quite applicable in practice. There are, however, some differences between the two. The e-government strategy of New Zealand states that the FEA requires a *full cooperation* to become operational whereas the federated model does not stipulate this requirement. This is probably due to the federal resources that have to be installed inside any participating agency. In contrast, the federated model only requires the presence of the agency's interface to allow for data exchange and thus interoperability. Any resource inside an agency or GE is considered internal even if it was developed or supplied by the federal government. In fact, the presence of two types of resources inside one agency is messy as it creates complicated authorities over data ownership for example. Autonomous or local authorities need just to exchange data through their interfaces in order to engage in shared services. The federated model in this sense is simpler and more manageable.

Referring back to Case 1 with all its variations and decentralisation, the Swiss case is quite typical for the implementation of the proposed model. The idea was to distribute the underlying system of the portal among the local communes. This is in line with the proposed model. Each commune was perceived as an autonomous entity very much similar the GEs described in our proposed model (see Figure 53 above). So, the communes are a collection of GEs in the terminologies of our model with each GE being able to provide some content to the portal (through its interface). The way the portal was planned and implemented corresponds to the propositions of our model. This proves that the proposed model is conceptually applicable even for the toughest and most complex cases like the Swiss case.

7.4   Implications of the Federated Model

I have proposed a model that simplifies implementation of e-government initiatives. It facilitates cross-agency integration. The idea behind the model was to encapsulate local governmental units of a democratic political system that is based amongst other things on distributing power and authorities. As we have seen, the model has the capacity to cut down huge expenses because it does not inflict replacement of legacy systems. Training costs are avoided as a result. In addition, it assures minimal changes in the working environment of government employees. They can still work on their familiar systems. This reduces risk of project failure dramatically. Research shows that unaccounted-for change is a primary reason for failure of projects of this kind because of employees' resistance to changing the way they used to work (Laudon, 2006).

The greater the diversity in terms of systems, language...etc inside a country the more indispensable the model becomes. If the model has worked for an extreme case like Switzerland with all its diversities and variation (Case 1) it would definitely work for less extreme cases.

The model supports encapsulation of GEs. Thus, a government agency can decide on how transparent it would become. They can expose more their internal processes and information and thus improve their transparency. If they are fierce bureaucrats, on the other hand, then they can hide their internal processes and information. Obviousy, bureaucracy in this fashion is neutralised. This makes the model less prone to faiure. The model can be a double-edged sword: on the one-hand, the model preserves bureaucracy but only if the LG wants to do that by constricting the *interface* (see Figure 54). On the other hand, the model welcomes the opening up of internal processes to enhance transparency. Of course, everybody wants more transparency but, unfortunately, it is not always promoted by some GEs. I did not want to create a model that imposes transparency on the technical level and then fails because of the possible conflict with bureaucracy. I tried to make it valid for all the GEs regardless of the level of transparency they espouse. The reason again is the workability potential for as many governments as possible.

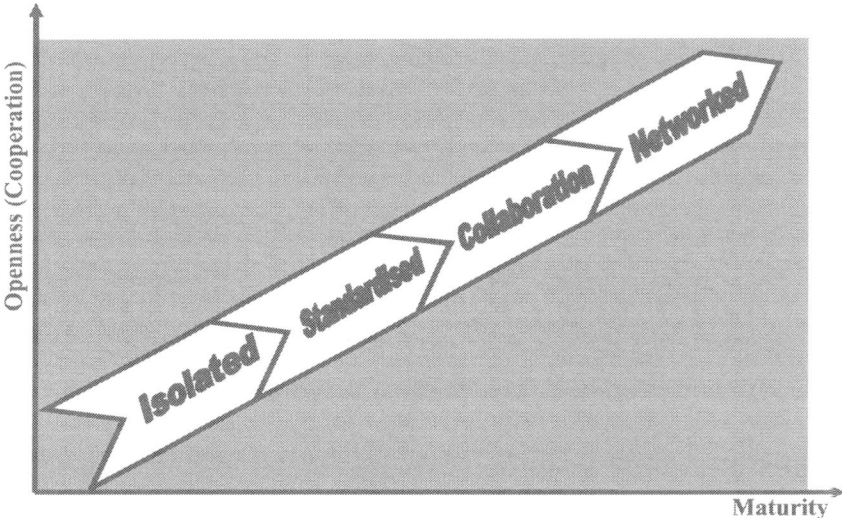

Figure 56: Impact of the federated model on service maturity

The model supports any level of integration among some or all GEs. The high-level abstraction the model provides makes it suitable for all GEs yet the implementation framework described above is a down-to-earth perfect realisation. Maximum efficiency is attained when there is maximum transparency in the GEs. This means that the more the openness and cooperation the maturity is of service delivery. As Figure 56 above shows, higher maturity levels of services delivery are achieved when there is more openness to work with the other agencies. Delivering shared services will certainly depend on the level of coordination demonstrated by the involved agencies.

A downside of the model, though, is that it may hamper innovation. As long as software and hardware are running properly, they will not be changed as often (when an interesting new technology debuts for example). As said previously, governments have priorities regarding their expenditure on projects. Because of that, they can be reluctant to replace systems that are working well enough.

7.5 Technical Implementation of the Model

A model that is not implementable is hardly useful. This section describes briefly the IT platform architecture that can underlie the federated model of e-government.

Each GE may have its own back office systems. These could be legacy systems that are very difficult to be integrated into other (normally new) systems. This, inarguably, entails that different GEs can have different data formats. This should not pose a problem to the federated model. The model was originally built around the idea of encapsulation of disparate systems. However, these systems should be able to "talk" to one another regardless of the hardware and software used in each of the GEs. The idea here is to make common interfaces among the GEs and not to make a common platform. This cuts down intricacies and lowers costs dramatically as mentioned earlier. This can be achieved fairly easily by using interfaces as described above in Figure 54.

But how can interfaces become common among disparate systems? A lot of research (e.g. Tambouris, 2001; Traunmüller & Wimmer, 2002; ICA Country Report, 2004; Bochicchio & Longo, 2004; Scholl, 2005; Punia & Saxena, 2004; Mugellini et al., 2005; Anthopoulos & Tsoukalas, 2005; Spahni, 2004; Klischewski & Jeenicke, 2004, Henriksen et al., 2004; IT Pro 2003; Smith & Adams, 2005) suggest the adoption of the eXtensible Markup Language--XML. The power of XML over the more traditional HTML format is that it describes not only the content and formatting but also the meaning and properties of each element (object) in the document. But these meanings are only readable using computer programmes tat are written to decipher the meanings as well as the structure of the document. This necessitates the need for standardisation of these programs. A government can come up with its own ontology in defining concepts, terminologies, meanings...etc. The advantage is quite obvious when searching through documents. Search results will be conceptual rather than simply matching out texts. For multi-lingual countries (e.g. Switzerland, Belgium...etc) this could be quite advantageous because the search will be concerned with concepts regardless of the original language used to write the document.

In this context, the World Wide Web Consortium (W3C) has developed XQuery, which is based on XML. XQuery was designed from the very beginning to support data integration. It works on data from different sources provided that it can be formatted in XML. Since XML is a highly structured format. XQuery can produce more useful results than traditional queries. Searching for a specific content can be based on concepts and not occurrences of the search string and independent of the language used for search. This should yield accurate and structured results. This can be quite beneficial for foreigners living in a country or community and who need to access governmental information or services where the official language is not their mother tongue.

Each government can come up with its own specific XML structure and formatting. A government-customised version of XML can be useful. These customised formats have common terminologies that describe all sorts of information a GE can work on. An example of such customisation is the Japanese G-XML project. G-XML project is currently being carried out by the Database Promotion Centre DPC in Japan. DPC is a non-profit organisation that works under the auspices of the Japanese government's Ministry of Economy, Trade and Industry (METI). G-XML project is aimed at creating a protocol for encoding data through extensions built upon XML. This project is to facilitate the adoption of common Geographical Information System.

The interfacing (bridging) required among GEs is achieved through unified data format and messaging protocols. Local implementations, however, can remain the same. Thus hardware and software can be left as is without alteration. There might be a need, though, for a middleware (*a software used to convert data formats from one format into another*) in case the installed software in one of GEs does not support XML format. In case the structure or meaning of data has been changed by the LG in charge to other formats (for the use in other LGs), then the translation will be done only once by updating the rules in the translator. The translator itself is part of the interface.

The federated model of e-government is indispensable when building a large-scale governmental portal. A governmental portal provides one-stop access to governmental services and information. One-stop government refers to the integration of public services from a citizen's point of view (Tambouris, 2001). Aseen seen in Case 1, a government portal can collect information from different GEs simply by sending messages to the interfaces of the GEs concerned. The local content is compiled by local GE(s). This makes it easy to manage complexities of hyperlinks and document formats. Hyperlinks and local URLs are maintained by the GEs. Document formatting, layout and style can then be standardised by applying Standard Governmental XLS to the received local content. More recently, OASIS (www.oasis-open.org) has provided a standard called Web Services for Remote Portlets (WSRP), which is aimed at standardising presentation-oriented Web Services. To standardise interactions, WSRP defines a set of interfaces and semantics. Using these standards, writing a unique code for interaction among the different Web Services is avoided.

7.5.1 Service-oriented Architecture

Since around 2004, there has been a trend among big enterprises towards using the Service-Oriented Architecture (SOA). The Organisation for the Advancement of Structured Information Standards (OASIS) defines SOA as the following:

> *A paradigm for organizing and utilizing distributed capabilities that may be under the control of different ownership domains*

SOA architecture has a tactical objective of achieving interoperability. SOA can be viable implementation architecture for the federated model of e-government. This architecture best fits loosely coupled systems. SOA facilitates interconnecting legacy systems. Most implementations use the XML standards.

Governments worldwide are accelerating their efforts to offer online services. Most have launched different programmes to move forward towards full electronic government implementation. One of the biggest challenges of e-government is interoperability. Most government agencies have back office systems installed. Development of such systems used to be carried out locally. Decision making in government agencies is decentralised. This has led to great diversities in back office systems. Application programmes, operating systems data formats and hardware specifications have little in common. The federated model of e-government guarantees interoperability among disparate systems. The model can roughly be based on SOA.

SOA is a concept, which is built around the notion of services. It came as a response to pan-enterprise integration challenge. Thus, it is possible to connect heterogeneous disparate systems regardless of operating systems, programming language, or hardware. Globalisation and intercontinental companies gave rise to thinking about such architecture. Many governments, as well, embraced the idea for they face the same challenges. In fact, SOA is currently the most conceivable implementation framework for our model as we shall see shortly. In their recent version of e-government strategies, many governments considered SOA as a platform for their networked operation (e.g. India, The Netherlands, Denmark, Australia, and Austria). Other countries have developed similar architectures that can be said to be SOA-inspired (e.g. Belgium).

SOA is not only a technical implementation or solution. It is also a managerial concept. SOA as a concept is technology independent. The following technical components are some potential examples of SOA implementation. Together, they can form a workable SOA solution:

- *Web Service Description*: this component utilises WSDL to describe the functionality of the Web Service. It provides name of the Web service, namespaces used, *port-types* which are essentially the publicly available functions the Web Service (WS) provides, message transmission protocol (SOAP), input and output messages. This detailed description enables clients to interact with and utilise a Web service

- *Web Service Registration*: a WS is more constructive if it is discoverable by clients otherwise, it will remain largely unknown. Universal Description Definition Interface (UDDI) is a standard WS discovery component. It provides pointers to WSDL documents attached to WSs. UDDI can be accessed manually by clients as well as programmatically. Although it is essential for a WS to be registered in the UDDI to become discoverable, some WS are meant to be hidden.

- *Messaging*: SOAP provides a common standard of communication between services. SOAP has in-built security and transaction functionalities.

- *Process Execution Language*: While WSDL describes operations the WS offers, PEL describes how these operations are correlated in the context of a process. They either choreograph or orchestrate the flow of messages across WSs depending on process paradigm.

Messages in the federated model of e-government can be easily implemented using the Simple Object Access Protocol (SOAP). SOAP is an XML-based protocol used for object invocation. SOAP can be thought of as an envelop that encapsulates a message transmitted among different applications across the Internet. This envelop has two parts: header and body. The header part describes the message format and how it can be decoded. The body contains the data to be communicated. The body can be a whole XML document. This technology facilitates communication among applications running on different operating systems, different platforms, and developed with different programming languages. SOAP fits the model quite nicely. Other countries have used custom protocols. An example from Belgium is the Universal Messaging Engine UME. It generally uses the same principle of having a unified messaging format across GEs.

Many back office or front office systems can easily be written to load a WSDL document. WSDL documents have pointers to local applications (operations) within the WS. Invoked local applications may have been written using different programming languages. They may also be running under diverse operating systems or hardware platforms. The ultimate advantage of SOA is it allows disparate applications to "talk" to one another. This platform utilises the portability of XML. PEL, WSDL, SOAP, and UDDI, which are all XML-based.

BPEL is used to execute clearly defined business processes. It is based on the orchestration paradigm (Juric, 2005). E-Government processes, by contrast, are choreographic in nature as alluded above. BPEL is thus best applied for centralised processes. It was built with business processes in mind as the title suggests. It definitely wasn't tailored for e-government implementation. Other standards, however, were introduced to fit the choreographic paradigm, which better superposes e-government processes. Among these were Web Services Choreography Interface (WSCI) and Web Services Choreography Description Language (WS-CDL). Unfortunately, they did not gain enough support by the business industry (Juric, 2005). Again, though, they are still not tailored for e-Government type of process execution.

When the number of systems integrated with SOA becomes larger and larger; processes become intricate and indistinct. Eventually logic behind these processes becomes even harder to maintain, update and understand. We know already that process ownership in governments is not as clear as that in business even before implementation of SOA. Moreover, process ownership is more important for governments.

It is important that process logic remains clear and human understandable by both public servants and clients. Process execution languages, today, are not human understandable. They are not even rule-based. My proposition is to use both rule-based and human understandable approach. I propose the use of the rule-based approach in two tiers of the Service-Oriented Architecture: on the Web Service level and across Web Services.

7.6   Rule-based Approach

Klischewski (2001) compared the service flow (which is now the articulated SOA) and workflow approaches. Service flow better fits governmental processes, as there is no central flow "engine" to coordinate the different services offered by the different government agencies. Processes in governments are decentralised. In other words, processes follow the choreographic paradigm. Process ownership changes continuously across different agencies involved.

SOA allows for citizen-centric processes. According to (Klischewski 2001) service flows constitute personalised sequence of interrelated activities. A process in service flow is considered as a means for personalisation rather than control.

Application development, however, mixes up process logic, application logic, GUI logic and data access logic (Tammet et al.). The obvious downside is that government processes become less understandable. This has its ramifications on the maintenance, reusability, and portability of process logic. It is the purpose of this section to propose a system that can keep the logic of governmental processes separate and clearly defined at all times.

A government process is a logic-intensive knowledge that is too intricate to be represented with traditional procedural programming or databases. Think about taxation for example. Traditional procedural programming tools are Omni-available. In addition, skilled programmers who can use these tools, outnumber considerable the logic programmers. These tools however fall short in representing logic knowledge. Logic rules exhibit non-procedural sequences of execution.

The role of a government is to practise governance and maintain the well-being of the society. In contrast, the role of business is to achieve maximum profit with least cost. This huge difference in role has its influence on processes. For a government process, a number of strict considerations are to be taken into account at design time and at run time.

Transparency in government processes, per se, is a public a constituency or public demand. Normally, an independent organisation conducts auditing of government operation including processes. In many cases, the auditors do not have the appropriate IT background. In this case, separate and simple rule-based representation of processes will be quite helpful for these auditors. Otherwise, auditing becomes ineffective.

Business process design, on the other hand, focuses on efficiency, cost reduction, and capitalisation on profit. Of course, business abides by law but the field of application though is very limited in comparison. Business processes generally produce products. Government processes, by contrast, aim to furnish citizens and businesses with services (e.g. issuing a permission to build a house or to start a new business). Clearly, government processes, in general, are more delicate and therefore should be represented accurately.

It is well known that logic languages are much more expressive than procedural languages. Generally, non logic-based programming languages use variables to represent facts. The extensive use of variables in complex structures (e.g. loops, branching…etc) causes a degradation in the readability of the programme which makes it harder to maintain or update. Whereas, logic languages provide a simpler and a declarative representation of facts and rules in a coherent manner and then use either forward chaining or backward chaining to execute the programme. Logic programmes are also pointer-free which makes them much more flexible than traditional programmes (Morozov et al. 1999).

Furthermore, a simple declarative representation of facts and rules makes them even easier to understand by humans. This representation has a self-describing nature. It makes it, thus, self-documenting. This is necessary on the long run. It is not very uncommon that software manuals get lost after a long time. In this case, it would be almost impossible to update the software without rewriting it. It becomes worse if the contract with the software developer has long ended.

In many cases, rules have time-frame validity. A specific rule or a collection of rules can be valid for a certain period of time. Other rules might apply afterwards. This means that different rules are applied across the time-line. In such cases, there is a need to keep track of which rules were applicable at a specific time-frame. One of the persistent problems of using traditional databases to store rules was the difficulty to express time-dependant rules. With the rule-based approach, it is much simpler and easier. Time validity is embedded within the rules themselves. All rules are kept in one separate place called "Knowledge Base".

Logic programming languages have the capacity to be used for natural language recognition. It allows clients to get recommendations on the best things to do to get a government service. The client can feed information to the system in natural language. The system then analyses what has been typed, recognises it, and responds accordingly by choosing the best process. Finding the best track or process for the client to go through is one aspect at which logic programmes excel. Logic languages are much more advanced in searching best solutions than traditional procedural languages.

7.6.1 Are Changes to Process Logic in Governments Common?

One thing for sure is that process re-engineering and streamlining is much more evident in businesses than in governments. This has to do with the fact that business is much more flexible than the government and that business environment changes quite rapidly due to micro economic factors and fierce competition. Still though, changes to government processes are more frequent than might seem to be. It seems that government processes are frequently reviewed. Reasons behind process re-design vary from policy shifting to enhancing transparency. Besides, we have seen in Chapter 4 that reform in organisational, operational and legal aspects of e-government was the number one success factor cited by the majority of governments. In addition, achieving internal efficiencies -which was also found to be the number one focus area of e-government- has its toll on processes, regulations and legislations.

There are many examples that took place in different countries. To give just one valuable example I will introduce in Case 3 below the Belgian initiative "Kafka".

Case Study 4 – The Kafka Initiative, Belgium

In 2003 the Belgian Secretary for Administrative Reform was assigned a specific task: cut the red tape (Kafka 2003). This initiative was meant to commence large-scale administrative reforms that will rid citizens and businesses of administrative rigmarole. Notorious bureaucracy caused great inefficiencies for citizens and businesses alike. In just four years some (200) laws and regulations were either simplified or even abolished all together (Kafka Report 2006). As a result administrative costs for businesses have decreased by 25%, a reduction of about (1.7) billion euros. This has put Belgium in first position among European countries where it is fastest to start a new business. According to the World Bank, "Belgium has developed the European Union's most innovative communication programme for cutting red tape".

This case makes one realise that changes to government processes can occur more frequently than one can imagine. This dictates that process implementation should be designed in such a way that allows easy update and maintenance.

7.6.2   Process Development

Each public agency sets its own processes. They design processes based on the services they offer. Their services, however, can use local processes within other GEs. This means that a process can span across many GEs that have their local rules to provide their service(s). A local service might charge one or more other processes. Rules, thus, will overlap. With traditional programming, this becomes too complicated. With my approach, the rules can be easily inherited using *Semantic Bridging* (Barnickel et al, 2006).

Figure 57: Semantic Bridging (Barnickel et al, 2006)

With a Semantic Bridge, Web Service with Ontology A can understand information passed by another Web Service with Ontology B and vice-versa. For example, different agencies might keep different formats for the same address of a person. Using semantic bridging, address and name formats can be translated transparently among these agencies as show in the following example:

(A hasStreet S), (A hasStreetNumber N) → (A hasStreetAddress S+N)

(A hasName N), (N hasGivenName G), (N hasSurname S) → (A hasRecepient G+S)

(Source: Barnickel et al, 2006)

Rules can also be backtracked in the hierarchy in case of any problem during implementation. Developing a governmental process requires analysis and design across multiple levels. There are standards and tools that can guide and carryout process development. The following subsection describes some of them.

7.6.3   Business Process Modelling Tools

A number of standard modelling tools can be used for process development. None of these tools, though, can fit alone all fields of application. Each tool has a specific field of application. Some modelling tools are still under development. The following is a list of the most standardised modelling tools:

- Process execution languages (PEL): these are XML-based languages that define business processes. They use the Web Services model for process execution. There are two types of PELs: choreographic and orchestration. Business Process Execution Language (BPEL); an orchestration language. It has become an industry standard. BPEL relies on the Web Services Description Language (WSDL) which is basically an XML document that describes the functionality of a Web Service (WS)

- Process automation analysis languages (PAAL): basically, PAA languages include Unified Modelling Languages (UML). UML 1.0 and 2.0 possess advanced graphical notations. They have been quite efficient in modelling object-oriented designs

- Organisation analysis and value chain analysis languages: these languages provide tools for organisation and value chain analysis. None of the previous languages was dedicated to these kinds of analysis. ISO 9000x was the first reference standard to address business processes. But the ISO 9000x is just a reference standard for the quality analysis and does not provide any graphical notations which has limited its spread

- Business Process Data Model (BPDM) and Business Process Modelling Notation (BPMN) provide tools for process automation analysis, value chain analysis and organisation analysis. These two however are still not finalised

The following table (Table 22) summarises current and proposed new standards:

Standard	Originator	Status	Application	Graphical Notation
XPDL	WFMC	Finalised	Process Execution Language	Not Supported
BPML	BPMI	Finalised	Process Execution Language	Not Supported
BPEL	OASIS	Finalised	Process Execution Language	Not Supported
UML 1.0	OMG	Finalised	Process Automation Analysis	Supported

Standard	Originator	Status	Application	Graphical Notation
UML 2.0	OMG	Finalised	Process Automation Analysis	Supported
BPMN 1.0	BPMI	Finalised	Process Automation Analysis	Supported
BPMN 2.0	BPMI	Underway	Process Automation Analysis Organisation Analysis Value Chain Analysis	Supported
ISO 9000x	ISO	Finalised	Organisation Analysis Value Chain Analysis	Not Supported
BPDM	OMG	Underway		Supported

Table 22: **Proposed new standards for process development (adapted from Lonjon 2004)**

The general note to make about the above languages is that they all mix rules and conditions with procedures which makes rules' logic less clear. More importantly, however, is that none of them is rule-based and therefore they cannot avail the benefits of a rule-based system. The following section, presents a short theoretical review of logic and knowledge representation systems.

7.6.4 Logic and Knowledge Representation Systems

Rule-based approaches are not something new. They follow one or another type of logic. According to Merriam Webster's dictionary, Logic is defined as:

"A science that deals with principles and criteria of validity of inference and demonstration, the science of formal principles of reasoning"

Unlike natural language, logic is precise. It is used to represent facts and rules accurately. In addition, it uses reasoning (interpretation, satisfaction...etc) in order to deduce new facts (conclusions or answers to problems). Historically, logic has philosophical roots. Aristotle, a Greek philosopher introduced two types of logic deductive and inductive reasoning based on syllogism (Cornwell 1998). It was only in the nineteenth century that Bertrand Russels and Alfred Whitehead have set formal logic as a foundation for Mathematics (William and Martha 1962).

There are several types of logic. Basic Mathematical logic is composed of Propositional and Predicate logic. Other types of complex logic followed (temporal, modal, higher order, and non-monotonic). Logical programming languages use mathematical logic to execute computer programmes. They are declarative in nature. Unlike procedural programming, the programmer sets facts and a logical model composed of rules.

A number of implementations of logic programming began in the sixties of the last century with Abys being the first language that was exclusively devised for assertions. Other languages followed (e.g. Planner, QA-4, QLISP, Prolog, Ether...etc.). Prolog has

---

gained the utmost popularity. Many siblings have evolved such as Visual Prolog and more recently HiLog, and λProlog that use high-order logic. Higher order logic is more expressive than the classical first order logic. It allows taking even other predicates as arguments, which allows for complex constructions.

7.6.5 Complexity of Rules in Government Processes

A legitimate question is now *are there really that much rules governing processes in governments?* In fact, there are plenty of them. For example, in Hong Kong's Civil Service, vacation requests of staff are governed by 200 different rules.

Besides, the nature of these rules can be very complex. They can exhibit a decision tree format as mentioned above. In other words, the process can go on taking one path across the rules and at some point; the process may stop for failure to fulfill a certain rule. The process has then to be moved up the tree to the previous node in order to check another path. Clearly, traditional programaring languages will not be able to handle such complexity using their nested if-then structures. It is simply ill suited for this purpose. The following are just three real rules from the Palestinian Territories that judge the particular shares of inheritors of the fortune of a deceased person:

- If no inheritors other than offsprings then they inherit all the estate. In this case, a son gets twice as much as a daughter. If the deceased has only one daughter and no sons then she gets half the estate. If the deceased has two or more daughters but no sons then they all get two thirds and each parent gets one sixth. If no offsprings then the father gets two thirds and the mother gets the rest. If the deceased has brothers then the mother gets one sixth, the father gets the rest and nothing for the brothers.

- A husband inherits half the estate of a deceased wife if she had no offsprings otherwise he inherits the quarter. A wife inherits one quarter of a deceased husband if he has no offsprings and one eighth otherwise.

- If the deceased (man or woman) has no offsprings but has a brother or a sister (of the same mother) then each gets one sixth. If the number of sisters and brothers (of the same mother) is greater then they share the third of the estate

Let us now see this scenario:

- Amre and Zeid are brothers from one Mother (Huda). Ahmed is their brother from their father (Ibrahim). David's mother is (Sawsan). Muna is their sister (from Huda).

- Jamal is married to Yasmine and has two sons Waleed and Haitham. The other brothers are not married. Muna is married to Ragheb and has one daughter (Laila).

- Rania is the daughter of Hassan the brother of Huda. Adam is the son of Hassan. Rani is the uncle of Muna.

Now, we need to automate the process and ask the following two simple questions

- Who is the brother of Sawsan?

- Who are the inheritors of Waleed? How much each of them gets?

Can this be done with a traditional procedural programme? Imagine if we talk about an old fortune of a hundred years back, many of the original inheritors have died, and their offsprings need to get their share. This is just one example of part of the logic of a government processes. There is an absolute necessity to use logic programming to approach their intricacies.

The power of logic programming is that it mainly captures fact and rules. The example below is part of a logic programme that captures part of the above facts and rules.

Facts	Rules

man(Amre).
 man(Zeid).
 man(Ibrahim).
 man(Waleed).
 man(Haitham).
 man(Adam).
 woman(Huda).
 woman(Sawsan).
 woman(Muna).
 woman(Laila).
 father(Ibrahim,Amre).
 father(Ibrahim,Zeid).
 father(Ibrahim,Ahmed).
 father(Hassan,Adam).
 father(Jamal,Waleed).
 father(Jamal,Haitham).
 father(Ragheb,Laila).
 Mother(Muna,Laila).
 ..
	son(X,Y) :- male(X),
	     father(Y,X).
	 son(X,Y) :- male(X),
	     mother(Y,X).
	 daughter(X,Y) :- female(X),
	     father(Y,X);female(X),
	     mother(Y,X).
	 uncle(Y,X):-mother(Z,X),father(F,Y),father(F,Z).
	 ...

Figure 58: Logic code snippets that capture some facts and rules from the inheritance example

As long as the rules and facts are entered correctly, the logic programme will handle the complexities with efficiency. Besides, entry of rules and facts can be automated.

7.6.6 The Proposed Approach

As mentioned earlier, there is a need to keep the logic of governmental processes separate, clearly defined and reusable. To achieve this, some assumptions must be made regarding the proposed approach:

- The proposed approach should be logic-based as processes themselves are logical (rule-based)

- Rules should be kept separate from procedures (application programmes) and not embedded in them

- Rules should be declarative, none procedural and intuitive

- Rules are understood/written by people who presumably do not have programming skill

- Rule-base development should take the least time

- It should be easy to maintain or update the rules

- Rules should be reusable (portable)

- The approach should allow explanation and reasoning to provide the sought level of transparency to the "customers"

Once a system possesses these qualities, it merits as being the answer for what we need to achieve. What is needed now is to compile the tools necessary to originate such a system. The following subsection describes the results of my rule-based prototype. This prototype is not meant to measure efficiency of the proposed approach in any scientific means whatsoever. It is just presented to prove the workability of the approach using some readily available programming tools.

7.6.7 Applicability of the Rule-based Approach

Procedural programming languages like Java, C++, Visual Basic…etc have dominated the Web development. They worked well for most applications. For some specialised applications, however, they fall short. An example is when relationships among objects are too complex to fit a database.

As mentioned earlier, such applications normally take the form of a tree of possible paths to find a solution. They are used when there are too many inter-related facts to be checked against a plethora of rules. A good example is a medical assessment of a disease based on patient's symptoms. I already mentioned that government processes are also rule-based. I have developed an architecture that uses logic programming to implement government processes. A prototype was created to test the architecture (Figure 60).

New tools were built in Web logic programming. On the server side we have systems like EMRM Knowledge Base (Szeredi et al. 1996), ECLiPSe (Bonnet et al. 1996) WebLS (Amzi 1999)…etc. In addition, many other client-side logic-based systems were developed. Among these are Win-Prolog, Jess (Friedman 1999), Jinni (Tarau 1999), NetProlog (de Carvalho 2001)…etc. Some tools offer server-side and client-side support like Visual Prolog and Amzi!Prolog.

Until recently, the most prominent logic programming language Prolog suffered from two major deficiencies to be used for Web development: embeddability and extensibility. Embeddability means the ability to embed Prolog code in other programming languages. In other words, providing APIs in other languages for Prolog programmes. Extensibility, on the other hand, refers to customising Prolog programmes by extending them with other programming languages. These two shortcomings were overcome with the creation of tools that bridges Prolog code with other procedural code like Java. An example of such tools is Amzi!Prolog which I used in sample application.

I would stress, at this point, my choice of Amzi!Prolog does not entail that it was the best among other languages. In fact, some other languages might have been more efficient. I chose Amzi!Prolog (Amzi, 2006) as a Logic Server because it was free for academic use. This Prolog engine supports the embedment of Prolog code into host languages like C++, Java…etc. I chose Java as my host language because of its wide use in Web applications. The use of Java and Amzi!Prolog is to prove a concept and not to advocate this particular solution over the others.

I compiled my sample Prolog programme, which serves as my *mini* Knowledge Base. A knowledge base is essentially a collection of facts and rules written in Prolog in this case (see Figure 58). I then used the provided Amzi!Prolog Linker to generate the loadable XPL file. After that, I utilised the readily available Java APIs to connect to the mini Knowledge Base. In other words, the Java programme was able to read read facts and rules from the mini knowledge base as seen from in the sample code in Figure 59. I followed the Amzi!Prolog guidelines to do that.

```
import amzi.ls.*;

class Legacy
{
    LogicServer ls;

    public static void main(String args[])
    {
        System.out.println("Inheritance Decision System");
        try
        {
            Legacy legacy = new Legacy() ;
            legacy.runDecisionMaker() ;
        }
        catch (LSException e)
        {
            System.out.println(e.GetMsg());
        }
    }

    ...

    public void runDecisionMaker() throws LSException
    {
        long term;
        String pred = "parents(X,Y,Amre)" ;
        term = ls.ExecStr(pred) ;
        String father = ls.GetStrArg(term,1) ;
        String mother = ls.GetStrArg(term,2) ;
        System.out.println("Father: " + father) ;
        System.out.println("Mother: " + mother) ;
        ls.Close();
    }
}

    public Legacy() throws LSException
    {
        ls = new LogicServer();
        ls.Init("");
        ls.Load("legacy");
    }
}
```

Figure 59: Sample code of the Java programme with Amzi!Prolog extension

Then, I installed Tomcat as a Web Application Container (Web server). Here, I wrote my sample Web application. Finally, I installed the Web Service extension facility. AXIS was used on top of Tomcat server (see Figure 60). In the end, I wrote the WSDL document to connect to the applications Web Server. With this, I had a fully functional Logic Web Service running.

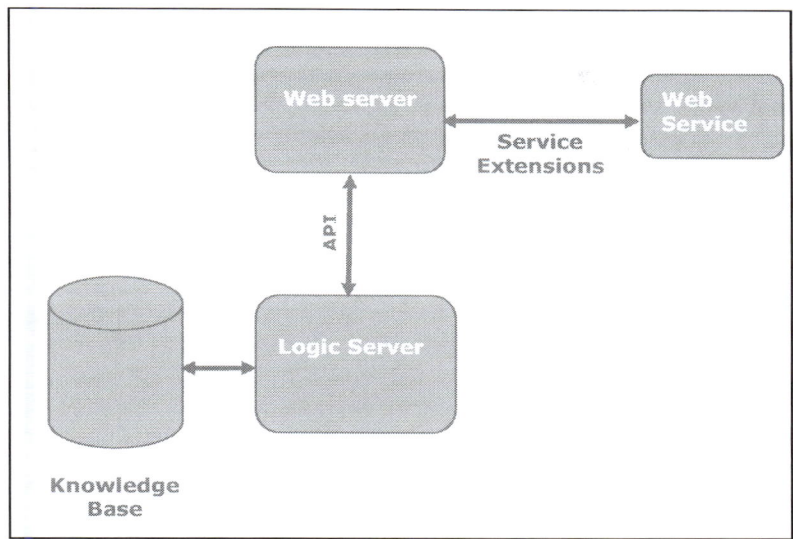

Figure 60: Schematic representation of an example application of a rule based approach

7.6.8   Conclusions

It is true that Prolog rules are not written in natural language. Still, they are more human comprehensible than traditional procedural languages. They are much simpler. Because of their simplicity, even those without IT background can understand. Besides, they are kept separate in the knowledge base, which satisfies my objective in this chapter. I needed to keep the logic of government processes both separate and understandable.

Prolog has the capacity to be used for natural language recognition. A citizen for example, can express his query in his own language over the Web and get accurate recommendation. By doing that, one can create an expert system, that is available twenty-four hours a day and seven days a week. This enhances government service dramatically. Moreover, the system can read the rules and facts in the knowledge base and easily generates a report about procedures, conditions, requirements…etc of a particular government service. The information in such a report will be up-to-date. The citizen or company can then know why the procedure is like that. This enhances transparency.

Work is underway to produce a natural language-like logic language. Extended Logical Mark up (ELM) language is both rule-based and human-understandable (Tammet 2004). The specification is still a work in progress. This is based on the RQL technology (Karvounarakis et al. 2002). ELM relies on the RqlGandalf rule solver, which provides interpretations of logic rules. This technology is promising because it also allows more client interaction in human language.

I produced an intra-WS prototype that implemented processes within a WS as rules and facts. Still though, I did not resolve the inter-WS rule-based implementation of processes.

What is needed to approach this is an XML together with a rule-based approach. I need it to be XML-based for portability. A choreographic language (e.g. WSCI which is XML-based) is needed but with ability to support logic rules. These rules can be either natural language-like or formal notation or even a mixture of both. I believe that this should be a direction for new research for better process implementation. A group of researchers from both academia and industry are working to come up with such a language. A new initiative called "The Rule Markup Language (RuleML) Initiative" is being launched (www.ruleml.org). It is about bringing logic and XML together. This stems from the necessity to have *inference rules* in a portable format. The advantage is obvious and inline my proposition. It also steps up the notion of Semantic Web.

I have presented a rule-based approach for implementing e-Government processes. In my crude sample prototype, I have managed to keep the logic of processes separate and well expressed. It is a promising approach to reduce complexities in Service-Oriented Architecture, which has received interest for e-government implementation. Typically, SOA supports a multitude of electronic processes of a government or a business. Part of these processes span across more than one Web Service. My approach helps to sort out the logic behind these processes so that it remains understandable and auditable.

The proposed approach bridged eloquent logic declarative programming with the power of procedural programming over the Web. This modus operandi has the best of both worlds. On one hand, we use the precise description of facts and rules of processes. On the other hand, we use the efficient and widely used procedural programming. In such approach, logic and operation are split apart. This has a unique effect on simplifying understanding of e-Government processes.

The rule-based approach is another step forward towards Semantic and Intelligent Web. Bringing logical representation of facts in its ultimate form can have total re-thinking of things like logical search, Web-based intelligent agents...etc. I hope this will become a new direction in research of both academia and industry towards a better process design and implementation.

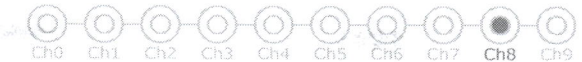
CHAPTER 8: PARTICULAR OPPORTUNITIES FOR THE LESS DEVELOPED COUNTRIES

8.1 Introduction

Broadly speaking, there are economic, political, cultural, and demographic differences between developed and underdeveloped countries. Additionally, there is an obvious difference in ICT readiness. On top of that, there are mild to severe differences in level of education and wealth. These differences reflect as well on development.

(Austin 1990) has studied this issue in detail in his book" Managing in Developing Countries - Strategic Analysis and Operating Techniques". He mentioned that developing countries are plagued by the following:

- Governmental controls
- Rampant inflation and devaluation
- Cumbersome bureaucratic procedures for obtaining import licenses
- Skill scarcity
- Difficulties with training new employees in new technology
- Lack of political stability
- Scarcity in logistics.

The latter point hinders any local outsourcing plans. There are fewer advanced and reliable industries or business in certain fields. For instance, if a company wants to outsource backup of its data chances are slim of finding a local company that can do that.

Any company willing to operate in an LDC must be aware of what the local environment can bring up. The hardest part in their quest is getting the right information from their credible sources. A major setback is to stumble across an unforeseen law or regulation that may draw an end to an investment in a project. This is where e-government can really be of great benefit to foreign as well as local investors. e-Government would presumably make all sorts of information easily accessible for investors. This is one good reason why e-Government can drive development in an LDC.

Differences in culture can bring some risks to business. Employees from different cultures working together must really understand each other's differences on the personal and on the professional levels. In addition, Level of service of each joint-venturing or outsourcing company must be compatible to some extent. If a company with a high level of service or maturity liaise with another of a lower level then expectations from each are different. In many cases, this leads to a standstill in operation. This can dangerously put a project on halt.

Besides, working in politically unstable environment adds a severe threat to the mix. Unlike in the developing countries, geopolitical situation must always be monitored closely as it affects directly operation of companies. Political risk assessment here is necessary.

Investing in an LDC must not be understood as retarding. On the contrary, there are important opportunities that companies need to hunt. Many LDCs have plenty of skilful workforces that are well trained and low-paid. This is a practical formula for maximising returns on investment. On the demographic front, many LDCs are heavily populated. Investing in low-priced but large volume products can be quite lucrative. The caveat here is to account the new different kinds of risk in advance and to curb them with appropriate measures.

8.2   The Learning Government

The World Wide Web knows no borders. Everybody can avail from the free information it has offer. Besides, it allows cheap communications. LDCs can use the Internet as a free learning tool and as a primary source of quality information. Many solutions to different kinds of problems have already been posted over the Internet waiting for the wise and motivated researchers to avail from. Numerous quality scientific journals publish articles online that are accessible for either free or at a low cost. Many of these articles provide solutions feasible for LDCs. It only requires considerate and serious officials from the governments assign committees to research them.

We have seen the impact of e-government on e-commerce. Nevertheless, there is just the opposite effect. e-Government can learn from businesses. In fact, many of the solutions adopted by e-governments today are the best-tested solutions that were implemented in businesses. Business solutions can form a testing environment for e-government. Despite my argument earlier in the previous chapter about differences between governments and businesses, I believe that government can at least benefit from experiences of the private sector. It is true that there are differences, but there are plenty of common solutions too. I do not call for directly implementing business solutions to governments, but rather to promote government learning from business. Albert Gore and Scott Adams argue in their book "Businesslike Government: Lessons Learned from America's Best Companies" that governments can learn a lot from business practices. The authors stress that innovation in e-government can stem from the working force (the government employees) who know risk, mistakes and opportunities of e-government. They call for the stimulation of government employees to innovate.

Some scholars have identified possible private sector's participation in operating e-government projects (e.g. Zukauskas & Kasteckiene, 2002). Private international companies can participate in building the infrastructure needed to support online services. For example, Microsoft has contracted the Jordanian government to develop e-government in the country. The private sector can also provide the public sector with their expertise. In addition, the private sector can directly carry out some less sensitive transactions on behalf of the public sector but with strict government monitoring. Another form of participation is to joint-venture projects with the public sector in the form of packaged public/private sector solutions. Finally, business can affect governments in an indirect way. Since citizens are now used to buying products and services over the Internet, they would expect something similar from their government. Hopefully, this would put some pressure on governments to offer online services.

8.3 Added Advantages of Using the Proposed Framework and its Underlying Model

We have seen the necessity of the developed strategic framework of e-government in Chapter 1. The framework has many benefits and values for any strategy of e-government. As mentioned earlier, the framework was built to be generic. Thus, the advantages are not limited to a group of countries with certain characteristics. Remember that various countries from different parts of the world were considered to achieve generality. However, there are some added advantages of this framework for LDCs in particular. This section introduces some of these advantages.

The framework provides a readily available prototype for e-government. A great effort has been made to make it the way it is. As mentioned in the introduction of this chapter, there is a lack of skills and financial resources in LDCs. This framework saves LDCs who are devising their e-government strategies some research efforts and resources and provides a quick answer of how the e-government framework should be like. I was personally involved in laying out strategy in my developing home country and we had to do first some research to figure out a baseline. Had such a framework been available would have saved us a lot of work. It would have also allowed us to focus efforts on our objectives rather than wasting a lot of time wandering about where to go or what methodology to adopt or even worse what case to follow. The framework serves as an initial guide for planning e-government strategies.

As cited previously, most countries tend to learn from best-practice example. The proposed framework provides a typical best-practice strategic framework of e-government. Every concept or element of it is based on best practice. Thus, shareholders of e-government in LDCs can avail from the experiences incorporated into the framework through structural, organisational and technical features.

The framework furnishes decision makers LDCs with the important principles, concepts and components of e-government. It bridges the gap between theory and practice. Many contributions and studies of previous researchers in addition to a plethora of cases from practice have been taken into consideration for developing the framework. The included concepts, principles and elements are today's de facto of the modern e-government. These components are necessary to understand the complete picture on the strategic level.

The findings reveal what is important to consider for developing e-government. The dissertation has clarified the e-government challenges, pillars, major focus areas, important initiatives…etc. This information should give a useful overview of e-government development.

The framework shows the trends in e-government. What the preponderance of countries is doing, where they are heading, what they are focusing on and so forth. This helps LDCs assess their own situation against the majority of countries. The provided strategic objectives maturity model is relevant this regard.

The above information is valuable for LDCs since these countries do not have *established* e-government pragrammes. The added values are met with a lack. These values have more value to an LDC with less developed e-government programme than a country with an advanced one. Yet not all the added values meet just the lack of skills in LDCs. There are other indirect benefits too. The framework and the underlying technical model exhibit a structure that supports democratic governance. Since one of the key pillars of e-government is reform, just by implementing e-government the right way as advocated in this thesis will result in a better governance overall. This is surely a step forward to fight corruption, which is more evident in LDCs.

8.4 Recommendations

8.4.1 E-Government as a Catalyst for Development

Undeniably, e-commerce plays an important role in development. It increases efficiency of the commercial transactions. It facilitates buying and selling over the Internet. The added convenience of conducting business online gives a strong boost for commercial activities of small and big business institutions as well as the customers. Such an environment is obviously attractive to investors. The business sector as a result will grow. For this reason, e-Japan (Japanese e-Government initiative) has set e-commerce the next priority after the establishment of an ultrahigh-speed network infrastructure. According to e-Japan, e-commerce is not just the digitisation of paper-based transactions but also a creation of new modes of transactions that are never thought of before.

Unfortunately, though, e-commerce does not come without irritants. There are many challenges that need to be overcome before e-commerce thrives. One such challenge is the technical infrastructure. An online business transaction is normally conducted between two financial institutions: typically the bank of the seller where the account is credited and the bank of the buyer where the account is debited. If we seek to have a real e-commerce system running nationwide then there must be a common infrastructure utilised by financial institutions.

Common financial infrastructure per se is not the ultimate remedy. It will not function efficiently and securely without regulations. To this, we believe that governments must actually lead on three fronts:

- Establishing the technical infrastructure
- Setting forth regulations in consultation with the private sector
- Piloting e-commerce operation

Central Banks plays the most important role in building the common infrastructure. It assures inter-operability, efficiency, trust, and accessibility through the common infrastructure and effectuated regulations and guidelines. In many LDCs, each private bank uses its own money transfer forms, bank number formats, communication protocols, modus operandi…etc. This diversity in similar bank functionalities makes it difficult for fast, accurate and efficient cross-operation on the national level. In the United States, for example, the central bank (The Federal Reserve) acts both as an operator and as a regulator of the e-payment system. Regulating the work of financial institutions is meant to reduce risks and build up trust in conducting online transactions. A security breach or operation failure can severely adversely affect customer's trust in e-payment systems. Proper legislations must be passed to regulate:

- Digital signatures

- Authentications certificates

- Privacy laws

- e-Payment and e-money guidelines etc…

The Canadian government has built a Secure Channel Network (SCNet) in order to provide secure access to online governmental services. Later on, a Common Services Roadmap was devised on top of SCNet to support e-commerce operation. In addition, the Canadian government has introduced its basic authentication system called e-Pass. e-Pass is basically based on Public Key Infrastructure (PKI) technology. The Federal Information and Communication Technology (FEDICT), which is responsible for realising the Belgian e-government programme, has also introduced similar authentication system, called (e-ID).

In fact e-government brings about efficiencies and cost reductions not only for internal government operation but also for businesses. They both become more responsive. In other words, the benefits are mutual. e-Government reach out to e-commerce has a dramatic positive impact on development. It allows the latter to grow quickly by facilitating operation and access to common ICT infrastructure.

8.4.2 Improving e-Government in LDCs

E-Government is a large-scale endeavour. It requires abundant resources to function properly. Unfortunately, many LDCs are plagued by scarcity of monetary resources. There is usually huge deficit in yearly budgets. The budget of an LDC is in many cases a fraction of the developed countries. For example, Egypt is a home of some 80 million people. It is about three times the geographical area of Germany, which has a population of 82 millions. Even so, the budget of Egypt was just (3%) of that of Germany for the year 2008 (World Factbook, 2008).

Despite abundant resources in many developed countries on the other hand, little is being shifted towards e-government. That is why we still see some developed countries with lower maturity level of e-government implementation.

Some LDCs (particularly in sub-Saharan Africa) suffer from famine. Clearly, these governments strive to furnish citizens with necessities. Little or nothing is virtually left in many cases for e-government. Yet, LDCs can still reach some basic level of e-government development with relatively little investments. The gains from such small investments can improve governance and facilitate operation to some extent. In this section, we will introduce some practical applications that can help both developed and under-developed countries.

Many LDCs are plagued with illiteracy. If locals are hopelessly illiterate then radio broadcasts that draw information from the Internet can be a forthcoming source of information. Information, after all, can take many forms and disseminated in different ways including radio broadcasting. Local radio stations are more popular than one can imagine especially in developing countries where not everybody can afford a computer at home. Prices of radio sets are much lower than personal computers. Besides, simplicity of operation is far more convenient. This makes it well suited for illiterates.

On the implementation level, the best policy is to follow the "Divde and Conquer" methodology. As e-government is a large-scale endeavour. It cannot be approached as a single project but rather as a collection of sub projects. This is to minimise the risk of failure. It is also advised to implement e-government in an incremental approach. This way, the results will be felt quicker. As soon as a sub-project is ready, it can be set operational regardless of the completion of other projects. Many governments actually perceive e-government as a collection of projects as in the case of Belgium. Nevertheless, it is very important that interoperability be always kept in mind. Each project must follow the same guidelines for integration. *Data portability* is key for any e-government project if we are to have a *connected* government.

Online Presence

Although online presence is the simplest form of e-government, it is essential since it makes information available for the public. It is simple and cheap enough to enrich static Web pages with database connectivity. This allows for customised and dynamic content. The Web pages in this case draw their content from databases.

e-Mail

The idea behind Electronic Mail or e-mail is very simple yet this is a very effective tool. It is so trivial that in many cases it is overlooked by system designers who look for more sophisticated solutions. Such sophisticated solutions, however, do not come without cost. Normally, they come at huge costs and require aggressive maintenance.

Email constitutes a major two-way communication channel of service delivery in e-government. Compared to other forms of communication, email is more formal similar to a fax in that sense. Its asynchronous nature makes it quite beneficial for e-government usage. It incurs huge savings nation-wide, as it replaces traditional phone calls. There is no need for amplified help desk staff to answer clients' phone calls. On the other hand, it costs almost nothing to send an email with all sorts of attachments. It is a service that is naturally accessible 24/7.

e-Mail systems are simple and easy to setup. A part from maintenance costs, installation costs are low particularly when using open source software. In comparison, it arguably requires fewer maintenance and updating costs than state-of-the-art communication systems. Furthermore, abundant hardware come email-ready out f the box (think about PDAs, Smartphones…etc). An e-mail system can be accessed across different hardware and software platforms. This tool can really be used to provide G2B and G2C interactions and vice-versa at reasonably low cost. This makes it a precious tool for LDCs.

Simplified Knowledge Management

State-of-the-art Knowledge Management Systems (KMS) are generally very expensive. A commercial KMS license can cost between US$ 150,000 to 1 million. Cost of ownership is even multiple times larger (Wagner et al, 2003). However, some simplified KMS can be both simpler and cheaper. They call for less maintenance and updates. For example, it is simple enough to create a directory of professionals with their field of specialty and expertise in a database and then make it accessible via Web pages. It is equally possible to make a list of requirements, conditions, exceptions…etc of a process. This helps cherish the government's unit memory and knowledge. In addition, information for investors can prove beneficial to draw investment. Also posting CVs for graduates with the same simple technique can contribute to the reduction of unemployment.

ICT can be utilised to build virtual communities (Wagner et al, 2003). A virtual community is a cyber aggregation of people who share common interests. Underlying technologies can vary from e-mail to chat rooms to online forums to work groups…etc. Virtual communities serve as a dissemination engine of information and knowledge. A government, after all, must find some way to disseminate information among employees in a fast, reliable and cheap manner.

Pubic Private Partnership

One way in which a government can enhance its online service offering is through Public-Private Partnership (PPP). Unlike outsourcing private companies, PPP means that both government and the private company(s) share profits as well as risk through a contractual agreement. Many countries face difficulties in approving budgets. PPP can help getting e-government projects across. PPP can rid governments from financing, maintaining and managing infrastructures of certain online services. It can also innovate online service offerings, as new ideas are likely to immerge from a business partner.

PPP is not something new, in many countries contractual agreements were signed between governments and private partners to build and run hospitals, prisons, power plants ..etc. Some other governments partner with private companies to support the formal army. For example, half the security personnel in Iraq belong to private companies. What is new, however, for PPP in e-government is service delivery. Institutions from the private sector can devise, run and maintain governmental online services. This leads to enhancing government services quite dramatically.

Private companies, however, seek profit. It is an imperative for PPP to be tempting. There are different sources of profit. The following are some opportunities:

- Revenues in the form of subscription fees for the automated services

- Revenues from transaction fees

- Advertisements on portal's Web pages.

There are two caveats that must be dealt with accordingly when drafting the contractual agreement. The government must make sure that no personally identifiable information can be disclosed either to or by the private partner. The rule of thumb is that privacy of customers must be preserved by the private partner as if the information or service is maintained by the government itself. In addition, it is important to make sure that the level of security provided is as high as the government itself would allow should it be in charge of the service.

An example of PPP is TexasOnline. This is the online portal for the state of Texas. The government of Texas has partnered a private company BearingPoint to devise, manage and run online services. With a $23 million investment, the company could achieve profits of $1 billion. This profit was shared by BearingPoint and the government on the basis of the agreed ratio.

In order to promote the use of e-government services further, some countries have set up e-Government Centres of Excellence (e-Gove COE). Such centres increase awareness through special campaigns. They provide piloting and spearheading of innovation. In addition, e-Gov COE encourage competitiveness among government units. e-Gov COE might be perceived as the factory for e-government development where research and testing can take place and if a system is ready, it can be populated to the other government units. This is where best practices churn out. This way such centres increase readiness for e-government. They can also be the glue for a strong public-private partnership.

When resources are available, many applications can be implemented to enhance e-Government. Among those are:

- Geographical Information Systems (GIS): Providing spatial services

- e-Procurement: Electronic management of public tendering

- Client-centric approach: Services are designed and implemented not according to government units' needs and constraints but rather clients' (citizens and businesses) needs

- Client Relationship Management (CRM): Managing relationships with clients electronically and offering customised services for individuals

- Increasing the number of servers

- Implementing Broadband Network

- Extending e-government with m-Government and u-Government

- e-Authentication (Smartcards)

- Enhancing Security

- Protecting privacy

- Identity Management projects

- …etc

ICT as an Enabler for e-Government

ICT for Business must go hand-in-hand with ICT development and fighting poverty. ICT must be available and affordable to the public in order to achieve development. Yet there are certain considerations to be taken into account. Introduction of ICT in LDCs must be carefully planed and managed.

These technologies must be market-driven as much as possible and wherever is possible. They will meet demands efficiently. They should have multi-stakeholders with vigorous government involvement. Government should perceive itself as a pioneer and a leader. This should be part of its strategy. This would achieve faster and concrete development. Governments of LDCs can adopt the following policies:

Open-source Software

People in LDCs are relatively low incomed. It is necessary for the implemented technologies to be affordable. There are certain technologies that are efficient enough to serve a certain purpose yet they cost far less than others do. Budgets of a typical LDC are only a fraction of that of Developed Countries as mentioned before. Not only money is scarce but also these countries are stifled by heavy deficits and debts. Procurement of ICT, therefore, must be considerate.

An example of such a technology is open-source software. The important thing about open source in this context is that the license is available to anybody or group without discrimination. The Open Source Initiative—OSI (www.open-source.org) was launched in order to set conformation guidelines for the open source community. According to the Open Source Definition (OSD) guidelines, which is promoted by the OSI, open source does not only mean access to the source code. Free distribution, coupling of source code with the compiled code, modifications to the sources code, integrity of the author's source code, distribution of licenses…etc are some examples of the OSD guidelines.

In comparison to OEM software, open source has virtually no cost to own the license. Open-source operating systems, programming languages, desktop applications…etc can generally be owned without paying extra money. Once acquired, the government or authority is free to make modifications and re-compilations. There are several advantages for adopting open-source strategies:

- LDCs need to buy many computers for schools, laboratories…etc. In many cases, software that is shipped with these computers can exceed the price of the hardware many times. Using open-source OS and office applications can cut down expenses sharply.

- Students studying computer science or IT can avoid paying a lot of money for owning commercial software. Java for example is an open-source programming language that is both powerful and free.

- Open-source software encourages innovation. An open-source OS like Linux for example can be tailored specifically for certain usage. Modules can be developed to provide extended functionalities.

- Locally developed solutions are more convenient with open-source. Buying locally developed solutions means less drain of precious hard currency.

Software Industry

It is industry that achieves sustainable development and prosperity for a nation. The new term to describe a developed LDC is "newly *industrialised* country" or NIC. Industry, however, can be in any field. Some countries have excelled in certain industries whereas others have developed other kinds of industries. Among traditional industries (machinery, high-tech, agriculture, medical...etc) software industry is conceivably the most profitable for LDCs. Software industry does not require any raw materials as input. It only needs innovative human brains.

There are many programmers graduating every year from universities in LDCs. These programmers are low salaried compared to their peers in the developed countries. Thus, LDCs can achieve better returns on investments as in the case of India.

Knowledge Economy

In today's economy, knowledge is a key component of any business or industry. To this, modern economy is referred to as "knowledge economy". Therefore, institutions employ knowledge management systems to capture and codify knowledge. The good news is that this knowledge has become easier to get thanks to the Internet. Knowledge is available in different and rich forms. It is easily transferable and storable. The Internet has made information equally accessible by all. Whether you live in an LDC or in a DC you will always be able to gain access to the same information. This opportunity has never been so abundant throughout history.

Quality information and knowledge can be utilised for development. One problem is that individuals in LDCs generally pay more to access the Internet than their counterparts in DCs. This has to do much with poor ICT infrastructures. Governments should work with private sector to lower access costs.

8.4.3   Technology Leapfrogging

Fortunately, LDCs have the opportunity to avoid the investments born by early adopters (typically developed countries) of less efficient or more expensive solutions. They can directly seek solutions that were found to be most effective through best practice

(Hobday, 1995; Lee & Lim, 2001). This theory of development is referred to as "leapfrogging". Perez (1988) observes that any country can be a beginner in terms of emerging socio-economic paradigms. This, in turn, gives latecomers the opportunity to leapfrog these primary adopters.

Leapfrogging can be performed in any field: technological, social, political...etc. For example Freeman (2005) discussed the prospects of Human Resources (HR) leapfrogging. He argued that LDCs could achieve a competitive advantage by utilising their huge low-waged working force of scientists and engineers. Quantity can in some cases of Research and Development (R&D), outweigh quality. Superiority of DCs stems from two factors: technological infrastructure and skilled labour. This skilled labour though comes at a price, as these workers are high-waged. If we are going to apply economics to R&D, which is attributed to produce new innovative products, then we can see that by employing more under skilled but low-waged workers LDCs can become quite competitive with DCs.

In this section, I will focus on technological leapfrogging. According to the technological leapfrogging theory,

> under certain social, economic, and technological conditions,
> communities or countries can jump several steps to reach a higher level of
> technology production and consumption and attain parity with countries
> at the top of the ladder in that particular domain.

(Brezis & and Tsiddon, 1998)

LDCs can perform technology leapfrogging by using the latest and most efficient technologies. Many LDCs have little or no technologies in place. This means they have little to ditch at worst.

Leapfrogging can be practiced by LDCs as well as DCs. DCs can leapfrog to new and efficient technological tools or systems. Even companies can leapfrog competitors to new technological solutions. After all, companies are about achieving maximum rate of return. If new proven solution is adopted by a small and fast-growing company then it can achieve a higher "rate of return" than an old company that had already invested in a less efficient solution. New mobile operators in a certain country find it easy to offer new services than old ones. This is because they do not have old systems installed. This is not always successful though. The company must have some input requirements to make the shift. Among these are availability of market niche, training, skills, leadership, vision, and commitment. The aim for LDCs, however, could be different. They may seek to build an efficient infrastructure that can bridge the divide with DCs or to reduce it to say the least.

Benefits of Technology Leapfrogging

There are a number of acclaimed benefits attained from practicing leapfrogging. Among these are:

- *Access to Information*: With the implementation of a new efficient IT infrastructure, it is contingent that the Internet penetration rate will be boosted. The government strategy must encourage this and become a catalyst for the private sector. There will be a great social impact on the population. Mentality shift of people of LDCs may accelerate pace towards modernisation. Now that people have access to transparent information through the net, they are arguably empowered to participate vigorously in the political process. Chances are higher for them to influence government policies.

- *Human Development*: The impact of ICT on human development is critical. Implementation of innovative ICT solutions in fields like education, health, economy, agriculture, transportation…etc can have great benefits on sustainable development. Distance learning can provide a good opportunity for people in remote areas. Video conferencing allows professors from universities in DCs to lecture students in universities of LDCs. This is particularly important for LDCs witnessing conflicts where students might not have the chance to leave their homes or villages.

- Farmers can benefit from the Internet to get relevant and timely information to help them in all stages of cultivation. Farmers will be more productive and efficient if they are more informed.

- Physicians can follow up their patients' conditions though cell phones whenever a local clinic is not available. Some gadgets available today can measure patients' blood pressure, sugar level, heart rate…etc and can transmit data wirelessly to medical centres.

- Technology leapfrogging has a huge impact on the economy. Businesses in LDCs can employ e-commerce and can thus have access to worldwide markets at lower costs. They can also better manage their supply of raw materials. e-Commerce allows local businesses to go global and joint venture multi-national companies. They can act as outsourcers to foreign companies with the help of technology.

- Employing new technologies to transportation can result in elevated safety and efficiencies. Hi-tech control systems in railways, airports, highways, waterways…etc can reduce accidents due to human errors. They can better handle congestions much more efficiently. Inside cities, the use of fully actuated traffic lights manages circulation much more efficiently and thus reduces green gas emissions preventing further degradation to the environment.

- *Conservation of resources by using the most efficient technologies*: Costs should now be decreased and revenues should be increased

• *Bridging the Digital Divide*: Now that both DCs and LDCs use the same, efficient technologies they can have better cooperation on different levels: economy, cooperation, information and skills interchange…etc.

Technology leapfrogging must be practiced carefully. If people affected are unprepared then this might lead to what is referred as "Technological Shock".

In the summary of the Third United Nations Conference on the Least Developed Countries held in Brussels 2001, it was stressed that the major challenge to for LDCs in embracing e-commerce was not technical. Technology and infrastructure were not found to be the most demanding challenges. Business culture and practices were simply inconsistent with successful e-business strategies adopted by DCs.

From this brief discussion, we can see how important technology leapfrogging is to human development. The list can go on and on for every sector in the LDCs.

8.4.4 Wireless Access Opportunities

Wireless communications provide a communication platform that can be setup quickly. They are cost and power effective because of wire elimination. This communications infrastructure can be utilised in many ways. In general, it helps establish a connected society. Broadband wireless communications can reach Internet access speeds of up to (1) Gbps towards 2009 (WiMAX 802.16m standard). These gigabit mobile networks can have many useful applications. They can be used for remote medication, distance education video conferencing…etc.

Availability of these highly capable mobile devices combined with broadband wireless communications allows new modes of interaction. Not only can wireless communications and the related technologies be used for development, but they can also support innovative business applications. As mentioned earlier, there is a high penetration rate of mobile phones even in LDCs. These mobile devices vary in complexity and applications they support. Simple DTMF (Dual Tone Multi Frequency) and SMS based applications can reach out the masses. In Jordan, for example, some parking services in the capital Amman have started to receive reservations via SMS. In addition, many banks offer SMS services to their clienteles. Similar e-government services can be setup for accessibility via SMS.

These are just some examples of mobile-based services. The list is endless. What is amazing about mobile–related services is that a mobile device is actually an incessant point-of-service (POS). This is not the case for traditional POSs. A customer cannot be at a retailer's place or in front of his or her computer or TV anywhere and any time. Yet the overwhelming majority of customers always carry their cell phones with them wherever they go. This means mostly a non-stop service channel for e-government.

8.5   Conclusion

This chapter has introduced some opportunities for LDCs to consider in order to cause some efficiencies in their e-government programmes. It showed that a learning and a considerate government should be motivated enough to spearhead the ICT development through it e-government programme. The chapter has also highlighted the particular benefits of e-government for LDCs. The chapter has clarified how LDCs in particular can utilise the developed strategic framework of e-government. It has also introduced some simple and cheap yet sufficiently effective technologies that can potentially enhance e-government in LDCs. Although many of the presented technologies were not originally built for e-government, they can still be utilised to achieve more for quite less. Governments in LDCs are urged to adopt and promote the use of these technoloies for better governance. This chapter is not directly related to the major contributions of this dissertation. However, its presence, I believe, will add even more value to the dissertation.

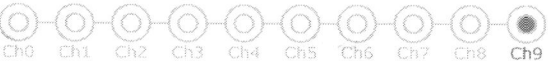
CHAPTER 9:   CONCLUSIONS AND RECOMMENDATIONS

9.1   Summary

This dissertation has addressed two major challenges of e-government: strategy and development. A considerable part of the thesis has been dedicated to clarify and conceptualise the e-government strategy. The scrutinisation of e-government strategies using comparative analysis has resulted in a formalised structuring of a generic strategy. Once the structured form of a typical e-government strategy was produced, it was possible to work out a framework that was originally missing from practice and literature. The strategic framework of e-government was developed based on best practice witnessed through replication of successful concepts, principles, components, methodologies and techniques.

The second major challenge that this dissertation has addressed is not less important than the strategic framework of e-government. Most failures occur during development. Complexity and multi-dimensional nature of e-government increase the chances for failures. Lack of cross-agency cooperation can result in patchy development of e-government. Binding the government together was found to capture the attention of many governments. The developed federated model of e-government was aimed at simplifying development of e-government and providing more manageability. The model diffuses the risks attributed to the seemingly long-lasting bureaucracy in governments.

The dissertation has discussed and clarified the different challenges that face the development of e-government. A number of important concepts of e-government have been introduced. Practical guiding principles have been exposed. The dissertation has uncovered key trends and aspirations. Common strategic objectives of e-government have been ranked based on their commonality among governments. The study has as well investigated the focus areas of e-government. Basic building blocks of e-government were figured out. In addition, critical success factors and pillars of e-government were identified from a practical point of view. The dissertation has also discussed public value creation as part of the developed strategic framework of e-government. It has also offered some allusions to the initial and basic projects of e-government. The purpose was to provide some initial guidance on what projects to start with when developing e-government.

These findings were either used as tools to structure the strategic framework of e-government or as an extension and further elaboration on the framework. They added value to the developed framework. Furthermore, the dissertation has dedicated a whole chapter to provide recommendations for development of e-government in the LDCs. Many of the potential opportunities were discussed. An explanation of how LDCs in particular can avail from the strategic framework of e-government was also provided. Despite the lack of financial resources in LDCs still they are able to enhance e-government through a number of simple and affordable technologies. Tips on these technologies were incorporated in the discussion.

Finally, when a new theory or concept was introduced, available and relevant literature was consulted and brought in for comparison and insight.

9.2   Contributions to the Body of Knowledge

In this dissertation there have both major as well as minor contributions to the body of knowledge in the field of e-government. The following is a summary of contributions per chapter:

Chapter 2: This chapter has discussed and clarified the different kinds of challenges that can potentially impede the development of e-government. Data from practice as well as literature were used to cluster these challenges into basically political, social, legal, economic, organisations and technical challenges.

Chapter 3: The contribution of this chapter was the provision of a deeper insight on the perception of e-government. In this chapter, I have developed a generic view of how e-government as perceived by the majority of governments. This view was a result deep analysis of numerous e-government strategies.

Chapter 4: The chapter is a deep exploratory study of e-government strategies of (21) countries in addition to that of the EU. This study was aimed at formulating a generic structured view of an e-government strategy. In the process, many interesting findings have surfaced, including:

- Ranking of strategic objectives of e-government

- Trends in guiding principles of e-government

- Focus areas of e-government

- Building blocks of e-government

- Ranking of ultimate goals of e-government

- Maturity model of strategic objectives of e-government

- The real drivers of e-government

Chapter 5: The core contribution of this dissertation was introduced in this chapter. The chapter presented the strategic framework of e-government.

Chapter 6: Major contributions in this chapter include:

- Critical, success factors

- Pillars of e-government

- Introduction of public value

- Prioritisation of e-government initiatives

Chapter 7: The second major contribution of this dissertation was introduced in this chapter. It is the federated model of e-government. In addition, the rule-based approach for government process design was also presented here.

Chapter 8: Chapter 8 explores particular opportunities of e-government development in LDCs. It provides simple ideas to enhance e-government in these countries.

9.3   Potential Implications

As mentioned earlier, e-government is actually more of practice than science. Given the nature of this research, there are implications for both theory and practice. The following two subsections summarise the implications for each of them. It must be said, however, that it is hard to set a clear cut between the two.

9.3.1   Implications for Theory

This study has filled a gap in a very important part of e-government. The study has clarified the development of e-government strategies. No previous research has been done to structure a strategic framework for e-government. The developed strategic framework of e-government furnishes researchers with a new perspective of e-government at the strategic level. It conceptualises e-government strategies. This bestows a new understanding. Researchers can build on this framework to produce new knowledge. For example, it can provide researchers with a solid base to conduct studies aimed more at efficient structures of e-government.

In addition, the developed strategic objectives maturity model provides a tool for researchers to validate new theories. It can be used to assess maturity of e-government based on the government's strategic objectives.

The dissertation has developed a better understanding of the real drivers behind e-government. In addition, the federated model of e-government and the rule-based approach can open new directions in e-government research.

Finally, the framework accentuates important concepts from practice. The study has resulted in interesting findings concerning a number of concepts and principles in e-government. Researchers can learn about the trends in e-government development.

9.3.2   Implications for Policy Makers and Practice

As revealed earlier, no country has developed a strategic framework for e-government as advocated by this thesis. The argued benefits of such a framework are significant. To recap the main advantages of including a similar framework in the national e-government strategies are:

- It abstracts the e-government strategy in graphical form

- It provides a quick reference to the strategy

- It facilitates discussion with decision-makers who are normally non-technical

- It shows the fit between e-government elements better than lengthy text and makes discrepancies easier to spot

- It makes it easier to disseminate and print

- It makes it easier to reflect the focus of the government

- It supports prioritisation of projects and public value addition

Additionally, the framework exhibits the following qualities:

- Customisability

- Simplicity

- Modularity

- Extensibility

On the other hand, the federated model of e-government was built to combat a number of challenges associated with e-government development. Generally, these challenges have to do with complexity and bureaucracy. The model allows for more manageability over e-government implementation. The federated model of e-government can preserve the autonomous status of local agencies and neutralise the seemingly long-lasting bureaucracy. In a nutshell, the model:

- Simplifies implementation

- Allows for incremental development of e-government

- Is technology independent

- Calls off the need to have identical processes, applications, or data format in the individual agencies as it encapsulates local implementations

- Reduces risk of failure associated with resistance to change, bureaucracy, and lack of cross-agency cooperation

Finally, the developed maturity model of strategic objectives of e-government guides any government particularly in LDCs on setting strategic objectives. As explained in Section 4.5.1, governments need to progress wisely across the levels of the model.

9.4   Further Research

I am motivated to continue to work in this field of e-government. A lot of opportunities lay ahead for exploration. Further extensions can be added to the framework Sub frameworks can add more value to this core framework. I would investigate these possibilities in the near future.

In my quest, I have studied only documentation of the federal governments. There are, however comparable strategies, visions, objectives…etc developed by local governments. It would be interesting to study the differences among federal and local e-governments. What I see particularly inquisitive is focus. *What constructs could be used to build the local framework?* It is also interesting to investigate in detail how to align local and federal strategies.

Furthermore, although the framework was created based on practice (using federal e-government strategies), yet interviews with practitioners for feedback on the findings might prove insightful. This qualitative research has revealed the important constructs to builds the framework. A quantitative research in the form of surveys targeting practitioners responsible for the development of federal e-government would reveal their impressions on the developed strategic framework. This however, can be challenging not because of complexity but rather because of the difficulty in making contacts and arranging for such a study with a large number of countries to prove statistically feasible. From my experience, getting cooperation from government officials is not an easy task.

9.5   Concluding Remarks and Recommendations

We have seen the importance and necessity of the developed framework and the accompanying development model of e-government. It is strongly recommended to incorporate a similar strategic framework in the national e-government strategies. It adds value to these strategies.

In response to a research question of Chapter 0, the findings tell us that there is much in common among the different e-government programmes. After all, governments are facing similar challenges and they employ comparable solutions as indicated earlier in the dissertation.

The dissertation has demonstrated that awareness of e-government benefits among constituents is necessary for pushing e-government development. Informed representatives of the society should put more pressures on governments to develop e-government.

As we have seen from Figure 15 government perception of what "e-government" really means is too simplistic. A holistic perception of e-government should prevail among practitioners and policy makers. Such perception is necessary for multi-dimensional understanding of e-government. Additionally, basic elements of e-government should not be thought of as just technical. There are managerial, organisational, social, political and other aspects, which are equally important. Misjudging these aspect, can lead to failures and disappointments.

Furthermore, governments need to address carefully the five elements, which were referred to in this dissertation as the *pillars of e-government*. These pillars are reform, technology, collaboration, leadership and people (review Figure 46). Any serious government must have suitable plans for each of these elements.

Organisational, operational and managerial reforms have to be enacted and implemented at an early stage of the development of e-government. The reforms include changes to incumbent inefficient laws and regulations. These changes should, as well, be accompanied by changes on the operational level. Process reengineering is likely to produce new efficiencies. These reforms must though be followed up by seamless change management to avoid the risk of failure associated with resistance to change that government employees are likely to manifest.

The government should procure and install the simplest technologies but which produce more efficiency. Choosing simpler technologies will reduce complexity. This dissertation has offered the federated model with its underlying technical platform to help in this regard.

The highest maturity level of e-government is referred to as "networked government". At this level, the government can offer shared services in a one-stop shop manner. To achieve this level of maturity cross-agency collaboration is required. This is hampered by bureaucracy and the tendency to keep local information private. This is a major dilemma democratic governments have to address. From one hand, public authorities need to work together in order to achieve maximum efficiency. On the other hand, democracy calls for the distribution of power and authority. An impeccable solution must strike the balance between the two.

As mentioned earlier, leadership is a key for success. Political leadership is necessary to provide support for financial resources allocation, inter-agency coordination, policy changes and human efforts (PCIP, 2002).

Administrators must be educated about the concepts of e-government. They should also be trained on new and efficient approaches of management. Government employees should have enough training on the new systems. It is absolutely necessary to bridge the digital divide and to train people about the new offerings. Public adoption of e-government reflects the overall success of e-government. Yet in its provision of modern and efficient solutions, the government must make sure that this would not widen the digital divide.

LDCs do not have to abandon e-government because of the related costs. With little investments, affordable technologies can be wisely installed to achieve fairly satisfying efficiencies. A few of these technologies have been discussed in Chapter 8.

Finally, academia and practice need to work together on e-government research. This cooperation produces scientifically valid and more accurate results. The benefits of such a liaison are mutual. From one hand, practice will avail from the readily available huge scientific work force that is motivated and interested to do research in e-government. On the other hand, academic researchers will get the more needed cooperation from public servants to carry out proper data collection. Further insight is provided in Section 3.4.

Appendices

APPENDIX A: List of Abbreviations

This brief appendix interprets the abbreviations used throughout this dissertation

PPP: Public Private Partnership

LDCs: Less Developed Countries

GE: Government Entity

LG: Local Government

PKI: Public Key Infrastructure

PDA: Personal Digital Assistant

UMPC: Ultra Mobile Personal Computer

GIS: Geographical Information System

APPENDIX B: Thesis Glossary

This appendix lists the definitions of some important terminologies used throughout the dissertation.

e-Government:

e-Governance: A way of describing the links between government and its broader environment - political, social and administrative Riley (2003)

e-Government strategy: A plan for e-government systems and their supporting infrastructure which maximises the ability of management to achieve organisational objectives (Heeks, 2006)

Best practice: A concept, technique, methodology, or solution that has proven reliable in achieving a desired objective, through experience, research and best available knowledge or technology and that has proven effective through replication

Digital divide: The gap between individuals, households, businesses and geographic areas at different socio-economic levels with regard to both their opportunities to access information and communication technologies (ICTs) and to their use of the Internet for a wide variety of activities. The digital divide reflects various differences among and within countries (OECD)

Client-centricity: Taking customer need as a premise for designing processes, systems or services

Identity theft: A cyber crime that involves the assumption of another person's identity

Leapfrogging: A theory of development in which developing countries skip inferior, less efficient, more expensive or more polluting technologies and industries and move directly to more advanced ones (Wikipedia)

Smartphone: An OS-equipped mobile phone that is capable of running third party programmes

Enhancing public sector/services: Efforts to modernise the public sector in terms of infrastructure, organisation and training

Networked Government: A maturity level of e-government implementation in which agencies are integrated

Operational/Cost Efficiency: Achieving maximum efficiency with fewest resources

Enhancing Accessibility: Making government services more accessible through better GUIs, addressing people with disabilities, providing new delivery channels and enhancing existing ones...etc

Simplifying Procedures: Reducing unnecessary steps in government processes and abolishing or modernising laws that are retarding for e-government development

Increasing Citizens' Participation: Pushing citizens for more political participation and enabling them to provide feedback through e-government

e-Commerce/e-business/market-based: Designing a business-aware and ready e-government

Simplifying/enhancing life: Raising standards of living through efficient and convenient e-government

Human capacity building: Increasing the level of skills within the government or within the society at large

Increasing public value: Increasing the value created by government through services, laws, regulation and other actions (Kelly et al 2001)

Networked society: A society in which communications among individuals are enabled through ICT

Knowledge-based society: A society where individuals rely heavily on accessible online information in their daily lives

Responsiveness: Speed of government reactions towards users' queries or requests for services

Distributed government: An interoperable government with no uniformity in local systems

Knowledge-based government: A government that relies heavily on quality, and fast information exchange for daily operation

Global readiness: Maturity in infrastructure to meet the new challenges of e-government against world index

Result-oriented: an e-government strategy that is focused on results. End results will judge the success or failure

Government transformation/digitalisation: Moving the government online through digitalisation of data, processes and operation

Shared services: Cross-agency cooperation to offer joint and more efficient services

Mutualism: Peer-to-peer development of systems

Portals: A one-stop gateway for offering government information ad services online

Interoperability: The capacity of distributed or disparate systems to talk to one another

Access channels: Traditional and electronic channels used to offer government services (e.g. government offices, portals, fax, email, SMS…etc)

Bottom-up cost calculation: Assessment of the necessary funding for e-government initiatives calculated by the local authorities who are the end beneficiaries

One-stop shop: The integration of public services from a citizen's point of view (Tambouris, 2001)

Mindset shift: Forming new perceptions of modern principles, procedures, organisation, systems…etc

Change management: A management imperative upon, before, during and after modifications to organisation, process, roles, systems…etc to guarantee smooth transition and avoid risk of failure through proper training and prior planning

Reusability: Coding or building once and using many times through populating across agencies

Openness: The opposite of reluctance to cooperate

Scalability: Capacity of ICT systems to handle the growing needs of an agency

Digital inclusion: Reducing the digital gap among individuals, communities or agencies

Leadership in e-government: The sense of responsibility and dedication to carry out new e-government initiatives

Government transformation: Development of e-government

Mobile government: strategy and its implementation by the government to provide information, deliver services, engage citizens and improve efficiency through mobile devices (Sang et al, 2006)

GIS government: A government strategy aimed at providing location-based information and services

Ubiquitous government: A term to refer to accessible government anywhere, anytime and by anything

Many agencies but one government: A description of a democratic connected government

Internal efficiencies: Achieving maximum value with fewest resources through reorganisation, process re-engineering, simplification…etc. The value is aimed at the government itself

External efficiencies: Achieving value aimed at the users or the society at large by offering timely and quality services

Channel of choice: Fast government response to requests regardless of the channel used to deliver services

Personalised services: Offering government services tailored for individuals through customisation and clustering of users

One-time information entry: Calling off redundant data entry during requesting services by individuals

No wrong door: No matter through which agency or channel the user asks for a service he or she will always receive the right response. In this manner, the user is shielded from the internal organisation of the government.

Service packaging: offering related services as one package

Government networking: interconnecting government agencies through ICT

Government entity: A local government unit or department that is responsible for doing one or more functions

Benchmark: A standard or point of reference against which things may be compared or assessed (Pearsall, 1999)

Abstraction of e-government: Perceiving government entities as separate entities having local characteristics (regulations, data, government processes...etc)

Encapsulation: Refers to the lack of rigorous integration among government entities where individual local characteristics are kept private

APPENDIX C: Initial Projects of e-Government to Start With

USA

Rationale: Choose high pay-off projects (that produce value to government and citizens) that result for example in integration (government value), one-stop and one-time data collection (citizen value).

Enabling E-Government Success		Value to Citizens	Value to Government
	e-Authentication	Secure, consistent method of proving identity to the federal government	Eliminate redundancy in electronic signature technology and policy operations, thereby reducing costs and employee time required
	Federal Architecture	Citizens are best served by an efficient and effective government	More efficient and effective government, reduction of redundancy
G2C		Value to Citizen	Value to Government
	Recreation One-Stop	A user-friendly single source of information save approximately 50 minutes by using this service	reduced duplication, increased sales and employee time savings
	Eligibility Assistance Online		Customer service calls will be reduced
	Online Access for Loans	Faster, easier access to loan information and transactions	Employees will save time in managing the loan process
	USA Services	Timely, consistent and helpful customer service	Elimination of redundancy
	EZ Tax Filing	reduction of automated tax preparation costs	Reduction of data errors and call centres burden
G2B		Value to Citizen	Value to Government
	Online Rulemaking Management	One-stop access to rule-making process, participation	Elimination of redundancy
	Expanding Electronic Tax Products for Businesses	Reduce the burden of compliance with tax laws for businesses	Increases the accuracy and reliability of tax data, as well as the costs associated with paper processing
	Federal Asset Sales	One-stop access, reduction of transaction costs	Cost reduction
	International Trade Process Streamlining	Increase of exports	Reduce redundancy and burden

		Value to Citizen	Value to Government
	One-Stop Business Compliance Information	Regulatory burden reduction on the private sector	reduction of agency costs
	Consolidated Health Informatics (business case)	Reduction of private sector's healthcare expenditures, health care improvement	savings in managing, transporting, copying and exchanging paper medical records
G2G		*Value to Citizen*	*Value to Government*
	Geospatial Information One-Stop	Standardised and reliable spatial data	Easier, more reliable access to spatial data, elimination of data redundancy
	e-Grants	Reduction of time spent preparing and searching for grants	Reduction of postage costs
	Disaster Assistance and Crisis Response	Accurate and timely data may result in saved lives and reduction in property damage.	Elimination of redundant programmes and administrative costs in agencies
	Wireless Public SAFEty Interoperable COMmunications/ Project SAFECOM	saved lives, as well as better-managed disaster response	Reduction in communications infrastructure, overhead, maintenance and training
	e-Vital (business case)	Elimination of burden imposed on citizens to obtain and deliver vital record information from local government to the federal government	, reduction of erroneous payments
Internal Efficiency and Effectiveness		*Value to Citizens*	*Value to Government*
	e-Training	Easy one-stop access to just-in-time training with more effective development and retention of high-quality, diversified work force	Low-cost delivery of effective training
	Recruitment One-Stop	Resume Posting	Gives agencies broader and faster access to resumes and the automated tools needed to select candidates

Enterprise HR Integrations e- Payroll/HR (Payroll Processing Consolidation)	Improves services and protects the rights and benefits of the federal workforce and provides faster security clearances	Reduces dependency on paper-based processes, Improves HR capabilities and communications
	Better Services	consolidate payroll operations to simplify and unify processes
e-Travel	One-stop integrated travel services for all federal employees	Reduced cycle time and improved travel and budget information at a lower cost
Integrated Acquisition Environment	Cost savings	Will make the purchase of goods and services faster and less expensive
Electronic Records Management	Easier process for creating information, with more reliable storage	More efficient operations

Korea

Innovating the way government works

> Establishing Electronic Work Processes
>> Electronic Document Processing
>> Consolidated Financial Information Systems for Central/Local Government
>> Local E-Government
>> e-Audit Systems
>> e-National Assembly
>> Integrated Criminal Justice System
>> Consolidated Personnel Administration System
>> e-Diplomacy System
>> Real-time System for National Policy Management
> Expansion of Administrative Information Sharing
> Government Business Reference Model Development

Innovating Civil Services

> Enhancing Citizen Services
>> Enhance Online Citizen Service
>> Integrated National Disaster Management Service
>> Consolidated Architectural Administrative Information System
>> Consolidated Online Tax System
>> Integrated National Welfare Information Service
>> Consolidated Food and Drug Information System
>> Consolidated Employment Information System
>> Online Administrative Trial System
> Enhancing Business Support Services
>> One-stop Business Support Service
>> Consolidated National Logistics Information Service
>> Electronic Trading Service
>> Comprehensive Foreigner Support Service

Support for Exporting E-Government Solutions
Expansion of Online Citizen Participation

Innovating Information Resource Management
Consolidating and Standardising Information Resources
Government-wide Consolidated Information Resources Management System
Enhancement of E-Government Communication Network
Application of Government-wide Information Technology Architecture
Establishment of Information Security Systems
Restructuring of IT Personnel and Organisations

Reforming the Legal System
Reform of E-Government Legislation

Denmark

Internal government initiatives
- Service communities across government levels
- Electronic records management systems for the public sector
- eDay – digital communication between government authorities
- Infostructurebase – seamless communication between databases
- IT architecture – setting the basic rules for government IT systems

Citizen and business oriented initiatives
- Online access to government services
- Digital signature to all Danish citizens
- Virk.dk – e-Portal for all government services to businesses
- Health portal for citizens and medical professionals
- Legal modernisation – removal of barriers to e-government

Malaysia

Pilot Flagship Applications
- Electronic Government
- Multipurpose Card
- Smart School
- Telehealth
- R&D Clusters
- E-Business
- Technopreneur Development

Brazil

Universality of Service
- Installment of all of the service and information by the Internet
- Small farms of service and information in the Internet
- Centres of Relationship
- Inventory of Service
- National net of Information in Health – RNIS
- Door of Support to the Micro and Small Farmer
- Programme of Computerisation of the Educational Actions

Best-Practice Framework for Developing and Implementing e-Government   188

- Door of Support to the Search of Job
- Public system Integrated of Security
- Door for Micro and Small Exporting
- Development of interfaces and content for the public terminals of access to Internet
- Electronic payments

Infrastructure
- Net Br@sil.gov
- Service of Mensageria Integrated of the Federal Government
- Modernisation of local nets
- Policies of local nets

Universality of Internet Access
- Service of Service to the Citizen - GESAC
- Tariff Internet
- Card of the Citizen
- Terminals of public access to Internet

Establishment of Norms and Standards for the Installment of Service
- Political of installment of information and service
- Catalogue of Information ("White Pages")
- New Human Resources Management System
- Plan of Investments in technology of the information
- Catalogue of Application and Bases of Facts
- Integration of Protocols
- Integration of Systems
- Civil Works Accompaniment system in the Public Sector
- Electronic trading
- Electronic documents
- Infrastructure of Public Keys

New Zealand

Convenience and Satisfaction
- Delivering Government Services
- Enabling Variety in Delivery
- Adding Value to Information
- Providing Authorities Data

Integration and Efficiency
- Delivering Value for Money
- Building Standards and Interoperability
- Building Foundational Infrastructure
- Addressing Collaboration
- Provide Collaborative Tools
- Fostering Innovation and the Use of Technology
- Building IC Professionalism

Trust and Participation
- Enhancing Public Engagement
- Strengthening Trust and Security
- Managing the govt.nz Space

India

Mission Mode Projects
  Central Government
- Income Tax
- Passport Visa & Immigration Project
- DCA1

- Insurance
- National Citizen Database
- Central Excise
- Pensions
- Banking

State Government
- Land Records
- Road Transport
- Property Registration
- Agriculture
- Treasuries
- Municipalities
- Gram Panchayats
- Commercial Taxes
- Police (UTs initially)
- Employment Exchanges

Integrated Services
- EDI (E-Commerce)
- E-Biz
- Common Service Centres
- India Portal
- EG Gateway
- E Procurement
- E Courts

UK

Citizen and Business-Centred Services
- Varney Review
- Systematic engagement
- Customer Group Directors
- Service design principles
- Modern channels

Shared Services:
- HR, finance and other corporate services

Common infrastructure
Information management
Identity management
Technical standards and architecture
Sharing culture
Portfolio management
IT profession in government
Reliable project delivery
Supplier management
Innovation
Data sharing
Engaging local authorities
Engaging the Devolved Administrations
Information assurance
Reliable project delivery

France

Services that are repetitive, easy to implement, and accessible by all at all times

Services intended for citizens

Employment and training life-long
- ADELE1. Portal for Empolyment
- ADELE2. Training portal
- ADELE3. Contest Portal, Employs and offers courses in the public function

Family, health and retirement
- ADELE4. Change of address
- ADELE5. Change of marital status
- ADELE6. Consultation of pention laws
- ADELE7. Development of Life Card
- ADELE8. The Daily-life Card
- ADELE9. Social Security Portal (securite-sociale.fr)
- ADELE10. Family allocations online
- ADELE11. Health inssurance
- ADELE12. Accommodation request and enhancement of living

Education
- ADELE13. Digital Spaces of pupils and students
- ADELE14. Opening up of schools for parents
- ADELE15. National debate of future of school
- ADELE16. Inscription portal of exams in teaching
- ADELE17. Candidacy portal and the inscription in superior teaching
- ADELE18. Shielding pupils interface from inappropriate content over the Internet
- ADELE19. Portal of agricaltural teaching techniques

Environment
- ADELE20. Information over the environment
- ADELE21. Infrastructure for prediction of floods

Information highway
- ADELE22. Information over inter-urban transportation network

Sports
- ADELE23. Sports portal

Administrative advancements
- ADELE24. Administration portal (service-public.fr)
- ADELE25. Civil State
- ADELE26. French abroad
- ADELE27. Driving licesence and navigation licesence
- ADELE28. Juridical aid requests
- ADELE29. Requests of Juridical File
- ADELE30. Attestation requests
- ADELE31. Military Archives

Polling
- ADELE32. Development of electronic voting

Relationship with the administration
- ADELE33. Personal Space
- ADELE34. My Public Service
- ADELE35. National Electronic Identity Card (CNIE)
- ADELE36. Enhancement of services for foreign nationals
- ADELE37. Unique telephone number 39 39 All public services

Taxation
- ADELE38. Taxation file

Services intended for Businesses

Life of the company
- ADELE39. Professional Space
- ADELE40. Identification Number of businesses online
- ADELE41. Taxation account of professionals
- ADELE42. Requests online for payment orders
- ADELE43. Residence clearance procedure

Economic development
- ADELE44. Portal privillages and authorisations
- ADELE45. Portal for information on line of public statistical inquiry
- ADELE46. Economic information for public enterprises
- ADELE47. Service-Public.fr, Administration Portal: Development of access for enterprises and independent professionals

The Sectors: solcial, health, and environment
- ADELE48. Creation of a Subscriber's File online
- ADELE49. Employment service enterprise
- ADELE50. Monthly declaration of working force movement
- ADELE51. Pursuit of the dématérialisation of the exchanges between the cash registers of health insurances, the health professionals, the suppliers and the businesses
- ADELE52. Unique office for health professionals
- ADELE53. Management of public health and social establishments
- ADELE54. Information of the veterinarians, laboratories of analyses and establishments subject to the checks of the veterinary services of the State
- ADELE55. Agricultural warnings, Previous Declaration of the Tests of Regional Knowledge, Collect Officially Recognised Essays

Services for professional profitability
- ADELE56. Reliable communication concerning the civil procedures
- ADELE57. Mortgage keeping
- ADELE58. Remote procedure of census of the businesses of transportations and of BTP in the framework of their obligations of defense (PARADES)
- ADELE59. Patent management, qualifications and services o the professional sailors
- ADELE60. Unique administrative office for the arrival of a vessel to the harbour (Traffic 2000)
- ADELE61. Inscription to the registers and title delivery to the businesses of road transportation (GRECO)
- ADELE62. Dangerous merchandise and exceptional transportations
- ADELE63. Vehicle Registration
- ADELE64. Driving schools: modernisation of the system of information linked to the driver's license

Services intended for associations
- ADELE65. Space Association
- ADELE66. WALDEC Projet (Web des Associations Librement DEClarées)
- ADELE67. Subsidies to the associations and to the professionals
- ADELE68. Associative check use

Services intended for territorial groups
- ADELE69. Co-marking deployment with service-public.fr
- ADELE70. Territerial information systems
- ADELE71. Dematerialisation in the local public sector
- ADELE72. Transmission statistics of civil state and electoral opinions of the city halls to the INSEE

- ADELE73. Burgundy
- ADELE74. Set up of an infrastructure of confidence allowing the dématérialisation exchange between the groups and the administrations

Modernisation of public services in collaboration with European partners and piloting development of eGovernment creating conditions for trust
Enhancement of public services
Services of public agents
- ADELE75. Public agent's space
- ADELE76. Public agent's card
- ADELE77. Public agents access to tele-services
- ADELE78. Evolution of electronic messaging
- ADELE79. Dolce/Vitamine
Modernaisation of information systems of the administration
- ADELE80. Dematerialisation and modernisation of public procurement
- ADELE81. SOLON 1 and 2 (system of online organisation of the normative operations)
- ADELE82. Generalisation of the application "Accord"
- ADELE83. Electronic handling of civil aviation
- ADELE84. Management of automobile park
- ADELE85. Renovation of the information system of the Direction of the official newspapers
- ADELE86. Information system of human resources (SIRH)
- ADELE87. Geographic information systems (GIS)
- ADELE88. Crisis Management
- ADELE89. Natural hasards and technological measures
- ADELE90. Management of receiving public establishment
- ADELE91. Collaborative database on the French community abroad
- ADELE92. Management of real-estate heritage
- ADELE93. Management of social logement
- ADELE94. Portals of the prefectures and services of the State
- ADELE95. Territorial info-centre
- ADELE96. Database of indicators on the manifistation of French living abroad
- ADELE97. Common system of management of the sanitary risks linked to the habitat (insalubrity, lead, asbestos, radon, carbon monoxyde, etc.) and associated procedures
- ADELE98. Creation of a data bank Life federal athletic and athletic Equipment and Renovation of the census of the athletic licenses
- ADELE99. COPERIA (COProduction En Réseau de l'Information Administrative)
- ADELE100. Driver of tele-procedures and workshop of genius software
- ADELE101. Development of video-conference over IP
- ADELE102. Multi-services public boundaries
- ADELE103. Archiving and proof server
- ADELE104. Electronic archival tools
- ADELE105. Creation of committee Europe of eGovernment
- ADELE106. Portal European structural funds
- ADELE107. Support the development of eGovernment for a **democratic governance**
Modernisation of educational information systems
- ADELE108. Information System of the EPLE (high schools and high schools)

- ADELE109. Information System of the 1st degree (elementary and maternal schools)
- ADELE110. ACCADEMIA
- ADELE111. Jury portal of contests

Change management and training
- ADELE112. Development plan of eGovernment
- ADELE113. Change Management
- ADELE114. eDevelopment

Reenforcement and of the security of information systems

Reenforcement and of the security of information systems plan (PRSSI)
- ADELE115. Mutualising security services of information systems
- ADELE116. Develop the competences in security of information systems within the administrations
- ADELE117. Provide security products developped by trust actors
- ADELE118. Obtain a series of priority equipment

Policies of the inter-sector security
- ADELE119. Policies of iter-sectoral security (PRIS)

Putting in place the necessary administrative certification for enhancing security, interoperability and mutualism of services
- ADELE120. Authorities of administrative certification

Access rights and authorisation management
- ADELE121. Management of Authorisation

Schema director of eGovernment
- ADELE122. Director Schema of eGovernment

Evolution of eGovernment
- ADELE123. Authentic dematerialised official journal

Constitution of referentials
- ADELE124. Referentials and associated directories
- ADELE125. Common standards of electronic cards
- ADELE126. Graphic charters and ergonomics
- ADELE127. Free software and collaborative development

Developing the know-how and mutualism of the initiatives
- ADELE128. Technical platform for collaborative development centre of technical resources
- ADELE129. AGORA
- ADELE130. Migration of work post

Development of infrastructure prior to setting up of functional services
- ADELE131. Infrastructure "Middle Office"
- ADELE132. Housing and followed by exploitation (of new interministerial services)
- ADELE133. Forms server

Enhancement of transportation infrastructure
- ADELE134. SETI Plus
- ADELE135. Interconnetion AdER - TESTA

User assistance
- ADELE136. Users Assitance

Communication tools and evaluation

Communication paln
- ADELE137. Communication plan

Observation and measurements
- ADELE138. Observation and measurement
- ADELE139. Governmental barometer Stat@Gouv

Development of networks
- ADELE140. Development of networks

Bibliography

A. A. Morozov, Yu. V. Obukhov, Yu. V. Gulyaev. (1999) 'On the Problem of Using Logic Object-Oriented Programming in the World Wide Web, Proceedings of the Special Russian Session', The Internet Developments in Russia. First IEEE/Popov Workshop on Internet Technologies and Services. pp 54-59.

Accenture (2003) eGovernment Leadership: Engaging the Customer. Accenture.

ADAE (2004) Enjeux stratégiques de l'administration électronique. Agence pour le développement de l'administration électronique. France.

Aichholzer, G. (2004) 'Scenarios of e-Government in 2010 and implications for strategy design', Electronic Journal of e-Government. Volume 2, Issue 1.

Åke Grönlund (2005). What's In a Field – Exploring the eGoverment Domain. Örebro University. Sweden ake.gronlund@esi.oru.se. 0-7695-2268-8/05 IEEE.

An International Look at Virtual Citizenship, Drew Robb, September, October 2003 IT Pro.

Antoine Lonjon. (2004) BPTrends. Retrieved 18 September, 2006 from http://www.bptrends.com.

Attewell, P. (2001) The First and Second Digital Divides. Sociology of Education, Volume: 74, Issue: 3. pp. 252-259. American Sociological Association.

Austin, J. (1990). Managing In Developing Countries - Strategic Analysis and Operating Techniques. Free Press. ISBN 0029011027.

Australian Government Information Management Office, (2006) Responsive Government - A New Service Agenda. e-Government Strategy. Australia.

BBeGov (2007). Breaking Barriers to eGovernment study, retrieved 7 August, 2008 from http://www.egovbarriers.org/.

Becker, J., Niehaves, B., Algermissen, L., Delfmann, P. & Falk, T. (2004) 'e-Government Success Factors' in ed (Traunmüller) Electronic Government. Lecture Notes in Computer Science. ISSN: 0302-9743 (Print) 1611-3349 (Online). pp503-506. Springer Berlin / Heidelberg.

Belgian Government Portal. Retrieved 8 May, 2008 from http://www.belgium.be.

Bellamy, C. & Taylor, J. (1998) Governing in the Information Age. Open University P., Buckingham, Philadelphia.

Berners-Lee, T., Hendler, J. & Lassila, O. (2001) 'The Semantic Web. A new form of Web content that is meaningful to computers will unleash a revolution of new possibilities', *Scientific American*.

Best, M. & Maclay, C. (2002). Community Internet access in rural areas: solving the economic sustainability puzzle. Retrieved October 14, 2006, from http://www.cid.harvard.edu/cr/pdf/gitrr2002_ch08.pdf.

Bhatnagar, S. (2004) E-government: From Vision to Implementation : a Practical Guide with Case Studies. ISBN 0761932607, 9780761932604. SAGE.

Bhatnagar, S. (2004) E-government: From Vision to Implementation : a Practical Guide with Case Studies. ISBN 0761932607, 9780761932604. SAGE.

Bicking, M., Brwoen, M., Cook, M. (2007) State of play in e-government research and implementation in Europe and worldwile, in Condanogne & Wimmer (ed.): Roadmapping eGvovernent Research: Visions and Measures Towards Innovative Governments in 2020. MY Print snc di Guerinoni Marco& C, Clusone.

Bonnet Ph., Bressan S., Leth L., Thomsen B. (1996) Towards ECLiPSe Agents on the Internet, Proceedings of the 1st Workshop on Logic Programming Tools for Internet Applications, Bonn, Germany, 1996 – pp 1-9.

Brazilian Government Portal. Retrieved 12 December, 2007 from http://www.governoeletronico.gov.br.

Brezis, Elise S. & Daniel Tsiddon (1998) 'Economic Growth, Leadership and Capital Flows: The Leapfrogging Effect', *Journal of International Trade & Economic Development*, 7 (September), 261-277.

Bundesministerium, des Innern (2006) E-Government 2.0. Das Programm des Bundes. Publikationsversand der Bundesregierung. Postfach 48 10 09 | 18132 Rostock. E-Mail: publikationen@bundesregierung.de. Artikelnr.: BMI06333. Germany.

BundOnline (2005) Implementation Plan for the E-government Initiative 2005. Progress Report on Implementation Cabinet Decision Dated 11 December 2002.

Cabinet Decision, (2002) Implementation Plan for the E-government Initiative 2005. Progress Report on Implementation. Dated 11 December 2002. Germany.

Cabinet Office (2000), Electronic Government Services for the 21st Century, Cabinet Office, London.

Cabinet Office, (2005) Transformational Government Enabled by Technology. Cm 6683. UK.

Cabinet Office, (2006) Transformational Government Enabled by Technology. UK.

Canadian Government Portal. Retrieved 14 June 2007 from http://www.canada.ca.

CceGov (2007) Citizen-centric eGovernment study. Retrieved 1 September, 2008 from http://www.ccegov.eu/

Centeno, C., Bavel, R. & Burgelman, J. (2004) eGovernment in the EU in the next decade: Vision and key challenges. Joint Research Centre. European Commission.

Centeno, C., Van Bavel, R. & Burgelman, J.C. (2005) 'A Prospective View of e-Government in the European Union', *Electronic Journal of e-Government*. Volume 3 Issue 2 pp. 59-66.

Central IT Unit, (2000) e-Government - A Strategic Framework for Public Services in the Information Age. ISBN 0 7115 0394.X. Cabinet Office. UK.

Chen, Y., Chen, H. Huang, W., Ching, R. (2006) 'E-Government Strategies in Developed and Developing Countries: An Implementation Framework and Case Study', *Journal of Global Information Management*. Idea Group.

Chowdhury, G., Wahidul, H. & Kushcu, I. (2006) Success and Failure Factors for e-Government projects implementation in developing countries. Proceedings of the EURO mGOV 2006.

Civil House of the Presidency of the Republic (2002) 2 years of Electronic Government Review of Achievements and Future Challenges. Ministry of Planning, Budget and Management . Presidency of the Republic. Council of Government. Executive Committee of Electronic Government. Brasilia.

Codagnone, C. & Wimmer, M. (2007) Roadmapping eGovernment Research: Visions and Measures towards Innovative Governments in 2020. eGovRTD2020 Project Consortium.

Cole, M. & Vivienne, J. (2005) Leadership in Customer Service: New Expectations, New Experiences. The Government Executive Series. Accenture.

Comitê Executivo do Governo Eletrônico (2002) 2 Anos de Governo Eletrônico Balanço de Realizações e Desafios Futuros. Casa Civil da Presidência da República Ministério do Planejamento, Orçamento e Gestão. Brazil.

Commission of the European Communities, (2006) i2010 e-Government Action Plan: Accelerating e-Government in Europe for the Benefit of All. SEC(2006) 511.

Compaine, B. (2007) 'The digital divide: facing a crisis or creating a myth?' MIT Press. ISBN 0262531933, 9780262531931.

Corrford, T., Smithson, S. (1996) 'Project Research in Information Systems', Macmillan Press, New York, NY.

Coursey, D. & Killingsworth, J. (2005) 'Managign e-Government in Florida: Further Lessons from Tranition and Maturity', in Garson, G. (ed.) Handbook of Public Information Systems. ISBN 0824722337, 9780824722333. CRC Press.

Cuellar, M.F., Drozdova, E., Elliott, D., Goodman, S., Grove, G., Lukasik, S., Putnam, T., Sofaer, A. (2001) The Transnational Dimension of Cyber Crime and Terrorism. The Board of Trustees of the Leland Stanford Junior University.

DADA, D. (2006) 'The Failure of E-Government in Developing Countries', iSChannel - *The Information Systems Student Journal.*

Daniels, M. (2002) E-Government Strategy: Simplified Delivery of Services to Citizens, Office of Management and Budget, Washington, DC.

Dawes, S. & Helbig, N. (2007) 'Building a Research-Practice Partnership: Lessons from a Government IT Workforce Study', *Proceedings of the 40th Hawaii International Conference on System Sciences.* 1530-1605/07 IEEE.

Dawes, S. (2008) 'Governance in the information age: a research framework for an uncertain future', *Proceedings of the 2008 international conference on Digital government research.* Montreal, Canada

Dawes, S. (2008) 'An exploratory framework for future e-government research initiatives', *Proceedings of the 41st Hawaii International Conference on System Sciences.* January 7-10, Waikoloa, Big Island, Hawaii, USA.

de Carvalho C. L. (2001) NetProlog Home Page. Retrieved 25 August, 2006 from http://netprolog.pdc.dk.

De la Porte, C. & Pochet, P. (2001) 'Social benchmarking, policy making and new governance in the EU', *Journal of European Social Policy*, Vol. 11, No. 4, pp. 291-307.

Delanghe H., Duchêne, V. & Muldur, U. (2004), "À l'aube d'une nouvelle vague de croissance ?", Futuribles, no. 300, 19-44.

Denzin, N. & Lincoln, Y (eds.) (1994) Handbook of Qualitative Research, Sage, Thousand Oaks.

Department of Information Technology (2006) National e-Governance Plan (2006).Ministry of Communication and Information Technology. Government publications. India

Department of Information Technology Website. Ministry of Information and Communication Technology. Retrieved 5 May 2008 from http://www.mit.gov.in.

Devendra K. Punia, Doctoral Student Management Development Institute, Gurgaon +91-124-2347585, fpm02_devendra_p@mdi.ac.in, K.B.C. Saxena, Professor Management Development Institute, Gurgaon +91-124-2341 190, bsaxena@mdi.ac.in (2004).

Managing Inter-organisational Workflows in eGovernment Services. 1-58113-930-6/04/10 ACM.

Dieter Spahni, Institute for Business and Administration IWV University of Applied Sciences. Berne, Switzerland Dieter.Spahni@iwv.ch. (2004). Managing Access to Distributed Resources. 0-7695-2056-1/04 IEEE.

Dutil, P., Howard, C., Langford, J., Roy, J. (2007) 'Rethinking Government-Public Relationships in a Digital World: Customers, Clients, or Citizens?', *Journal of Information Technology and Politics*. Volume 4, Number 1.

Easterby-Smith, M., Thorpe, R. & Lowe, A. (1991) Management Research: an Introduction, Sage, London.

E-awareness Survey (2003). Retrieved Nov 2008 from http://www.e.govt.nz/archive/resources/research/eval-survey-results-200310/.

E-awareness Survey (2003) Final Results. New Zealand. Retrieved 18 June 2008. from http://www.e.govt.nz/archive/resources/research/eval-survey-results-200310/listing_archives.

Ebrahim, Z. & Irani, Z. (2005) 'E-government adoption: architecture and barriers', *Business Process Management Journal*. Vol. 11 No. 5, 2005. pp. 589-611.

EC (2000) Creating a Safer International Society by Improving the Security of Information Infrastructure and Combating Computer-related Crime. Commission of European Communities. Brussels.

ECOTEC (2008) Organisational change for citizen-centric eGovernment: Issues, Policy and Strategy. ECOTEC Research and Consulting Ltd. UK.

Efthimios Tambouris (2001). An Integrated Platform for Realising Online One-Stop Government: The eGOV Project. Archetypon S.A., 236 Sygrou Ave., 176-72 Kallithea, Athens, Greece, tambouris@archetypon.gr. 1529-4188/01 IEEE.

eGEP (2006) Compendium to the Measurement Framework, eGovernment Economics Project, European Commission, Brussels.

e-Government 2.0. Das Programm des Bundes (2006). Bundesministerium des Innern | IT-Stab Alt-Moabit 101D | 10559 Berlin, Germany. Retrieved 1 September 2008 from http://www.verwaltung-innovativ.de.

e-Gov Coordination Mission (2006) PA e-Government Project, EOI Workshop. E-Government General Directorate. Ministry of Telecommunication and Information Technology, Palestinian National Authority.

e-Government of Finland Web Site. Retrieved 11 July 2008 from http://e.finland.fi/eGovernment.

e-Government Overview. Retrieved 15 January 2008 from http://www.american.edu/initeb/ym6974a/egovernment.htm#E-Government%20Overview.

e-Government Programme, (2007) Jordan e-Government Architecture Vision. Government of the Hashemite Kingdom of Jordan.

e-Government Programme, (2007) Jordan e-Government Target Architecture (Central Platform). Government of the Hashemite Kingdom of Jordan.

e-Government Programme (2008) E-government - A Vision for New Zealanders. Retrieved 15 March 2008 from http://www.e.govt.nz/about-egovt/vision.html. New Zealand.

E-government Unit of the State Services Commission, (2003) The e-Government Component Architecture. Version 1.1. New Zealand.

e-Government Unit, (2005) e-Government Interoperability Framework. Version 6.1. Cabinet Office. UK.

e-Government Unit. Transformational Government – Implementation Plan, Retrieved 3 May, 2008 from http://archive.cabinetoffice.gov.uk/e-government.

Eisenhardt, K. (2002) 'Building theories from case study research' in Huberman ,A. and Miles, M. (ed.) Doing and writing qualitative research, London: SAGE Publications Ltd.

Enterprise Operations Division, (2000) Texas Electronic Government Framework. USA.

ePractice.eu (2008a) eGovernment in Austria. E-Government Factsheets. European Commission.

ePractice.eu, (2008b) eGovernment in Belgium. e-Government Factsheets. European Commission.

ePractice.eu, (2008c) eGovernment in Finland. e-Government Factsheets. European Commission.

ePractice.eu. Retrieved 17 February 2008 from http://www.epractice.eu.

Europen Commission, (2004) Framework to Reinforce the Exchange of Good Practices in eGovernment A contribution to eEurope 2005.

Evangelidis, A. (2004) 'FRAMES – A Risk Assessment Framework for e-Services' Electronic Journal of e-Government Volume 2 Issue 1 pp. 21-30.

Evangelidis, A., Akomode, J., Taleb-Bendiab, A. & Taylor, M. (2002) 'Risk Assessment & Success Factors for e-Government in a UK Establishment' in ed (Traunmüller)

Electronic Government.ISSN: 0302-9743 (Print) 1611-3349 (Online). Volume 2456/2002. Springer Berlin / Heidelberg.

Federal Chancellery, e-Government Section. Retrieved June 1, 2006 from http://www.ch.ch.

Federal Enterprise Architecture Program Management Office, (2007) Value to the Mission. FEA Practice Guidance, OMB. USA.

Federal Information and Communication Technology (FEDICT), (2007) Fertile Soil for Customer-Friendly e-Gov. Activity Report 2001-2006. Belgium.

Federal Planning Bureau Economic Analyses and Forecasts, (2002) Towards E-Gov in Belgium. Situation in August 2002. Working Paper. Belgium.

Finger, M. & Pécoud, G. (2003) 'From e-Government to e-Governance? Towards a model of e-Governance', *Electronic Journal of e-Government*, Volume 1, Issue 1. pp. 1-10

Flak, L., Olsen, D., & Wolcott, P. (2005) 'Local E-Government in Norway - Current Status and Emerging Issues', *Scandinavian Journal of Information Systems*, 17(2):41–84.

François-Xavier Chevallerau (2005). eGovernment in the Member States of the European Union. IDABC Programme.

French Government Portal. Retrieved 17 December 2007 from http://www.service-public.fr.

Friedman-Hill E. J. (1999) JESS: The Java Expert System Shell (Version 5.0, alpha. Retrieved 27August, 2006 from http://herzberg.ca.sandia.gov/jess.

Gartner Dataquest (May 2007).

Gáspár, P. & Jaksa, R. (2008) eGovernment in the EU New Member States: Drivers, Barriers and Challenges of Development. Information and Communication Technologies: From Theory to Applications, 2008. ICTTA 2008. 3rd International Conference. ISBN: 978-1-4244-1751-3.

Gazdar, G, Mellish, CS, Natural Processing in PROLOG: An Introduction to computational Linguistics, Addison Wesley. 0 201 18053 7.

Gichoya, D., HepWorth, M. & Dawson, R. (2006) Factors Affecting Success and Failures of Government ICT Projects in Developing Countries. Proceedings of the 2nd International Conference on E-government.

Gil-García, J. & Pardo, T. (2005) E-government success factors: Mapping practical tools to theoretical foundations. Government Information Quarterly. Volume 22, Issue 2, pp. 187–216.

Glaser, B. & Strauss, A. (1967) The discovery of theory: Strategies of qualitative research. London: Wiedenfeld and Nicholson.

Government of the Netherlands (2006) Progress Report 4 e-Government. The Netherlands.

Government On-Line, (2004) From Vision to Reality and Beyond. Government of Canada.

Government On-Line, (2005) From Vision to Reality and Beyond. Government of Canada.

Government On-Line, (2006) From Vision to Reality and Beyond. Government of Canada.

Government Portal of New Zealand. Retrieved 12 July 2008 from http://www.e.govt.nz.

Grant, G. and Chau, D. (2006) 'Developing a Generic Framework for e-Government' in Felix, B. (ed.) Advanced Topics in Global Information Management. Idea Group Inc (IGI). ISBN 1591409233, 9781591409236.

Gregory Karvounarakis, Sofia Alexaki, Vassilis Christophides, Dimitris Plexousakis, Michel Scholl. (2002) RQL: a declarative query language for RDF, Proceedings of the 11th international conference on World Wide Web. pp 592 – 603. ISBN:1-58113-449-5.

Grönlund, Å. (2005) State of the art in e-gov research: surveying conferences publications, Idea Group Inc.

Guido Bayens (2006). e-Government in the Netherlands - An architectural approach. Retrieved 1 January 2008 from http://www.via-nova-architectura.org.

Hans J. (Jochen) Scholl (2005). Interoperability in e-Government: More than Just Smart Middleware. The Information School University of Washington jscholl@u.washington.edu. 0-7695-2268-8/05 IEEE.

Heeks, R. (2001). 'Understanding e-Governance for development'. i-Government Working Paper Series, Institute for development Policy and Management, University of Manchester.

Heeks, R. (2006a) Implementing and Managing EGovernment: An International Text. ISBN 0761967923, 9780761967927. Sage.

Heeks, R. (2006b) Understanding and Measuring eGovernment: International Benchmarking Studies. UNDESA workshop, E-Participation and E-Government: Understanding the Present and Creating the Future, Budapest, Hungary.

Helle Zinner Henriksen Department of Informatics Copenhagen Business. School hzh.inf@cbs.dk, Volker Mahnke Department of Informatics Copenhagen Business,

School vm.inf@cbs.dk, Jens Meiland Hansen Local Government Denmark (LGDK) jmh@kl.dk. Public eProcurement adoption: Economic and political rationality. Proceedings of the 37th Hawaii International Conference on System Sciences – 2004.

Hobday (1995) Innovation in East Asia: The Challenge to Japan, Edward Elgar, Hants.

Hoffman, D. & Novak, T. (1998), 'Bridging the Racial. Divide on the Internet', SCIENCE, Volume: 280 (April 17), pp. 390-391.

Holliday, A. (2002) Doing and writing qualitative research, SAGE Publications Ltd, London. ISBN: 0 7619 6391 X.

HoReCa1 (2007) One-stop-shop for Hotel Restaurant Café licences. City of Amsterdam - Urban Program on Regulation and Enforcement. The Netherlands.

Huberman, M. (1990) 'Linkage between researchers and practitioners: A qualitative study'. *American Educational Research Journal.* Volume 27, Issue 2. pp. 363-391.

ICA Country Report Switzerland, ICA 38th CONFERENCE Limassol, Cyprus, October 2004

ICT Strategy Unit, (2007) Administration on the Net - An ABC Guide to E-Government in Austria. Federal Chancellery. Austria.

ICT Strategy Unit, (2008) i2010 Austria – Strategic Framework. Federal Chancellery. Japan.

Information Society Programme (2006) The National Knowledge Society Strategy: A renewing, human-centric and competitive Finland 2007–2015. Prime Minister's Office. Finland.

International Economic Affairs Division, (2007) Japan's New IT Reform Strategy and u-Japan. Deputy Director. Telecommunications Bureau. Ministry of Internal Affairs and Communications of Japan. Japan.

IT Strategy Headquarters, (2001) e-Japan Strategy. January 22, 2001. Japan.

Janssen, D., Rotthier, S. & Snijkers, K. (2004) If you measure it they will score: an assessment of international e-government benchmarking, Information Polity, 9(3/4), 121-130.

Janssen, M., Wimmer, M., Bicking, M. & Wagenaar, R. (2007). Scenarios of governments in 2020. In. M.A. Wimmer & C. Codagnone. Roadmapping eGovernment Research. Visions and Measures towards Innovative Governments in 2020 (ISBN: 978-88-95549-00-2), pp. 55-84.

Japanese Ministry of Internal Affairs and Communications. Retrieved 1 January 2008 from http://www.soumu.go.jp.

Jenny Y.Y. Wong, Dickson K.W. Chiu, Kai Pan Mark. (2007) Effective e-Government Process Monitoring and Interoperation- A Case Study on the Removal of Unauthorized Building Works in Hong Kong, Proceedings of the 40th Hawaii International Conference on System Sciences. 1530-1605/07, IEEE.

Jeremy Millard (2003). ePublic Services in Europe: Past, Present and Future, Research Findings and New Challenges. Final Paper, Prepared for the Institute for Prospective Technological Studies (IPTS). Retrieved 12 Oct 2007 from ftp://ftp.cordis.europa.eu/pub/ist/docs/epublic-services.pdf.

Jim A. Cornwell. (1998) 'History of Philosophy Ancient times Sixth to third century BC', *The Alpha and the Omega*, Volume III.

Joint Research Centre, (2004) e-Government in the EU in the Next Decade: the Vision and Key Challenges. Technical Report Series. EUR 21376 EN. European Commission. Directorate General.

Juric, M. (2005) BPEL and Java. Retrieved 29April, 2007 from http://www.inf.ed.ac.uk/teaching/courses/ec/miniatures/bpel-up.pdf.

Kafka Report (2006). Retrieved 1 March, 2007 from http://www.kafka.be.

Kearns, I. (2004) Public Value and E-Government, Institute for Public Policy Research, London.

Kelly, G., Mulgan, G. & Muers, S. (2001) Creating Public Value: An Analytical Framework for Public Sector Reform, Cabinet Office, London.

Kenneth C. Laudon & Jane P. Laudon (2006). Management Information Systems, 9/e. ISBN-13: 9780131538412.

Kenniscentrum bouwt mee aan de e-overheid, (2007) NORA 2.0 Netherland's e-Government Reference Architecture. The Netherlands.

Klischewski, R. & Jeenicke, M. (2004) Semantic Web Technologies for Information Management within e-Government Services. Proceedings of the 37th Hawaii International Conference on System Sciences. 0-7695-2056-1/04 IEEE.

Kneale, William, and Kneale, Marth. (1962) The Development of Logic, Oxford University Press, London, UK.

Korean Government Portal. Retrieved 3 February 2008 from http://www.korea.go.kr.

Kumar, V., Mukerji, B., Butt, I. & Persaud, A. (2007) 'Factors for Successful e-Government Adoption: a Conceptual Framework', *Electronic Journal of e-Government* Volume 5 Issue 1 pp. 21-30.

Layne, K., Lee, J. (2001) Developing fully functional E-government: A four stage model. Government Information Quarterly, Volume 18, Issue 2. Pages 122-136.

Lee, K. & Lim, C. (2001). Technological regimes, catching-up and leapfrogging: findings from the Korean industries. Research Policy (ISSN: 0048-7333). volume: 30, issue: 2.

Lenk, E. & Traunmüller, R. (1999) Öffentliche Verwaltung und Informationstechnik - Perspektiven einer radikalen Neugestaltung der öffentlichen Verwaltung mit Informationstechnik. R. V. Decker's Verlag, Heidelberg.

Lenk, K. & Traunmüller, R. (2000) 'A Framework for electronic government', *Proceedings of the 11th International Workshop on Database and Expert Systems Applications*. pp. 340-345.

Leo Anthopoulos, Department & Ioannis A. Tsoukalas (2005) 'A Cross Border Collaboration Environment, as a means for offering online public services and for evaluating the performance of Public Executives', *Proceedings of the 2005 IEEE International Conference on e-Technology, e-Commerce and e-Service (EEE'05) on e-Technology, e-Commerce and e-Service.* ISBN: 0-7695-2274-2.

Löfstedt, U. (2005) 'E-Government – assessment of current research and some proposals for future directions', *International of Public Information Systems*. Volume 2005:1. pp. 39-52

Lowery, L. (2001). Developing a Successful E-Government Strategy. (p. 7). San Francisco: Department of Telecommunications & Information Services - City/County of San Francisco, CA.

Mahrer, H. & Brandtweiner, R. (2004) 'Success factors for implementing e-government services: the case of the Austrian e-government service portal', *International Journal of Information Technology and Management*. Issue: Volume 3, Numbers 2-4. pp. 235-245.

Makolm, J. (2006). 'A Holistic Reference Framework for e-Government: The Practical Proof of a Scientific Concept', *Proceedings of the 39th Hawaii International Conference on System Sciences.* 0-7695-2507-5/06/$20.00. IEEE.

Malakooty, N. (2007) 'Closing the Digital Divide? The $100 PC and Other Projects for Developing Countries'. Personal Computing Industry Center (PCIC). The Paul Merage School of Business. California, USA. Retrieved April 24, 2007 from http://pcic.merage.uci.edu/papers/2007/100PC.pdf.

Marche, S. & MacNiven, J. (2003) 'E-government and e-Governance: The Future Isn't What It Used To Be'. *Canadian Journal of Administrative Sciences*. pp. 74-86.

Marijn Janssen, Anthony M. Cresswell (2005) 'An enterprise application integration methodology for e-government', *The Journal of Enterprise Information Management*. pp. 531-47.

Marinos Themistocleous and Zahir Irani (2005) Developing E-Government Integrated Infrastructures: A Case Study. Department of Information Systems and Computing, Brunel University, Uxbridge, UB8 3PH, UK {Marinos.Themistocleous; Zahir.Irani@brunel.ac.uk, Peter E.D. Love, I-B Centre. School ofManagement Information Systems, Edith Cowan University. Joondulap, WA 6027, Australia p.love@ecu.edu.au. 0-7695-2268-8/05 IEEE.

Mario Bochicchio, Antonella Longo, Software Engineering and Telemedia Lab (SET Lab) Department of Innovation Engineering, University of Lecce – Italy mario.bochicchio@unile.it, antonella.longo@unile.it (2004). Conceptual Modeling of Data Intensive and Information Intensive Web Applications. 0-7695-2084-7/04 IEEE.

Miles, M., & Huberman, A. (1984) Qualitative data analysis: A source book of new methods, Beverly Hills, CA: SAGE.

Millard, J. & Horlings, E (2008) Current eGovernment trends, future drivers, and lessons from earlier periods of technological change. Interim Report of the eGovernment 2020 Vision Study for the European Commission, DG Information Society and Media, eGovernment and CIP Operations Unit, May 2008.

Millard, J., Warren, R., Leitner, C., Shahin, J. (2006) Towards the eGovernment V sion for the EU in 2010: Research Policy Challenges. Joint Research Centre. Directorate General. European Commission.

EISI (2004) The Egyptian Information Society Initiative for Government Services Delivery. e-Government Programme. Ministry of Communication and Information Technology. 7/3/04 AD-1/11. Egypt

MCIT (2006) Information Technology Annual Report 2005-2006. Ministry of Communications and Information Technology. Government of India.

MCIT (2007) Information Technology Annual Report 2006-2007. Ministry of Communications and Information Technology. Government of India.

MCIT (2008) Information Technology Annual Report 2007-2008. Ministry of Communications and Information Technology . Government of India.

Ministry of Government Administration and Home Affairs (MOSTI), (2007) Korea E-Government. Ministry of Government Administration and Home Affairs. Korea.

Ministry of Government Administration and Home Affairs, (2006) Annual Report for e-Government. South Korea

Ministry of Telecommunication and Information Technology, (2005) The National Strategy of Telecommunications and Information Technology 2005-2008. Final Edition. Palestine.

Miranda, R. (2000) The Building Blocks of a Digital Government Strategy. Government Finance Officers Association. Volume 16. Issue 5. Page 9.

Modernisation.gouv.fr, (2006) Le Schéma Directeur de l'administration électronique 2006-2010. Principes. France.

Mofleh, S. & Wanous, M. (2008) 'Understanding Factors Influencing Citizens' Adoption of e-Government Services in the Developing World: Jordan as a Case Study', *INFOCOMP Journal of Computer Science.* ISSN: 1807-4545. Volume: 7, Issue: 4.

Mohrman, Susan, Gibson, C., Morhrman, A. (2002) 'Doing research that is useful to practice: a model and empirical exploration'. *Academy of Management Journal.* Volume 44, Issue 2. pp. 357-375.

Mossberger, K., Tolbert, C. & Stansbury, M. (2003) 'Virtual inequality: beyond the digital divide'. Georgetown University Press. ISBN 0878409998, 9780878409990.

MSTI (2004) Architecture for e-Government in Denmark Challenges and Initiatives. Postscript to the Nyborg Conference, March 2004. Ministry of Science, Technology and Innovation. Denmark.

Mugellini, E., Abou Khaled, O., Chiara, M. & Kuonen, P. (2005). eGovSM Metadata Model: Towards a Flexible, Interoperable and Scalable eGovernment Service, Marketplace. Proceedings of the 2005 IEEE International Conference on e-Technology, e-Commerce and e-Service.

Murakami, T. (2005) Japan's National IT Strategy and the Ubiquitous Network. No. 97. Government of Japan.

Myers, M. (1997) Qualitative Research in Information Systems. Retrieved 23 April, 2006 from http://www.misq.org/discovery/MISQD_isworld.

Namatame, M., Kitajima, M., Nishizaki, Y. (2007) 'Utility of Labeled Pictograms for Improving Performance in Directory-Based Information Search Tasks at e-Commerce Sites', *Proceedings of the IADIS International Conference e-Commerce* 2007. ISBN: 978-972-8924-49-2 © 2007 IADIS. 7-9 December. Algarve, Portugal.

Nils Barnickel, Matthias Fluegge, and Kay-Uwe Schmidt. (2006) Interoperability in eGovernment Through Cross-Ontology Semantic Web Service Composition, Workshop on Semantic Web for eGovernment of ESWC 2006, 11-14 June 2006, Budva, Montenegro. pp 37-47.

Norris, P. (2001) Digital divide: civic engagement, information poverty, and the Internet worldwide. Cambridge University Press. ISBN 0521002230, 9780521002233.

O'Brien & Marakas (2008). Management Information Systems. Eight Edition. Mc Graw Hill.

OECD (2003), Challenges for E-government Development, 5th Global Forum on Reinventing Government, Mexico City. Retrieved 17 August, 2007 from http://unpan1.un.org/intradoc/groups/public/documents/un/unpan012241.pdf.

Office of e-Government, (2008) Citizen Centric Government Electronic Service Delivery Strategy for the Western Australian Public Sector. Department of the Premier and Cabinet Government of Western Australia. Australia.

Office of Information Technology (2001), The Government of Manitoba: E-government by Design, Manitoba Finance, Manitoba.

Office of the Chief Information Officer, (2003) e-Government Plan, 2004 – 2007. Ministry of Management Services. British Colombia.

OMB, (2002) Implementing the President's Management Agenda for E-Government - E-Government Strategy. Simplified Delivery of Services to Citizens. Version 60. Office of Management and Budget. USA.

Papantoniou, A., Hattab, E., Afrati, F., Kayafas, E. & Loumos, V. (2001) Change Management, a Critical Success Factor for E-government, dexa,pp.0402, 12th International Workshop on Database and Expert Systems Applications,

Pardo, T & Scholl, H. (2002) Walking Atop the Cliffs: Avoiding Failure and Reducing Risk in Large Scale E-Government Projects. Proceedings of the 35th Hawaii International Conference on System Sciences. Hawaii, USA.

Park, R. (2008) Measuring Factors That Influence the Success of E-government Initiatives. Proceedings of the 41st Hawaii International Conference on System Sciences. 1530-1605/08, IEEE.

PCIP (2002) Roadmap for E-government in the Developing World- 10 Questions E-Government Leaders Should Ask Themselves. The Working Group on E-Government in the Developing World. Pacific Council on International Policy. April, 2002. Los Angeles, CA 90089-0035.

Pearsall, J. (1999) (ed.) The Concise Oxford English Dictionary, 10th edn. Oxford: Oxford University Press.

Perez, C. (1988) 'New technologies and development'. In: Freeman, C. and Lundvall, B., Editors. Small Countries Facing the Technological Revolution, Pinter Publishers, London.

Performance and Innovation Unit. PIU Electronic Service Deliver Project (2000). Electronic Government Services for the 21 Century. UK.

Peterson, S. (2005) 'Finding a way'. *Government Technology Journal.* Volume 18, Issue 9. pp. 18-34.

Plummer, A. (2001) 'Information systems methodology for building theory in health informatics: the argument for a structures approach to case study research', *Proceedings of the 34th Hawaii International Conference on Systems Sciences*. Maui, Hawaii, USA.

Project e-Government (2004) The Danish eGovernment Strategy 2004-06. Denmark.

Project Steering Committee, (2006) Singapore e-Government 2006: From Integrating Services to Integrating Government. Report by the iGov2010. 2006 Report on Singapore e-Government. Ministry of Finance. Singapore.

Projekt Digital Forvaltning Den Digitale Taskforce, (2002) Towards e-Government – Vision and Strategy for the Public Sector in Denmark. Denmark.

Public Works and Government Services Canada (2005) Evaluation Framework for the Government On-line (GOL) Initiative. Audit and Ethics Brach, 2004-613 Final Report. Canada.

Pucihar A., Bogataj K., Wimmer M. A., Janssen M., Malinauskiene E., Bicking M., Petrauskas R., Klein M., Ma X., Amadori G. & Traunmüller R. (2007) Gap analysis: the process and gap storylines. In: Roadmapping eGovernment Research: Visions and Measures towards Innovative Governments in 2020. / Eds. Cristiano Codagnone and Maria A. Wimmer. Printed in Italy – MY Print snc di Guerinoni Marco & C, Via San Lucio 47, 24023 Clusone (BG), ISBN 978-88-95549-00-2, p.85-121.

Ralf Klischewski (2006). 'Information Integration or Process Integration? How to Achieve Interoperability in Administration'. University of Cairo. Egypt.

Ralf Klischewski, Hamburg University, Informatics Department, Vogt-Kölln-Strasse 30, D-22527 Hamburg, klischewski@informatik.uni-hamburg.de. Semantic Web for e-Government.

Ralf Klischewski, Martti Jeenicke, Hamburg University, Department of Informatics, Vogt-Koelln-Str. 30, 22527 Hamburg, Germany, Tel: +49-40-42883-2299, {klischewski, jeenicke}@informatik.uni-hamburg.de. Semantic Web Technologies for Information Management, within e-Government Services.

Ralf Klischewski. (2001) Infrastructure for an e-Government Process Portal, European Conference, MCIL, reading, UK, 2001, pp 233-245.

Richard Freeman (2005). Human Resource Leapfrogging. The Globalist. Retrieved 24 June 2007 from http://www.theglobalist.com/StoryId.aspx?StoryId=4759. Last visited.

Riedl, R., Roithmary, F. & Schenkenfelder, B. (2007) 'Using the structured case approach to build theory in e-government', *Proceedings of the 40th Hawaii international Conference on Systems Sciecnes*. 1530-1605/07. Hawaii, USA.

Riley, T. (2003) E-Governance vs. E-Government .ICT for Development. Retrieved 13 January, 2008 from http://www.i4donline.net/issue/nov03/pdfs/egovernance.pdf.

Roland Traunmüller and Maria A. Wimmer (2002). Web Semantics in e-Government: A Tour d'Horizon on Essential Features. Institute of Applied Computer Science University of Linz. A - 4040 Linz {traunm, mw}@ifs.uni-linz.ac.at. 0-7695-1393-X/02 IEEE.

Rule Markup Language. Retrieved February 13, 2007 from http://www.ruleml.org.

S.W. Smith, sws@cs.dartmouth.edu, Carlisle Adams (2005). Building Secure Web-Based Environments: Understanding Research Interrelationships through a Construction Metaphor, Secure Systems, Editor. University of Ottawa, PU BLISHED BY THE IEEE COMPUTER SOCIETY   1540-7993/05IEEE, IEEE SECURITY & PRIVACY

Sang M. Lee, Xin Tan, & Silvana Trimi (2006). 'M-government, from rhetoric to reality: learning from leading countries', *Electronic Government, an International Journal*. Issue: Volume 3, Number 2/2006. pp.:113-126.

Schuppan, T. (2009) 'E-Government in developing countries: Experiences from sub-Saharan Africa', Government Information Quarterly, Volume: 26, Issue: 1, Pages 118-127.

Secrétariat d'État à la Réforme de l'État, (2004) Plan d'Action de l'Administration Electronique (P2AE). Ministère de la Fonction publique, de la Réforme de l'État et de l'Aménagement du territoire. France.

Semantic Web Technologies for Information Management within e-Government Services, Ralf Klischewski, Martti Jeenicke (2004). Hamburg University, Department of Informatics Vogt-Koelln- Str. 30, 22527 Hamburg, Germany, Tel: +49-40-42883-2299 {klischewski, jeenicke}@informatik.uni-hamburg.de, Proceedings of the 37th Hawaii International Conference on System Sciences – 2004

Shahkooh, K., Abdollahi, A. (2007) "A Strategy-Based Model for E-Government Planning. International Multi-Conference on Computing in the Global Information Technology (ICCGI'07).

Sharma, S. (2007) 'Exploring best practices in public–private partnership (PPP) in e-Government through select Asian case studies'. The International Information & Library Review. Volume 39, Issues 3-4, September-December 2007, Pages 203-210.

Sharma, S, Gupta, J. (2003) 'Building Blocs of an E-Government—A Framework', *Journal of Electronic Commerce in Organisations*. Volume 1 Number 4. pp. 1-15. Article No. ITJ2487.

Sharma, S. & Gupta, J. (2002), "Transforming to e-government: a framework", paper presented at *2nd European Conference on E-Government*, Public Sector Times, pp. 383-90.

Signore, O., Chesi, F., & Pallotti, M. (2005) 'E-Governmen: Challenges and' Opportunities. CGM Italy - *XIX Annual Conference*. Florence, Italy.

Silverman, D. (1993) Interpreting Qualitative Data, Sage Publications, London.

Sorrentino, M. & Virili, F. (2004) Socio-technical Perspectives on e-Government Initiatives. Lecture Notes in Computer Science. Springer Berlin / Heidelberg. 978-3-540-40845-9.

State of Alabama, (2002) Electronic Government Framework and Strategy. State of Alabama e-Government program. USA.

State Services Commission, (2006) Enabling Transformation A Strategy for e-Government 2006. November 2006. ISBN 978-0-478-30302-5. New Zealand.

State Services Commission, (2006) State of the Development Goals Report 2006. ISBN 0-478-24473-8. New Zealand.

Statistics Belgium. Retrieved 18 September 2008 from http://www.statbel.fgov.be.

Stone, D. (2001) Getting research into policy? paper presented to the third Annual Global Development Network Conference on 'Blending Local and Global Knowledge', Rio De Janeiro.

Sutton, R., & Callahan, A. (1987) 'The stigma of bankruptcy: spoiled organizational image and its management'. *Academy of Management Journal*.

Swedish Agency for Administrative Development, (2005) IT-Architecture the Art of Communicating Visions for IT-related Change Processes. Dnr 2004/55-5. Sweden.

Szeredi P., Molnar K., Scott R. (1996) Serving Multiple HTML Clients from a Prolog Application, Proceedings of the 1st Workshop on Logic Programming Tools for Internet Applications. - Bonn, Germany, 1996. - PP. 81-90. Retrieved 14 November 2007 from http://www.clip.dia.fi.upm.es/miscdocs/lp-internet/iqsoft/multiple.html.

T. Tammet. (2004) Extended Logical Markup Language (ELM) Model and Syntax Specification. Retrieved January 18, 2007 from http://deepthought.ttu.ee/it/elm/elm.html.

Tammet, T., Hele-Mai Haav, Marko Kaaramees. (2006) A Rule-Based Approach to Web-Based Application Development. IEEE 1-4244-0345-6/06.

Tarau P. (1999) Java Inference Engine and Networked Interdictor. A Prolog Interpreter in Java for Mobile Agent Scripting and Internet Programming. Retrieved 19 February, 2007 from http://www.binnetcorp.com/Jinni/index.html.

Technical Committees, (2004) Strategic Planning Workshops. Consolidated Report. Executive Committee of Electronic Government.

Teorsana Oy (2008) Ubiquitous Information Society. Ubiquitous Information Society Advisory Board . ISBN: 978-952-201-727-7. Finland.

The Danish government, Local Government Denmark (LGDK) and Danish Regicns, (2007) The Danish e-Government Strategy 2007-2010 - Towards Better Digital Service, Increase Efficiency and Stronger Collaboration. Denmark.

The Economic Planning Unit (2001) Eighth Malaysia Plan (8MP, 2001-2006). Prme Minister's Department, Putra Jaya, Malaysia.

The Economic Planning Unit (2006) Ninth Malaysia Plan (9MP, 2006-2010). Prime Minister's Department, Putra Jaya, Malaysia.

The Egyptian Government Portal. Retrieved 22 June 2007 from http://www.egypt gov.eg.

The German Government Portal. Retrieved 5 September 2007 from http://www.deutschland-online.de.

The Jordanian Government Portal. Retrieved 22 April 2007 from http://www.jordan.gov.jo.

The Netherlands Government Portal. Retrieved 8 August 2007 from http://www.e-overheid.nl.

The Norwegian Ministry of Government Administration and Reform, (2006) An Information Society for All. Norway.

The Office of e-Envoy (2002) Online Annual Report (2002). Cabinet Office. London, UK.

The Official Web Site of the President's e-Government Initiative. Retrieved 23 April 2008 from http://www.whitehouse.gov/omb/egov.

The Open Group (2007), The Open Group Architecture Framework (TOGAF). Version 8.1.1, Enterprise Edition. Exeter: Author.

The Palestinian Government Portal. Retrieved 12 January 2007 from http://www.egov.ps.

The Portal of Government of Singapore. Retrieved 6 March 2007 from http://www.igov.gov.sg.

Thomas, R. & Walport, M. (2008) Data Sharing Review Report. Ministry of Justice UK.

Treasury Board of Canada Secretariat, (1999) Strategic Directions for Information Management and Information Technology: Enabling 21st Century Service to Canad ans. Catalogue No. BT53-10/1999. ISBN 0-662-64526-X.

Tronti, L. (1998) Benchmarking Labour Market Performances and Policies 1. Available from http://www.iasberlin. de/ersep/imi61_uk/00140002.htm.

United Nations (2001) Benchmarking E-government: A Global Perspective - Assessing the UN Member States. United Nations. Retrieved 1 August, 2007 from http://www.park.cz/soubory/egov-un2001.pdf.

Undheim, T. (2008) 'Best practices in eGovernment: on a knife-edge between success and failure'. *European Journal of ePractice*. Issue 2. ISSN: 1988-625X. Retrieved 17 May 2008 from http://www.epracticejournal.eu/articles/1234.

United Nations (2003) World Public Sector Report: E-government at the Crossroads, New York: United Nations. Retrieved 19 June, 2008 from http://unpan1.un.org/intradoc/groups/public/documents/un/unpan012733.pdf.

United Nations (2008) From e-Government to Connected Government. UN E-Government Survey. Retrieved 13 Oct. 2007 from unpan.un.org/intradoc/groups/public/documents/UN/UNPAN028607.pdf.

UNKE (2007) UN E-Government Readiness Knowledge Base. Retrieved 2 Nov 2007 from http://www2.unpan.org/egovkb.

US Department of the Interior, (2007) e-Government Strategy FY 2008 – FY 2013. USA.

Van Dijk, J. (2005) 'The deepening divide: inequality in the information society'. SAGE. ISBN 141290403X, 9781412904032.

Van Mannen, J. (1988) Tales of the field: on writing ethnography. Chicago: University of Chicago Press.

Vanvelthoven, P. (2003) Note stratégique du Secrétaire d'Etat à l'Informatisation de l'Etat. Belgium.

Wagner, C., Cheung, K., Lee, F., & Ip, R. (2003). 'Enhancing E-Government in Developing Countries: Managing Knowledge through Virtual Communities', *The Electronic Journal on Systems in Developing Countries*. Volume 14, Issue 4, 1-20.

Walk, K. (1998) How to Wite a Comparative Analysis, Writing Center, Harvard University. Retrived 12 December, 2007 from http://www.fas.harvard.edu/~wricntr/documents/CompAnalysis.html.

Warschauer M (2003) Social Inclusion and Technology, MIT Press: Mass.

Wimmer M., Bicking M., Bogataj K., Bowern M., Codagnone C., Dawes S., Janssen M., Klein M., Ma, X., Malinauskiene & E., Pucihar A. (2007) Research themes and roadmap charts. In: Roadmapping eGovernment Research: Visions and Measures towards Innovative Governments in 2020. / Eds. Cristiano Codagnone and Maria A. Wimmer. Printed in Italy – MY Print snc di Guerinoni Marco & C, Via San Lucio 47, 24023 Clusone (BG), ISBN 978-88-95549-00-2, p.123-147.

Wimmer, M. & Traunmüller, R. (2003) 'KM for Public Administration: Focusing on KMS Feature Requirements', *Proceedings of the 14th International Workshop on Database and Expert Systems* Applications (DEXA'03) 1529-4188/03. IEEE.

Wimmer, M. (2002) Towards Knowledge Enhanced E-Government: Integration as Pivotal Challenge. Johannes Kepler Universitat. Retrieved 14 August 2008 from http://www.iwv.jku.at/aboutus/wimmer/habilschrift.pdf.

Win-Prolog. - LPA, 1999. Retrieved Aug. 27, 2006 from http://www.lpa.co.uk.

World Factbook (2008). Retrieved Aug. 27, 2008 from https://www.cia.gov/library/publications/the-world-factbook.

Yin (1994) R.K.Case Study Research, Design and Methods, 2nd ed. Newbury Park, Sage Publications.

Yin, R K, 1993, Applications of case study research, Newbury Park: Sage.

Yin, R. & Moore, G. (1985) The utilization of research: Lessons for the natural hazards field. Cosmos Corp, Washington. USA.

Zhang, J. (2006) 'Good Governance Through E-Governance? Assessing China's E-Government Strategy', Journal of E-Government, Volume: 2 Issue: 4, ISSN: 1542-4049 , Pages : 39 – 71.

Zukauskas, P., & Kasteckiene, A. (2002). The Role of E-Government in the Development of the New Economy in Lithuania.

List of Publications

Rabaiah, A. & Vandijck, E. (2009) 'Maturity Model of Strategic Objectives of e-Government', International *Journal of Electronic Government Research.* [Submitted and awaiting comments from the reviewers].

Rabaiah, A. & Vandijck, E. (2009) 'A Strategic Framework of E-Government - Generic and Best Practice', *Electronic Journal of e-Government.* Volume 7, Issue 2, ISSN 1479-439X. [Forthcoming].

Rabaiah, A. & Vandijck, E. (2008). 'E-Government and its Impact on E-Commerce in LDCs'. In Rouibah, M. & Khalil, O. (ed.) Emerging Markets and E-Commerce in Developing Economies, Hard Cover Publisher: Information Science, USA. October 2008. ISBN: 978-1-60566-100-1.

Rabaiah, A. & Vandijck, E. (2007) 'Towards Efficient and Transparent E-Government Processes', *Proceedings of the IADIS International Conference E-Commerce* 2007, 7-9 December 2007, Algarve, Portugal, pp. 236-240, ISBN: 978-972-8924-49-2.

Rabaiah, A. & Vandijck, E (2007) 'Federation of E-government: A Model and Framework', *Information Systems Control Journal*, July 2007, Volume 4.

Rabaiah, A., Vandijck, E. & Musa, F. (2006) 'Abstraction of eGovernment', *Proceedings of the IADIS International Conference E-Commerce* 2006, 9-11 December 2006, Barcelona, Spain, pp. 27-34, ISBN: 972-8924-23-2.

Biography

Abdelbaset Rabaiah was born in 1973 in Meithalun in the northern part of the West Bank, Palestine. He has received his primary, elementary and secondary education in Meithalun's local schools. He later pursued his undergraduate studies at An Najah National University in Nablus/West Bank. He was awarded a degree in Civil Engineering in 1999. Mr. Rabaiah has worked in East Jerusalem with a German consultancy company for two years as a local civil engineer. He then joined the Arab American University (AAU) in Jenin/West Bank to work as a research assistant.

In 2003, Mr. Rabaiah was awarded a BTC scholarship to pursue his graduate studies at the Vrije Universiteit Brussel (VUB). He graduated with great distinction and received a Master degree in Business Information Management in 2004. He then headed back home to work on a case study in the Palestinian Territories in 2005/2006. There, he joined the e-Government Project team. That team was responsible for laying out the strategy of e-Government and ICT at the Ministry of Information and Telecommunication Technology – Ramallah. He gained a hands-on experience of how things are managed at the strategic level. Mr. Rabaiah has produced the Arabic version of the Palestinian ICT Strategy. At that time, he was doing research under the supervision of Prof. Farouq Musa of AAU.

In 2008, Mr. Rabaiah has joined the ePractice community (e-Government, e-Healh, and eInclusion) which was created by the European Commission (www.ePractice.eu). He later established the Community of Researchers of E-Government within ePractice.eu. Mr. Rabaiah has participated in workshops organised by ePractice and the Interoperable Delivery of European eGovernment Services to public Administrations, Businesses and Citizens (IDABC).

Finally, Mr. Rabaiah has published a number of papers in proceedings of some conferences and Journals dedicated to e-government. He has also co-authored a book in which he drew the connection between e-government and e-commerce in the Less Developed Countries.